THE
MUCKRAKERS

Evangelical Crusaders

Edited by
ROBERT MIRALDI

PRAEGER

Westport, Connecticut
London

Library of Congress Cataloging-in-Publication Data

The muckrakers : evangelical crusaders / edited by Robert Miraldi.
    p. cm.
    Includes bibliographical references and index.
    ISBN 0–275–96915–0
    1. Journalists—United States—Biography. 2. Journalism—Social aspects—United
States—History—20th century. 3. Investigative reporting—United States—History—20th
century. I. Miraldi, Robert.
    PN4871.M83 2000
    070'.92'273—dc21
    [B]   00–025129

British Library Cataloguing in Publication Data is available.

Library of Congress Catalog Card Number: 00–025129
ISBN: 0–275–96915–0

First published in 2000

Praeger Publishers, 88 Post Road West, Westport, CT 06881
An imprint of Greenwood Publishing Group, Inc.
www.praeger.com

Printed in the United States of America

The paper used in this book complies with the
Permanent Paper Standard issued by the National
Information Standards Organization (Z39.48–1984).

10 9 8 7 6 5 4 3 2

To the memory of Rich Katims,
A wonderful teacher

To Mary Beth Pfeiffer,
An ever-passionate reporter

Contents

Introduction: Why the Muckrakers Are Still with Us

Robert Miraldi

The first time I was accused of being a "muckraker" was in 1975. I was reporting for the *Staten Island Advance*, a daily newspaper in New York City that circulated to 80,000 people. New York City was then embroiled in a scandal involving dozens of nursing home owners who, indictments had begun to show, were stealing millions of dollars in taxpayer money. My job for many months, as the scandal had unfolded, had been to determine if the story had any connections to the local community. How were the dozen or so Staten Island nursing homes and their hundreds of patients affected by the scandal? Were their owners involved in the money tricks that seemed so widespread? One local owner, who operated Staten Island's best nursing home, ironically, had already been charged with stealing public money. A number of others had been linked to the one owner who had been identified as the mastermind of the money schemes and the kingpin of a cartel of nursing homes.

A special office within the state attorney general's office had been created. Sources there told me that the owner of Staten Island's largest nursing facility, who had not yet been implicated, was the target of their criminal investigation. A grand jury had been impaneled to hear evidence of his alleged wrongdoing. I was closely following the grand jury in search of leads, but I had come up blank and had written no stories that could explain where the investigation might be heading or what crimes had been committed. I decided I would simply write a profile, a biography of sorts, of the owner who was under investigation. For that, I would comb public documents he had filed with various government agencies, conduct interviews with residents and relatives of residents, and meet with him at his nursing home for a lengthy interview. Although I was not completely candid about what kind of story I was researching, he had to know what kind of story I was putting together. Most of my stories had been about nursing home problems and the owners' misdeeds. Nonetheless, the owner agreed to a meeting that we both likely saw as a showdown of sorts.

When our meeting day arrived, the owner had prepared a show for the reporter. Staff greeted me at the door, residents had been groomed and prepped for my visits to their rooms, floors had been scrubbed, linens had been changed, and posters had been hung on walls. I later learned all of this from talking to employees. Of course, I wasn't much interested in inspecting the building. I wanted information on the facility's finances. I wanted to hear how he had understood and had implemented the complex reimbursement formulas that the government employed in the reimbursement of nursing home operators. Who really owned the real estate? Who really owned the business? What were his ties to the various companies that supplied thousands of dollars of linens, food, and medical equipment? Other owners in New York State were running various scams, and my goal was to see if this owner was involved—or if he might tip his hand. After repeated questions about his finances, which he would not answer, the owner stood up, glared at me, and ended the interview. "You," he yelled, "don't care about the truth. You are just a muckraker. A smelly muckraker."

I left the interview wondering if I had been insulted or praised. Surely he meant his comments as damnation; that I knew. To him, I was a gunslinger, looking for notches on my reportorial belt. To him, muckraking was akin to "yellow journalism," a tawdry form of headline-seeking mudslinging with commercial, but no social, purpose. Of course, the fact that he was my target might have colored his view. But something told me that his attack was high praise. After all, the muckraking journalists who wrote exposés about corruption during the first two decades of the twentieth century were a courageous band of enterprising writers, rightfully praised in various histories as crusaders for change.[1] They were America's first investigative reporters. Acting as preachers, detectives, social workers, educators, and yes, entertainers, the muckrakers revealed an underside of America, an "invisible government" that both entranced and alarmed their reading public. Their exposés of political wrongdoing and corporate excesses in America's first national mass-circulation magazines were a key factor in fueling the Progressive Era reform movement that dominated the first decade of this century and ushered in modern America. At times, of course, as Stephen Whitfield makes clear in his chapter on Lincoln Steffens (chapter 5, "Lincoln Steffens: The Paradoxical Muckraker"), the muckrakers were not sure exactly what kind of change they wanted during a period when social options were many, when changes were head-spinning, and when reform efforts were culminating. Like Steffens, they leaped from local to state to federal issues, educating themselves and the public as they went along—and at times they were not sure what they had found or what to do about it. Confusion aside, however, the muckrakers, angry at the problems they found and working with an evangelical fervor, did set out to find and expose evil and injustice, and in the end, seek to institutionalize their moral indignation. In 1906 when David Graham Phillips unleashed his fusillade called the "Treason of the Senate," a look at how corporate money ruled the U.S. Congress, he was said to be so angry that even publisher William Randolph Hearst, not known for his moderation, asked him to tone down the articles. The muck-rakers were motivated—at least to a great degree—by a moral, almost reli-gious, belief that the exposure of ills would lead to cures. Phillips wanted his exposé to make clear that citizens needed to elect directly their senators and not leave the job to often-corrupt and partisan state legislatures. He got his way in 1912 when the 17th Amendment to the Constitution passed.[2] The formula was simple: Diagnose, prescribe, then watch solutions unfold. If all that was so, if muckraking was and is a noble pursuit, then to be accused of muckraking could and should be taken as a badge of honor, a noble job in an often-besmirched profession, a calling of a higher order.

When Charles Edward Russell, the grandson of a preacher and son of a crusading midwestern editor, wrote articles about the slum housing owned by the world's richest church in 1908, church elders struck back and accused him of "muck-raking." Russell responded, almost gleefully: "I am glad to be called 'a muck-raker,' " he said. "The only thing I object to is living in a world full of needless horrors and suffering without uttering one word of protest, however feeble and unheard."[3] However, certainly on that after-noon in 1975 when the nursing home owner asked me to leave his building, I was not being complimented, just as President Theodore Roosevelt was not praising the group of writers who he first labeled in April 1906 as "muck-rakers." After reading Phillips' "Treason" articles and Upton Sin-clair's protest novel, *The Jungle*, Roosevelt felt he had to counterattack, in part because he feared the muckrakers were fostering a revolutionary air in the country. These "wild preachers of unrest" only look downward, he said accusingly, into the muck of society, and in doing so they obscure the view to the sky, missing the wonders of democratic America and misleading the public.[4]

Roosevelt was quite wrong about this band of about two dozen or so writers who penned nearly 2,000 articles in soap opera-like serial install-ments that had the public gasping at their revelations. The muckrakers' gaze was neither up nor down; it was squarely straightforward—at a reading pub-lic that was both enthralled and dispirited by their exposés. With a supreme faith that an aroused public would respond to what they were revealing, the muckrakers—perhaps naively—trusted public opinion in the same way that investigative reporters today often believe in the power of fact.[5] The late Meg Greenfield, who edited the *Washington Post*'s editorial page for many

years, wrote that journalists continue to muckrake today with the same di-
agnostic mentality that the earlier muckrakers had. "We are morally certain
that if we yank open just one more door that the corpse will fall out" and
the public will respond, says Greenfield.[6] What is true today—and what was
emerging also at the turn of century—is that government, more than the
public, responds especially and vigorously to journalistic exposés. In fact,
Progressivism, the political movement that dominated American politics
right up to the onset of World War I, was premised on journalistic exposé
coupled with government response. As historian Richard Hofstadter points
out, Progressivism was a journalistic mentality, a mentality of exposé and
awareness. "The fundamental critical achievement of American Progressivism," Hofstadter points out, "was the business of exposure."[7] The muckraking exposés of the excesses of industrialism—from the bucket shops of
Wall Street to the sweatshops of the steel mills—made clear the need for an
organized response to the abuses that had been building up since the Civil
War. As David M. Chalmers points out, "The prime collective achievement
of the muckrakers was to point out the conflict between the growth of large-
scale private economic power and the needs of the new national American
society."[8] In chapter 6, "Small-town Editor, Big-time Fight," James Kates
locates this conflict on a rural local level where it might least be expected
to be found. Kates details the crusading efforts of Alfred E. Roese, the son
of a minister, who used his small Wisconsin newspaper to alert the public
to the mean-spirited behavior of a lumber company against a lone citizen
who resisted their corporate might. The David and Goliath battle spilled
out of Roese's pen and his news pages.

Kates' look at the alliance between Progressivism and journalism, albeit
at a local level, shows again that much is still to be uncovered about journalism at the turn of the century. Despite numerous scholarly works that
have chronicled the muckraking movement and the various biographies that
continue to appear about the most well-known muckraking writers, more is
yet to be uncovered and learned.[9] This anthology sheds light on four new
episodes of crusading, evangelical, and muckraking journalism. While most
attention has been focused on Ida Tarbell, Lincoln Steffens, Upton Sinclair,
Ray Stannard Baker, and Samuel Hopkins Adams, others were using their
pens and their publications in pursuit of reform and social justice. In chapter
2, Michael Dillon chronicles publisher Edward Butler's newspaper crusade
on behalf of Polish immigrants living in squalid tenements in Buffalo, N.Y.
The journalistic crusade was once thought to be the sole province of New
York City newspaper publisher Joseph Pulitzer. However, Dillon makes clear
that muckraking and exposé journalism did not reside with Pulitzer nor did
it start, as is often repeated, with Samuel McClure when he published Tarbell and Steffens in October of 1902 in *McClure's*, the most famous of the
exposé magazines.[10] In addition to showing how Butler, who was also the
son of a preacher, put together the nuts and bolts of his crusade, Dillon

suggests that the Buffalo expose also helped to define, or perhaps redefine, what it meant to be part of a community.

To Roosevelt, who thought that the muckrakers were tearing down and eating away at American values, the muckraking journalists were trouble-makers, not community builders. For many years, Eugene Roberts was the chief editor of the *Philadelphia Inquirer*, one of America's best newspapers, when it regularly won the Pulitzer Prize for its muckraking and investigative reporting. He sees enterprising and activist forms of journalism as a defining and shaping force in any community. "It explains to readers things they should know and will find important in their lives," he says. It is "a cohesive force, a constant that holds together" a community, he points out.[11] At the very least, investigative reporting sets the agenda for what is important and what needs thorough and dispassionate analysis in any community. It opens windows that otherwise would remain shuttered. When most effective, it sets in motion the deliberative governmental responses that will solve a problem; at other times, it mobilizes or enables reformers to point to ex-posés as buttressing the need for changes.[12] Such was the case with Charles Edward Russell, the most prolific of the muckraking writers who wrote on the widest variety of topics. As my chapter on Russell shows (chapter 3, "Muckraking the World's Richest Church"), Russell's three articles on the slum housing of Trinity Church capped a forty-year effort by tenement re-formers to force Trinity to clean up its properties. His angry articles provided the final blow that the church could not withstand. For Russell, who grew up in a small city in Iowa, community was especially important. He could not believe the way people living in tenements were treated and/or ignored by the surrounding community, especially by a church so integral to the lifeblood of lower Manhattan. Moreover, without attention to the needs of the thousands of people living in New York's growing slums, Russell be-lieved crime and disorder would be encouraged. Environment, Russell ar-gued, would not only be a breeding ground for disease, but also would produce a community of antisocial toughs. The goodness in man's heart would be overwhelmed by the evil of neighborhood conditions. Typical of Progressives, Russell was optimistic that the environment could be re-made and re-formed.[13] A dose of facts in front of the public would do the trick.

The optimistic muckrakers seemed to be motivated by a variety of inspi-rations beyond faith in the public, however. Agnes Hooper Gottlieb shows in chapter 4 ("Women and Exposé: Reform and Housekeeping") that the environment on a much smaller scale propelled some of the muckrakers, women who saw needs around their homes, needs that affected their chil-dren, needs that, if exposed, would help their households and protect their families. The community, in essence, was bounded and centered by the home. Bruce J. Evensen, in chapter 1 ("The Muckrakers as Evangelicals") finds religious ideals in much of the muckrakers' work, located in an even smaller community, one found in the heart, that had the potential to radiate to a larger universe. According to mythology, news people are hard-boiled cynics who prefer liquor to salvation. But Evensen finds evidence to the contrary. The fire in the belly that motivated the muckrakers often came from a spiritual core, sharply contrasting with the cruel principles that emanated from a science-based Social Darwinism. He sees the muckrakers as interested in moral regeneration and moral consensus as much as in political and social change.

Religion played a more important role in people's lives at the turn of the century than it does today. While journalism was not a religious calling, many journalists had begun to see it as a profession where they could not only hone their writing skills in preparation for producing fiction but also do important work in service of democratic values and social justice. It becomes problematic, therefore, to reconcile Thomas Leonard's chapter (Chapter 7, "Did the Muckrakers Muck Up Progress?") with the noble and spiritual goals of the muckrakers. Leonard finds that despite their evangelical fervor—or perhaps because of it—the muckrakers painted a bleak picture of the corporate-political alliance in the early 1900s. So bleak was the picture, Leonard argues, that citizens began staying away from the voting booths, a far cry from Roosevelt's fear that people would storm the government gates. Why participate in a system so riddled with moneyed influence? Instead of promoting civic participation, the muckrakers' work became anticivic and dispiriting, he argues. Instead of bringing the public to democracy, journalism was driving people away. As experts seek to explain why voting turnouts for major elections dipped below 50 percent in the 1990s, the Teddy Roosevelt criticism about journalism continues to be voiced today. Maybe public alienation and cynicism is more the fault of the "smelly muckrakers," rather than the fact that government and political leaders have disappointed for four decades. Sensitive to this criticism and fearful that if readers disengaged too much from public affairs they would lose their audience, a segment of the press responded in the 1980s with a call for a new activism. A movement known as civic or public journalism emerged to combat the problem of citizen alienation. A new activism needed to be found, so the argument went, to reenergize the public and foster citizen involvement.[14] This activism would come in the form of a press that was more proactive than reactive in setting the agenda for public discussion, taking the initiative rather than awaiting events.

One could suggest, as I would, however, that a return to the values of the Progressive Era and the sensibility and spirit of the muckrakers—who were indignant, outraged, and passionate—might better help to awaken a sleeping and disinterested public. Already, as sociologist Herbert Gans has found, Progressive Era values continue to endure in journalism. The advocacy of honest, meritocratic, and antibureaucratic government; antipathy to political machines and demagogues; responsible capitalism; celebration of an antiurban pastoral society—all are Progressive ideals that Gans found when he studied the ideology of journalism today. "The Progressive movement is long dead, but many of its basic values and its reformist impulses have persisted," Gans points out.[15] What seems to be missing often, however, is the passion and anger of the muckraking era, replaced, at least in part, by the notions of balance, temperance, and objectivity. Ben Bagdikian, a former editor and ombudsman at the *Washington Post*, is rightfully fearful that timidity and commercialism may have replaced evangelism in the contemporary newsroom. Reporters, he laments, look more like bankers these days, and often view one newsroom simply as a stepping stone to a larger newsroom.[16] How can community be fostered if the journalists simply hop in and out of a community? For that matter, how can community be fostered if the owner is an absentee landlord with dozens of properties and no roots in the community?

Perhaps the solution to both those problems lies in first understanding and then reinvigorating a tradition of journalism that belies and defies profit-oriented publishers and tabloid headline-seeking journalism. That tradition can be found in this book about a 100-year-old journalism movement known as "muckraking." When something is good and important, as well as endlessly interesting, it is worth recalling and understanding. Moreover, more episodes of exposé journalism are still to be unearthed and further connections to the confused quilt that makes up American culture are still to be made. Despite numerous scholarly attempts, a consensus on how to understand and interpret both muckraking and Progressivism has yet to emerge. However, some facts and principles about journalism are clear: When we look at the muckraking era, we find a time when publishers and journalists did not fear rolling up their sleeves and crusading for causes they believed in. We find individuals who were willing to take on rich and powerful interests, at times at their own peril. We find journalists who were fueled by anger at social injustice. We find alliances and blurred lines between journalism and reform politics. We find a public responsive to a stylized written account of corporate and political abuses. We also find confusion about goals and solutions—as well as about journalistic style—befitting the contradictions of both American capitalism and American journalism. The picture of the era of the muckrakers is, in the end, one that is still slightly out of focus. The one thing that *is* clear is that the muckrakers were principled, purposeful, powerful, and progressive—and worth recalling.

NOTES

1. There are various accounts of the muckraking movement. The most reliable and readable is Louis Filler, *The Muckrakers* (University Park: University of Pennsylvania Press, 1976), published originally in 1939 as *Crusaders for American Liberalism*. See also C. C. Regier, *The Era of the Muckrakers* (Chapel Hill: University of

North Carolina Press, 1932), and David M. Chalmers, *The Social and Political Ideas of the Muckrakers* (New York: Citadel, 1964). A good summary of the views and interpretations of muckraking is Harry H. Stein, "American Muckrakers and Muckraking: The 50-Year Scholarship," *Journalism Quarterly* 56 (spring 1979): 9–17, and Filler, "The Muckrakers in Flower and Failure," in *Essays in American Historiography*, ed. Harvey Shapiro (Boston: Heath and Co., 1968).

2. Phillips' articles are reprinted in *The Treason of the Senate*, ed. George Mowry and Judson A. Grenier (Chicago: Quadrangle Books, 1964), which has a fine introduction by Mowry and Grenier. The articles are analyzed also in Robert Miraldi, "The Journalism of David Graham Phillips," Ph.D. diss., New York University, 1985, 242–275, and Miraldi, "The Journalism of David Graham Phillips," *Journalism Quarterly* 63, 1 (spring 1986): 83–88.

3. Russell makes this comment in a letter to the *New York Times*. "Trinity's Tenements," May 8, 1909, 279. On Russell's father the editor, see Russell, *A Pioneer Editor in Early Iowa: A Sketch of the Life of Edward Russell* (Washington, D.C.: Ransdell Inc., 1941).

4. The speech is reprinted verbatim in Mowry and Grenier, *The Treason of the Senate*, 216–225. A good discussion of the speech's development is in Grenier, "Muckrakers and Muckraking: An Historical Definition," *Journalism Quarterly* 37 (autumn 1960).

5. The muckrakers, wrote Chalmers, "believed that the system was sound and that, with various amounts of tinkering, it would continue to work well." The public simply needed to have the facts set before them and be aroused, he notes in *The Social and Political Ideas of the Muckrakers*, 51.

6. Meg Greenfield, "Why We're Still Muckraking," *Newsweek*, March 25, 1985: 94.

7. Richard Hofstadter, *The Age of Reform: From Bryan to FDR* (New York: Vintage Books, 1955), 23.

8. Chalmers in his introduction to David M. Chalmers, ed., *The Muckraker Years* (New York: P. Van Nostrand, 1974), 27. A similar theme is found in Samuel P. Hays, *The Response to Industrialism, 1885–1914* (Chicago: University of Chicago Press, 1957).

9. See, for example, various new works on muckraking: Samuel V. Kennedy, *Samuel V. Hopkins and the Business of Writing* (Syracuse N.Y.: Syracuse University Press, 1999), and Kennedy's "The Last Muckraker: Samuel Hopkins Adams," Ph.D. diss., Syracuse University, 1993, Edd Applegate, *Journalistic Advocates and Muckrakers: Three Centuries of Crusading Writers* (Jefferson, N.C.: McFarland, 1997); Ellen F. Fitzpatrick, ed., *Three Muckraking; Landmark Articles* (New York: Bedford Books, 1994), and Jessica Ann Dorman, " 'Deliver Me from this Muckrake': The Literary Impulse Behind Progressive Era Muckraking," Ph.D. diss., Harvard University, 1996. As this work was in progress, Steve Weinberg of the University of Missouri was completing a new biography of Ida Tarbell.

10. That muckraking was a continuation of ideals and practices begun before the turn of the century can be seen in Warren T. Francke, "Investigative Exposure in the Nineteenth Century: The Journalistic Heritage of the Muckrakers," Ph.D. diss., University of Minnesota, 1974.

11. Eugene Roberts, "The Finest Reporting Is Always Investigative," *IRE Journal* (winter 1988): 14.

12. The literature on contemporary investigative reporting is still emerging. However, see David L. Protess, et al. *The Journalism of Outrage: Investigative Reporting and Agenda Building in America* (New York: Guilford Press, 1991), and Margaret Jones Patterson and Robert H. Russell, *Behind the Lines: Case Studies in Investigative Reporting* (New York: Columbia University Press, 1986).

13. The literature on the Progressive Era is vast, and it is an oversimplification perhaps to say that there was a typical Progressive. Overview accounts of the Progressive Era include William O'Neill, *The Progressive Years* (Chicago: University of Chicago Press, 1957), and Irwin Unger and Debi Unger, *The Vulnerable Years: The United States, 1896–1917* (New York: New York University Press, 1977).

14. There are various discussions of public or civic journalism. See Jay Rosen and David Merrit Jr., *Public Journalism: Theory and Practice* (Dayton, Ohio: Kettering Foundation, 1994); Arthur Charity, *Doing Public Journalism* (New York: Guilford, 1996); Jay Black, ed., *Mixed News: The Public/Civic/Communitarian Journalism Debate* (Mahwah, N.J.: Erlbaum, 1997); and Jay Rosen, "Community Connectedness: Passwords for Public Journalism," *Poynter Papers* 3 (St. Petersburg, Fla.: The Poynter Institute for Media Studies, 1993): 1–21.

15. Herbert Gans, "The Progressive Spirit Today," *The Quill* 72, 10 (November 1984), 22.

16. Ben Bagdikian, *Media Monopoly*, 4th ed. (Boston: Beacon Press, 1992), 212–216.

1

The Muckrakers as Evangelicals

Bruce J. Evensen

Newspaper reporters have long had the reputation of being hard-boiled cynics, boisterous, irreverent, full of themselves and whiskey. They are suspicious of those in power and too critical of those who operate the wheels of commerce. On a Sunday morning, they are more likely to be found sleeping it off than attending religious services. What motivates them, it is said, is a notch in the reportorial belt and a blaring yellow headline. So much for the clichés. Enter a different reality, as pictured by Bruce J. Evensen who meticulously combs the writings, letters and papers of seven selected turn-of-the-century muckraking writers—Upton Sinclair, Lincoln Steffens, William Allen White, Edwin Markham, Ida Tarbell, Ray Stannard Baker, and S. S. McClure. What he finds confounds the clichés about journalistic motivation for Evensen finds a deep spirituality—and lifelong conflicts about God's desire for mankind—in the muckraking journalists. In the end, Evensen concludes that the crusades and exposés of the muckrakers were not motivated by the cash register or personal gain, but by an evangelical fervor. For many muckrakers, journalism was a higher calling. This chapter appeared originally in 1989 and is reprinted with permission of *American Journalism*, a publication of the American Journalism Historians Association.

"Oh, God, give me faith. Oh, God, lead me out of this valley of depression. Oh, God, I am fearful and downcast, help me today to do my work bravely. I try to do large things, too large for me; I am not willing to be simple, straightforward, humble. I am terrified to speak generalities, to judge men and women by appearances, not realizing that they too, are having a bitter struggle within themselves. I am tempted to attack, not to press forward with positive faith. Oh, God, take me out of this. Oh, God, let me see and feel thy constant presence, let me feel my connections with thee and through thee with all of my neighbors."[1]

The prayer is that of Ray Stannard Baker, one of the most prominent of the muckrakers, and the meditation appears in a 1908 notebook, which was written at the height of muckraking agitation for a better America. What makes the statement so illuminating is not its moral thrust, for historians have seen that impulse at work in the reformers' call to action. What chroniclers have paid insufficient attention to is the vital struggle of faith that appears at the center of many of the muckrakers' personal lives and how this warfare became externalized in their writings.

This essay analyzes the private and public writings of seven muckrakers in the context of the evangelical origins of this remarkable group of men and women. In doing so, the researcher is reminded of the dangers of over-simplification, of Lincoln Steffens' warning to Upton Sinclair on the occasion of Edmund Wilson's muckraking of the muckrakers more than fifty years ago. "The fact that he lumps us is a bad sign," Steffens wrote, joking that they consider killing the critic and pleading self-defense.[2] Fearing a similar fate, this research will attempt to portray seven of these muckrakers as individuals, who shared a common context, which in turn produced a literature as rich and complex as the men and women who wrote it.

A half-century's research on the muckrakers has found no shortage of opinions on who they were and what they intended.[3] Historical interpretation of the muckrakers' work basically has divided over the question of whether the muckrakers were "liberal social reformers" or "conservative advocates of middle-class values and interests." The debate arose in the post–World War II generation of historians who placed the muckrakers in the broader context of the debate then underway over "consensus" and "class conflict." The effect of the discussion was to diminish the role of the muckrakers as moral crusaders and to see them instead as self-interested defenders of the status quo.[4]

What these frames of reference have tended to overlook is what the muckrakers saw themselves doing and the deeply personal struggle over faith that informed their work. Two historians, Richard Hofstadter and Harold Wilson, have argued that the muckrakers were attempting to achieve an "unselfish consensus" based on "Protestant and Social Gospel norms."[5] But the Hofstadter hypothesis, later developed by other historians, saw this popular appeal as a pretext through which the muckrakers attempted to fend off changes brought by industrialization and immigration, which threatened their social positions.[6] Wilson similarly sees a sociological explanation behind muckraking agitations. They were driven as well, he writes, by a morality of absolutes which confused the fragmentation stemming from immigration, the concentration of wealth, and the rise of the cities, with a deterioration in the old order familiar to them.[7]

Wilson attempts to show that this "morality of absolutes" stemmed from the muckrakers' abandonment of the faith of their fathers and their conversion to Social Darwinism. This transformation, he suggests, took place with "remarkable ease" and led to a "radical social Christianity" which was the synthesis of Darwinian determinism and the altruism of the Golden Rule. The muckrakers "swept divinity" and "inspiration" aside in "heralding a new social order" which was essentially mechanistic. Human society, led by a divine "force," was evolving progressively. The purpose of law and governments was to recognize this transformation and to develop policies and institutions to move matters along.[8]

An analysis of the diaries, notebooks, and private papers of several leading muckrakers casts doubt on whether they embraced Social Darwinism with "remarkable ease" and brings into perspective the inner conflicts which lay behind the public proclamation of their progressivism. The battle they waged was not so much that people should have faith but to describe what that faith should be. For some of the muckrakers the higher criticism of the Bible had shaken the certainty of the old-time religion. Their challenge then became finding an absolute to substitute for a belief in the Bible as the inspired Word of God, something that could arouse a generation to right thinking and right conduct. It is perhaps the final paradox of the progressive period that those who tried to teach others how to live were forever searching for the same answers themselves.

S. S. McCLURE: A PROGRESSIVE PILGRIM

The process of spiritual seeking and uncertainty is nowhere more apparent than in the life of Samuel Sidney McClure, the founder of the progenitor muckraking magazine. McClure remembered only three books from his Ulster home—a Bible, *Foxe's Book of Martyrs*, and *Pilgrim's Progress*. His Presbyterian parents, he writes in his autobiography, had been caught up in a revival that had swept Northern Ireland in 1859. The experience had changed their lives by returning them to the "simple teachings of the early church." His father's death and his mother's poverty weighed heavily upon him when he arrived in Galesburg, Illinois, with fifteen cents in his pocket. At Knox College he would find a "Purpose" for his life.[9]

"Forms wax old and perish," he wrote in his class notes. "Principles are eternal." Principles of "right and wrong" necessarily had their foundation in teaming up with God in the battle over His creation. "We see that we are engaged in a terrible conflict," he wrote, following his studies of the Apostle Paul, "not with flesh and blood, but with principalities and powers and the rulers of the darkness of this world." He was sure that "though strife be long, yet slowly and surely it will end with the glorious triumph of the right."[10]

There were two great facts of civilization as McClure saw it—the individual and the state. The latter existed solely for the former, even as the human soul existed only for God. God would equip the "sensitive, shrinking, quivering soul" to fight His battles for Him. For God had placed into the hearts of those who followed him an "enthusiasm" for service. It was only through such service that one's self was brought into proper view. Individuality consisted of following "enthusiastically" the pathway of service God had for man.[11]

It was in June of 1893, the month the bottom dropped out of the stock market and the panic spread westward from Wall Street, that McClure published the first number of his monthly magazine. Though it would be a decade before the publication would take on the appearance of a muckraking journal, McClure saw it as having a high purpose from the outset. In April 1894, while in Paris searching for literary material for the magazine, he wrote his wife that he saw himself "playing for high stakes." He reported that he was in an "awful condition" and owed "heaps of money everywhere." He had not even paid his church dues, yet he felt himself on the edge of a great breakthrough. The Lord had some "great work" for him to do.[12]

As McClure sifted through various ideas to make the magazine more attractive, his wife warned him to be true to his high ideals and not to sacrifice the magazine to commercial interests. McClure's statement of policy throughout this period remained high-minded. His May 1894 issue, which featured a piece on American evangelist Dwight L. Moody, told readers the magazine was endeavoring to "reflect the moving spirit of this time" by setting forth the achievements of the "great men of the day" and the "human struggle for existence and development."[13]

It was not only McClure's wife, but also his mother, Elizabeth, who expressed concern that the magazine aim for still higher purposes. In January 1895, she wrote him that her time on the earth was now "short." She therefore encouraged her son to publish only the work of men "sound in God's word." If her son wanted to bring "honor and glory to God" there was "only one way to do it." And that was "God's way." Her son needed to find "God's will." The magazine could be an instrument for that will, but she feared her son might miss this chance through lack of prayer and failure to "study God's will." Her greatest delight would be to have her son "if possible" follow the steps of his parents, so that whatever he did, he would do it "for God."[14]

By the end of the year, McClure could boast that circulation had risen from 45,000 to 80,000. Along with John S. Phillips, an old college classmate and now his chief editor, he promised "noble entertainment" and "worthy knowledge" designed to "uplift, refresh and encourage all who read it."[15]

While it has been suggested that McClure turned to muckraking to boost circulation, his greatest gains in readership had taken place years earlier, thanks in large part to Ida Tarbell's series on Abraham Lincoln. Tarbell's writing, readers were promised, would be both "entertaining and carefully considered." It would rely on materials that had been gathered directly from "original sources," from Lincoln personally as well as from the president's own writings and correspondences.[16] *McClure's Magazine* sold out in November and December 1895, having shown a gain of 175,000 in circulation since the series started and closing out the year with a readership of over 300,000. McClure wrote that his soul seemed finally "at rest." The "days of struggle" seemed over. He was now happy with his God.[17]

Tarbell's Lincoln portrait and the publicity surrounding the series idealized him as a perfect type while satisfying McClure's need to offer his readers a leader worthy of emulation. The piece celebrated Lincoln's pioneering origin and made much of the fact that he came from the stock of a "pioneering race of men and women." He had emerged from an ideal past where "lessons learned in early school out in the forest were grand and good." Everything around and about Lincoln "was just as it came from the hands of the Creator." It produced a remarkable President, who had celebrated democratic sacrifice at Gettysburg and the ideal of liberty when he emancipated the slaves. It was then, *McClure's* reported, that "God knew that he was good."[18]

McClure's Lincoln series was more than a circulation-building device. It was McClure's effort at constructing an ideal type, someone who had "striven with God" in the "glorious triumph of the right." When McClure returned to Knox College after his election to the board of trustees, he remarked that it had been thirty-eight years since Lincoln had last addressed a Galesburg audience. "What a legacy to our people," he commented, "was the memory of Lincoln." Soon the time would come when "no one living shall have seen Lincoln." That is why it was necessary to remind this and future generations what he stood for. Integrity, honor, and truthfulness had emanated from "his very soul." This generation needed heroes like that.[19]

Just after the Lincoln series, McClure wrote Phillips an excited letter. He reported "stumbling on" what would probably be "the most important publishing venture of our time." A long-awaited new translation of the Bible had just appeared. Its whole purpose had been to "re-discover the Bible, to make it really understandable . . . an indispensable book to all who believed in the Bible."[20] As originally conceived, the Bible series would run in twenty parts over four years.

Within weeks, McClure booked passage to Palestine ostensibly to find background material for the series. His letters to his wife reveal the journey to have been a personal odyssey of faith. Passing through each of the seven gates of the Old City of Jerusalem, McClure marveled that "God was here as a man, and I can't get away from that." Days later he reported that he was "reading and re-reading the gospels." He never knew the Bible to be "so fascinating." He was now convinced as never before that "God approves of our work."[21]

The years leading up to McClure's muckraking were filled with this endless stream of hope balanced by periods of ambivalence and skepticism. His ceaseless efforts at entering into fellowship with men of like-minded faith finished only in frustration. "I attended a Salvation Army preaching service," he wrote his wife. "It was bad." Booth's great army kept shouting "that God was there and at work, though they didn't seem to really believe it. It made me sad."[22] Throughout what remained of the nineties, the magazine described its purpose as offering month-to-month "transcription" of the times, encouraging the building up the nation's "moral self-respect." McClure wrote that while his was not a "religious magazine," no "Christian family" should be without it. McClure advertised himself as offering the family something to live by and for.[23] At century's end, McClure wrote his wife how "aware" he had been of God's blessing. And she wrote him how convinced she was that there was yet "some special work" he would do to "help bring the world back to God."[24]

McClure was now poised at the beginning of his career as the country's greatest muckraking publisher. It was a period of acute financial and personal hardship that would ultimately lead to his surrender of the magazine and the dashing of his hopes to build a publishing empire through it. "The year 1902 has been the most prosperous in the history of *McClure's Magazine*," he told his readers, while writing his wife the magazine was "starved" for funds.[25] Muckraking had made no immediate impact in circulation patterns and was expensive to do properly. "I'm having my usual breakdown," he wrote his wife, in another of his talent hunts in Europe. Ida Tarbell, he later told his wife, would be her "mainstay" in the event of his death.[26]

McClure proved a very lively corpse. The next decade would see muckraking cause a minor sensation, and McClure for a short time rode the crest of it, dining with President Roosevelt and Alexander Graham Bell, while addressing large audiences on the dangers that lurked all around them. In January 1904, he told the Twentieth Century Club in Brooklyn that nationwide those who broke the law conspired to put in office those "who let them." Machines existed in nearly every American city, and they operated to benefit some at the expense of others. Machine politics had left America "at the bottom of all civilized countries." Major corporations led in the "lawlessness." The people needed to rise and "protect" themselves. And that was what *McClure's* was in business to help them do.[27] Years later he told the New York branch of the YMCA the same thing. "The whole function of government," he observed, had been "to protect those who could not protect themselves." Beginning with Tarbell's attack on the Standard Oil Trust, he told them, "we have fought for those unable to defend themselves."[28]

A generation later, as historians began to write their summaries of the Progressive period in American history and the magazine which had tirelessly promoted its program, McClure wrote Tarbell that critics had gotten it all wrong. His "overwhelming passion" with the magazine had been to make it "as perfect as possible" by laying out a series of principles through which partial men could be made whole.[29]

TARBELL'S "RELIGION"

McClure maintained a lifelong friendship with Ida Tarbell, the first of the muckrakers, and a woman whose spiritual sensibilities were closest to his. Like McClure, Tarbell wrote extensively about the forces that formed her. She described herself as having been raised in a God-fearing western Pennsylvania family, rigorous not only in its church attendance, but also prayer meetings and revivals. She had received Christ at age 11. The life of prayer which followed aroused "self-observation," and this took her to the literature of Darwin and Spencer.[30] After serving as preceptress at the Poland Union Seminary in Poland, Ohio, where she taught geology and botany, she went to France, to continue both her studies and her spiritual search. The early nineties found her still attempting to reconcile her "need to feel and to know."[31]

On the eve of McClure's offer to join his staff, she remembered that she was "continuing [her] search for God in the great cathedrals of Europe." She later explained the impact this spiritual quest had on her muckraking career. It grew out of a childlike "conviction of divine goodness at work in the world." Despite the growing sense of life's injustice and ugliness, she could not shake an "inward certainty" that the "central principle of things is beneficence." This "serene, stable self-assurance" had a "hold" on Tarbell. It remained even as she embraced Darwinian evolution and lost the sense that God had a "human outline."[32]

Tarbell expressed little patience with the fundamentalist-modernist argument then permeating the church. She thought herself "outside" that quarrel. One's works and character reflected "true spirituality." Christianity was simply the "best system" because it was based on the "brotherhood of man." Political institutions consistent with that divine purpose were good. Those that operated on the basis of a different set of ethics were dangerous.[33] When she accepted McClure's offer and returned to America, she was immediately struck by the changes that had taken place during her absence of several years. What she most feared now, she wrote, was that "we were raising our standard of living at the expense of our standard of character." She was convinced that "personal human betterment" necessarily rested on a "sound moral basis" as well as a "personal search for the meaning of the mystery of God."[34]

Tarbell's personal search for answers to that mystery was at the center of her muckraking. It shaped her notion of how a "decent and useful person" could be formed and later could learn to function in a social system antagonistic to individual dignity. Her "History of the Standard Oil Company" serialized in *McClure's Magazine* was a revelation of the evil at work in human society. John D. Rockefeller employed "force and fraud, sly tricks and special privilege to get his way." His activities were only a symptom of a phenomenon that went deeper. Blackmail was becoming a "natural part" of business practice. The result, she found, was not only a "leech" on the public pocket, but the "contamination of commerce." Only the principles of Christian fair play, she argued, could transform business practice and make it a "fit pursuit for our young men."[35]

Biographers might charge that Tarbell's "greatest miscalculation" was that she relied on the Golden Rule too much and the law not enough in bringing about change, but what they fail to appreciate fully is how Tarbell, McClure, and other muckrakers understood their primary role and the intensely spiritual environment in which that fervor arose. Tarbell was not indifferent to the need for legal reform; but like her fellow muckrakers, she understood the central importance moral regeneration and moral consensus played in creating a human community in which democratic institutions could be allowed to work. Amelioration of "human sufferings, inequalities, greed, ignorance," she wrote, did not come through law alone, but was as well a fundamental matter of the human heart.[36]

She saw her whole life as having been spent in "striving in solitude and silence to enter into a fuller understanding of the divine." But that understanding, she insisted, was the only means by which the "moral diseases" which so afflicted the age—pride, greed, hypocrisy, cruelty, irreverence, and cowardliness—could be overcome. If the Bible gave men and women anything, it gave them a conception of how they ought to live. What is more, it showed them a way in which "the essential brotherhood of man" could be brought into being. She was convinced it came by bearing witness to an "Inner Light" that, if encouraged to develop, was solely capable of binding men to other men. Men would either "hunger and thirst after righteousness, mercy, meekness, and purity of heart," she wrote, or give way to the "poisonous" selfishness implicit in modern living. Her writing had been to call people to righteousness and to show them a means of how they might establish "right conduct" for themselves and their communities.[37]

BAKER'S SPIRITUAL UNREST

McClure's publication in January 1903 of the third installment of Tarbell's series on Standard Oil coincided with Lincoln Steffens' exposé on Minneapolis political practices and Ray Stannard Baker's attack on corrupt labor practices. The edition was billed as an analysis of the American "contempt" for law, and it was to do much in igniting Baker's forty-year fire for progressive causes. It was a career that would take him from *McClure's* to the *American Chronicle*; to a career as the author of best-selling fiction; and finally, to a career as aide to, and biographer of, Woodrow Wilson. This extraordinary progression was punctuated by flashes of both spiritual certainty and unrest and a life consciously led in service to God.

Baker recalled that in the Bible with which he had been brought up in St. Croix Falls, Wisconsin, his parents had highlighted the phrase, "in the sweat of thy face thou shalt eat bread." Rigorous self-discipline became a life's commitment. "I read. I studied," he wrote. From an early age he felt, as Tarbell did, "the essential truth of the teachings of Christ."[38] His father, educated at Oberlin, helped matters along. Ray earned a silver dollar from his father for finishing *Pilgrim's Progress* while in grade school.[39]

Perhaps no future muckraker had a firmer foundation laid in religious life than did Baker. Sunday in St. Croix Falls was a day entirely set apart. Sunday school and church in the morning were followed by a study of the scriptures in the afternoon, and, at six o'clock, an evening service. In addition, there were weekly Thursday evening prayer meetings in which the Bakers took the leading role.[40] "Plow deeply, till thoroughly," he recalled his father telling him as he prepared to begin his career in journalism. "Scatter the seed with care and the harvest will be all you hoped for."[41]

Like other muckrakers, Baker fought a "spiritual unrest" in his lifetime as he attempted to reconcile his old familiar faith with the higher criticism then engulfing much of the church. Like Tarbell, he sought the silence of personal rumination, even sequestering himself in an Arizona desert for a time, to carry on in private his crisis in personal faith. "I was brought up a Presbyterian," he later observed, "but I liked being a Quaker best. When the talk began I was usually not so certain. I found myself descending from the high places." Darwin's theories of evolution and natural selection had put him "much at sea as to what I should believe." The serpent, he said of his mental confusion, "began to tempt me."[42] Baker traced his "literature of exposure" to his encounters with William T. Stead in Chicago.[43] The evangelist's efforts to "clean up" that city mobilized Baker's "spirit of service" and put him on a muckraking path of "earnest endeavor." Baker's biographer sees the whole of that career as stemming from a moralism which was "deep-seated, almost inexplicable, and which remained the basis of a lifetime of action."[44]

Baker's muckraking attack on the churches of his day along with his own private notebooks and papers gives the clearest idea of how his personal "journey of faith" formed a framework for his public writing. His criticism of New York City's Trinity Church, the nation's wealthiest congregation, was broadened into a critique of the "malaise" which had fallen over the

Christian community. The problem was that the churches "lacked a moral vision" and did not know what they believed. They knew nothing of "social justice" and as a consequence had "no message for the common man." Baker's visits to many of the leading churches convinced him that they had a "passion for efficiency" but "no real purpose." The churches had come to appreciate the "crisis" they were in and were now trying to "get back to the people." They were throwing money at the problem of community relations when it was not money but "the human touch" that was required.[45]

Wilson has suggested that Baker and many of his fellow muckrakers became good Social Darwinists and "swept aside" the need for a personal, active faith. But Baker states explicitly in *The Spiritual Unrest* that the churches had a dual mission—both to the individual and to the community. This recognition is reiterated throughout his notebooks, where he argues that "individual salvation" and "community salvation" are "complementary and reciprocal."[46]

Publicly, Baker held up the work of Walter Rauschenbusch as a theology that could lead to the church's acceptance of its "new social mission" which sought to "save man and his society." Baker's criticism of the old evangelism was that it had not been "selfless" enough. Rauschenbusch's message had been to show that sin not only affects an individual's relationship to God but also his relationship to others. Repentance required turning away from sin not for the sake of oneself alone but for the sake of the community in which one lived. In this human community, Christ was the ultimate exemplar. His life alone gave the pattern upon which the church could hope to "magnify" itself. That pattern called for a church which "touched its neighbors" thereby strengthening the community's "fragility of faith."[47]

Baker's own efforts show how seriously he took the question of community worship in the moral upbuilding of his society. Here his "righteous indignation," as Tarbell called it, could be put to work providing communicants a sense of shared values and mutual responsibility. How could men be their brother's keepers, he wondered, if they did not know that they were brothers? What the church now needed were "Elijahs" willing to "imitate the life of Christ." This required risks and "sacrifice."[48]

Baker saw Woodrow Wilson as an Elijah offering Americans a course of action rooted in communitarian responsibility. Baker wrote that he was bewildered by the "fixity" of the president's "immovable faith" while feeling at the same time a certain "envy." He saw in the "certainty" of Wilson's "rock-like faith" the "creative impulse" with which the new administration could defeat the powers of "bossism" and "venality," as well as the "wretched conditions which had become the American way of life."[49]

In one of his notebooks, Baker admitted to a certain lifelong agitation behind the creative energy of his work. He had never denied the "reality of spiritual things" or the "essential unity" of the "inner voice" available to all men; but what did that have to do with Christ's personal call on his life,

and the lives of others? It appeared that Christ "depended on us" for doing
his work on the earth, he wrote. Christ had obtained a "unity with God"
which Baker had desperately sought in his own life and which he had sought
to make possible in the lives of others. A year before his death, he wrote
that the effort had not been without its frustrations. "Each age," he supposed, "must worship its own thought of God." Baker remembered that as
a boy, the "face" of God had ever been before him. As an adult, he feared,
he would never see His face again. In old age, he saw God's handiwork
everywhere about him.[50]

LINCOLN STEFFENS AND THE McNAMARA CASE

"I have been contending all my life," Lincoln Steffens wrote at the end
of his autobiography, "and always with God." The man considered the preeminent muckraking writer saw all the cities and states he had muckraked
as being part of but a single story. "They had different names, dates and
locations," he wrote, "but the essential facts were all described by Christ in
the New Testament." Jesus had known the "worthlessness of the good people," Steffens was sure. Like Christ's, his had been a lifelong mission to save
a world indifferent to life-giving instruction.[51]

Steffens, a veteran newspaperman when he came to the *McClure's* group,
crucified municipal government in "The Shame of the Cities" series. He
reported how he had soured on the "best people" when he saw that "the
law-abiding backbones of our society, in city after city, start out for moral
reform, but turn back" when they saw it would cost them something. Christianity alone, he became convinced, provided the only possibility of real
reform. It conveyed a faith, a hope, but more crucially a "vision" of how to
act.[52]

As was the case with many of the other muckrakers, Steffens came to his
moral sensibility early in life. His conversion seems to have skipped a generation. Contemporaries described his grandfather, the Reverend Joseph
Steffens, as a "bold defender of the faith once delivered to the saints." The
parents of Lincoln Steffens, however, appear to have been nominal Christians who went to church out of "social habit." Nevertheless, Steffens took
a liking to Sunday school and, under the moral instruction of a California
neighbor, read the Bible seriously in his early and midteens, even planning
a career in the ministry.[53]

Steffens' parents "followed his conversion patiently" as his intellect led
him away from the institutional church. He was beginning to find that "even
though the music was wet, the sermon was dry." Like Tarbell, he went to
Europe, ostensibly to study, but not incidentally to find a more satisfactory
basis for his faith. In Berlin, he attended a nondenominational American
church and wrote home that he was becoming suspicious of "hot-house
Christians." Those who had a "thoughtful comprehension of the full mean-

ing and true spirit of Christ" had come to the knowledge gradually and reasonably. The following year, he wrote his father from Heidelberg that he had received a letter from his sister, asking about becoming a Catholic. He urged restraint. She was in greater danger of rejecting the divinity of Christ, he wrote his father, than of turning to the Catholics.[54]

The day before he died, Steffens, writing a preface to a collection of his works, said he always understood himself to be a "teacher." In the days when he had "breathed the news" he had in mind giving his readers life-saving instruction. Speaking for the historical record, he argued that Old Testament writers were the original muckrakers. The trouble was, in New Testament times, ministers had never taught the true message of Christ to the Christians.[55]

Muckraking, Steffens once observed, had not gone far enough in proposing solutions to the corruption of the nation's political system. The problem was not to replace "bad men" with "good men" but to work for fundamental economic reforms that would prevent the perpetuation of a government of privilege. Steffens chafed under McClure's admonition to "find the facts" and to leave the interpretations to others. His career at *McClure's* and the *American* was characterized by his continuing efforts to have his colleagues recognize what he saw as fundamental to any campaign of reform.[56]

In December of 1909, he wrote his mother that he was finally coming to terms with the "self-doubts" that had so long plagued his work. He was now working on the "biggest thing I've ever tackled"—a series of articles on the life of Jesus. "I want to tell Christians," he wrote her, "what their Christ said they should do." He admitted that while he could not "accept it all myself," he was prepared to show how Christ could "solve" the problems of the cities and their corrupt administrations. "I can't expect to convert the Christian Church to Christianity," he told her, "but I can show what would happen if they would but believe."[57]

The articles were never written, but Steffens' intentions are important in understanding his involvement in the McNamara case and its aftermath. The McNamara brothers had gone on trial in the fall of 1911 for bombing the *Los Angeles Times* building which killed twenty-one persons. Steffens appears to have intervened on the brothers' behalf in part because of his friendship with their attorney, Clarence Darrow, but also because he thought by doing so he could focus international attention on the causes of the bombing and his plan to prevent future episodes of similar violence.

Steffens succeeded in obtaining a confession from the brothers, in exchange, he thought, for a ruling that all charges be dropped against them. His real scheme had been to lay before the court and the assembled press his notion that the "application of the Golden Rule" was crucial to future labor-business relations, for without it, the country ran the risk of perishing in civil strife. But the deal fell apart: James McNamara received a sentence of life imprisonment and his brother John, who had headed the Structural Iron Workers, received a sentence of six to twelve years. Steffens bitterly blamed the outcry from the churches on the eve of sentencing for turning public opinion against him and spent the rest of his life seeking pardons for the McNamaras.[58]

Before the trial he had observed that his "drift toward Christianity" had been triggered by his "systematic search" for remedies to the problem of city management. He had studied socialism; anarchism; the single tax; and, from time to time, the Bible. He was "amazed" at the teachings of Jesus which seemed "new" to him. Jesus saw and understood, he wrote, what Christians did not. He knew the "evils" of society, and he knew their "cure." What was needed was spiritual renewal of the individual, leading to the application of the Golden Rule to society.[59]

But the McNamara case had shown him he had misunderstood the enemy. Steffens' attack on the institutional church was far more severe than that of Baker and far more personal than that of his friend Upton Sinclair. The "Christian world" leaps on men when they are down, he sadly wrote. "We meant to have them forgiven," he said of the McNamaras, but "all the church wanted was their blood. It makes me sick." At the height of his disillusion, Steffens wrote his family, "I'm getting lots of letters from clergymen. They may be right. It is possible that Christianity will not work. I may have to admit it. If I must, I shall, you know."[60]

Steffens was now muckraked in the press under the title "Golden Rule Steffens." He retaliated by wearing a small gold cross from his watch chain, calling himself "the only Christian on earth." Even from his vantage point, many years after the experience, Steffens observed that Christianity could not be found in its churches. What they preached instead was "hate and disappointed revenge."[61]

Steffens' remaining years were spent courting communism, finding it the only "true" Christianity, and in defending its "necessary" violence. His project on the life of Jesus remained unfinished, and an anticipated work on the life of Satan hardly was begun. He saw a consistency of outlook in the trail he had taken from muckraking to Marxism. "Religion" remained forever central to his thinking and work. "From religion my reason would never be emancipated," he observed late in life. "By it I was conformed to my generation and made to share its moral standards and ideals." Early assumptions concerning "good and evil," "virtue and vice," remained his mind's measure of all things and the framework for his entire endeavor.[62]

THE MAN WITH THE "CHRIST COMPLEX"

Shortly after the publication of Lincoln Steffens' *The Shame of the Cities*, the author received a visit in his office from Upton Sinclair. "What you report," Sinclair told him, "is enough to make a complete picture of the system, but you seem not to see it. Don't you see it? Don't you see what you are showing?"[63]

Over the years, the two men's programs for reform were perhaps more closely alike than any of the other muckrakers. While Sinclair stopped at socialism, Steffens went on to advocating communism as a means of solving the structural problems of capitalist society. Despite the divergence, the men maintained an active and respectful correspondence for more than thirty years. From the first, they had shared a certain spiritual kinship. Still early in his career when Sinclair sent Steffens a copy of his *Cry for Justice*, Steffens understood it to be a "Bible for the faithful."[64] Of the criticisms Sinclair suffered in his long career, the one he received most gladly was the charge he suffered from a "Christ complex." Sinclair reportedly answered without embarrassment, "The world needs a Jesus more than it needs anything else."[65]

Like McClure, Tarbell, Baker, and Steffens, Sinclair lived into old age and left an autobiography to describe the impulses that formed his muckraking and led to the publication of *The Jungle*, his sensational indictment of the meatpacking industry. Though he had always considered ancestors a "bore," Sinclair's relatives claimed royal descent from English roots and his great-grandfather was apparently Commodore Arthur Sinclair, who had fought in the first American naval battle after the Revolution. Sinclair commented that a history of his ancestors read a little like "the history of the American Navy."[66]

By the time Sinclair was born in September 1878, the family's fortunes had faded through the ravages of the Civil War and on "a sea of liquor." Sinclair's father came from a family in which four "gentlemen of the Old South" had turned drunks. His earliest memories were of his father going off as a whiskey salesman and coming home drunk. Sinclair remembered his boyhood homes as a succession of "sordid" rooming houses he shared with a status-seeking mother, who appeared determined to make him an Episcopal bishop. "I became a dreamer," he wrote. "When I was 17 I came to the conclusion that Providence must have some special purpose in keeping me in the world."[67]

It was a horrific world tied to his father's unending drinking cycles. Upton remembered the father's constant prayers seeking forgiveness, the father's ongoing promises that he would stay sober, and his heart-rending debacles. As an adolescent, Sinclair remembered fishing his father out of bars and hearing the old man say his salvation had been "lost," because he had "fallen again."[68]

Sinclair saw those early years through the eyes of faith, and it made him in life, by his own admission, a hopeless idealist. By 15, he was an "ardent little Episcopal boy" teaching Sunday school classes at a church in New York. He went to church every afternoon during Lent, "not because I was told to," he later wrote, "but because I wanted to." He had read his Bible "straight through," and while writing in his seventies remembered that "its language and imagery" had ever been "a part of me." The church gave a "moral earnestness" to the problems of human life that formed the basis of his lifelong struggle for social justice.[69]

Sinclair had supported himself as a writer since the age of sixteen. In these early years he wrote his mother that he would see to it that they never again lived in vermin-infested rooming houses, making her a promise that he could keep. He assured her, "Whether you believe it or not, God's in heaven, who made this world." Sinclair wondered if He knew "what this life is all about anyhow." He hoped that there might be "a higher motive in this world than the love of money" and "a higher end than getting it."[70]

He wrote dime novels for cheap magazines to help finance his schooling at the City College of New York and Columbia University. There he began his lifelong "lover's quarrel" with the church, producing in 1918 *The Profits of Religion*. Whether muckraking the churches or the meatpacking industry, Sinclair measured all men by his "impossibly high standards of honor, continence, honesty, Christianity and truthfulness." He observed, "We have a continent with a hundred million educated people, materially prosperous but spiritually starving. I would be willing to wager that if I announced I had a visit from God last night and I communicated a new revelation from it, I could have a temple, a university, and a million dollars within five years at the outside."[71] Sinclair privately wrote that he felt he had been born "to reform." He told fellow muckraker Edwin Markham, "I want to give every second of my time and of my thought and every ounce of my energy to the worship of my God and to the uttering of the unspeakable message that I know he has given me." His muckraking attack in *The Jungle* was a part of that message. He "poured" into it all the "tears and anguish and pain" that he had known in life. His *Cry for Justice*, written in 1915, was an anthology of social protest that could serve as a "Bible" for the "discouraged and wounded" in their struggle against the economic institutions that oppressed them.[72]

One of those institutions, as he saw it, was the church. While Sinclair never abandoned his belief that organized religion was a bastion of "predatory, capitalist interest," this opinion never led him to abandon his personal faith in God, nor his certainly that Christ's teachings were the ultimate way to social betterment. Sinclair believed God had given him "a vision real to my fellow men," a vision of a better world, in which "courage, resolution and hope" animated the activities of men in their behavior to other men. That was the only real hope for civic betterment. Sinclair was sure God had put him on earth to share that vision with his fellow men.[73]

THE MAN WITH THE HOE

"I have a deep interest in your social gospel," the muckraking poet Edwin Markham wrote Upton Sinclair in May of 1910, "but I think you push it a little too far into the front of the stage."[74] Despite the admonishment,

Markham shared the thrust of Sinclair's social criticism and agreed with Baker and William Allen White that God "required cooperation" in bringing about change in the relations between business and labor and that central to that teaming was the application of the Golden Rule. The publication of his "Man with the Hoe" in 1899 won him worldwide recognition as a fighter on behalf of the working man. The poem itself was heralded as the "battle-cry of the next thousand years."[75] It led to the publication in 1900 of a collection of Markham's poetry and a separate volume which included the famous poem and his commentary on it. Both publications reflected the underlying assumptions of much of the muckraking press in its infancy.

Clearly, Markham saw himself in Millet's depiction of a worker "bowed by the weight of centuries" and leaning over his hoe with the "emptiness of ages in his face" and the "burden of the world" on his back. The youngest child of pioneering parents, Markham never knew his father and quarreled with his mother during "lonely years" of farm and ranch work in Lagoon Valley, California. He saw himself one of the "hoemanry" who worked under "hard and incorrigible conditions." The "smack of the soil" and the "whir of the forge" had ever been in his blood.[76] What the hoeman represented to Markham, and by extension to other muckrakers, was a "type of industrial oppression" found in "all lands and labors." The hoeman was the "symbol of betrayed humanity, the toiler ground down through ages of oppression, through ages of social injustice." His stooped image became a rallying cry for abolishing the "awful degradation of man through endless, hopeless and joyless labor."[77]

It was not the mere poverty of the industrial worker that Markham deplored "but the impossibility of escape from its killing frost." The only solution lay in the recognition of "Christ's work of public and organic righteousness." It was through that work that He sought to save both man and society from themselves. Men had achieved political liberty, but now they had to follow the example of Christ if they were to achieve "industrial freedom" that would only come when "we realize that I am my brother's keeper." Out of that realization would come "cooperation," which Markham, and then White after him, would describe as the "logic of Christianity."[78]

In a thirty-five year career as lecturer following the publication of "Man with the Hoe," Markham called for moral regeneration as the fountainhead for greater social justice. What had been the "purpose of Christ," he asked, "if not the realization of fraternity." That was the "holiest of all words," the word that carried with it the "essence of the gospels" and the "fulfillment of all revelations."[79]

In forty years of writing, Markham never achieved the impact he had with his critique of industrial relations. His work on "Lincoln, the Man of the People" and his crusade against child labor in *The Children of Bondage*, continued his passionate call for social justice. Collections published through

1920, particularly *The Shoes of Happiness* and *The Gates of Paradise*, reflected his continuing assertion that man needed to cooperate with a "divine strategy" if he hoped to live a better life.[80]

In a private notebook, Markham recorded that it was "injustice" that he had "detested most." Men must learn that the only solution to the problem was the "carrying of the Christ-purpose in the heart" or what he called the "inbrothering of men for the common good." He was sure that "in a generation" the application of just such a principle would "cure all our social sorrows." The church should join the writers of the day in pushing a "spirit of reform." He observed, "the saving of men's souls is very closely connected with the amelioration of their social and industrial conditions." The church in the new century needed more than anything else "a baptism of the Holy Spirit," which he believed was the same as saying "Social Spirit."[81]

A THEORY OF SPIRITUAL PROGRESS

Nowhere does the social spirit find a greater champion than William Allen White, the sage of Emporia, Kansas, who first came to the McClure group in 1897 with the publication of his "Boyville" stories and stayed on the national scene as a publicist for progressive causes for more than forty years. It was during his first trip to the East that White had lunch with Theodore Roosevelt at the Army and Navy Club, quickly falling under "the Great Man's spell." What followed was a highly public twenty-year career that White understood as service to the "moral vision" the two men shared. This vision recognized that a "social evolution" was already underway in America and needed to be encouraged by national policymakers. White saw it as a "step-at-a-time process to secure for the working classes, better environment in playgrounds, schools, housing, wages and shop conditions." He reasoned that "after a generation or two of workers bred in the newer, cleaner environment, a new vision will come to the workers—a vision which will justly solve the inequalities of the capitalist system." Unlike Steffens and Sinclair, White remained convinced that "capital may be harnessed for the common good as well as for private" greed.[82]

How that "harnessing" would occur is best described in White's epistle, *A Theory of Spiritual Progress*, published in 1910. White wrote that although the world was hardly a "chocolate éclair," there could be no denying that life on the planet was "outward bound." The choice between life as an "eternal grind" and an "eternal journey" was lived in the context of a society where "the public sense of evildoing was widening." This was a good sign, because "cruelty becomes intolerable as men become aware that it exists." As the "sensibilities" of the common man grew, his capacity for "kindness" grew. His goodwill broadened. His fellow man benefited. People insisted on the passage of laws more closely approximating patterns of social justice. This was the core of White's theory of "spiritual progress."[83]

The theory visualized Darwinian evolution working itself out in societal terms based on the Golden Rule and the character of Jesus Christ. In 1914, White wrote that he believed the world was "growing better" because it was becoming "more and more capable of understanding the social and spiritual message of Jesus Christ." It seemed to him that society was coming to recognize what he had long seen—"that Christ is not only the living God, but the only true growing God in all the world."[84]

White's spiritual intensity appears to have come from his mother, even as his spiritual unrest appears to have been drawn from a conflict lived out between his parents.[85] White's mother had been an early convert to anti-slavery Republicanism, who had moved while a teenager to Galesburg, Illinois. There she witnessed the Lincoln-Douglas debate, falling "platonically in love" with Lincoln. It took ten years of hard work to get her education at Knox College, where she studied under Dr. Albert Hurd, whose daughter married White's sometime boss, S. S. McClure.[86]

White's father was a lifelong Democrat, interested in the political life of Kansas. For a time, he had even served as the mayor of a small town. He had little use for his wife's campaign to civilize their only child, by encouraging his church activities and by reading to him out of the Good Book at night. White idealized his schooling on the Kansas plains. "We sang gospel hymns every morning," he wrote, "and the teacher read a chapter in the Bible. There was no nonsense about that. For we were all little Protestants. She made us say the Lord's prayer after Bible reading, and then we were all started off right for the day. At noon we sang another gospel hymn and loved it."[87]

White's own conversion—his "night of the light"—came during his college days. It left him with a sense that even if the higher criticism was right, and much of the Bible a "myth," there was no getting around who Jesus Christ was: the "greatest hero in history." Human happiness was achieved only to the degree people "made His philosophy a part of human institutions." Jesus had died to save the world by "demonstrating through His crucifixion and the symbol of his resurrection the indestructibility of truth."[88]

The essence of White's social gospel appears to have stemmed from his conviction that the simple application of the Golden Rule in human affairs would regenerate the social order. "I think the job of the church today," he wrote, "is to make a public opinion that will so revolutionize our industry, commerce, and political life that it will be possible for a man to live a generous, useful Christian life without hurt or harm to himself or his family."[89]

While he preached a message of spiritual reconciliation, White, like many of the publicists for progressivism, had a hard time reconciling the old familiar faith with the relativism of the new moral order. The churches were failed institutions. He had only gone to them as a lad, he snapped, to meet pretty girls, and had continued going as a father because he thought it might be good for his children. But a preacher's business was not "any more exalted" as a "calling" than was the work of the newspaperman. The purpose of both, he charged in *The Old Order Changeth*, was to recognize that in the "daily struggle for existence" God was nevertheless "fulfilling himself" in the affairs of man. The growth of democratic institutions had been "God-inspired." The "upward direction" of social change had proved there was a "director."[90]

Theodore Roosevelt was "God's man" because he had "kept the faith" while serving as a role model for how the twentieth-century man should act in his relations to other men. He had encouraged the development of the "hero" in every person and in so doing had demonstrated that the "kingdom of God is within us." The revolution from "kings to capitalism" had been but one step in an evolutionary process at work in the human community.[91] Now democracy was "seeking to control capital." Roosevelt had shown a way of "expanding people's vision" of democracy. Democracy was the playing out of the "self-abnegation of the Christian life" and was the greatest movement "in all of our national life."[92]

PROGRESSIVISM AND PESSIMISM

White's prewar assertion that the "worker for good will is paid in eternity" and that "righteousness exalted a nation" as the "divine spark" burned "in every soul" may have seemed like wearied rhetoric to the generation of the twenties. White continued to chronicle the great men and movements of his time, always reshaping them in his image of the past. "What a God-damned world this is!" he wrote Baker, following Warren Harding's election. "Starvation on the one hand, and indifference on the other, pessimism rampant, faith quiescent, murder met with indifference, the lowered standard of civilization faced with universal complaisance, and the whole story so sad that nobody can tell it. If anyone had told me ten years ago that our country would be what it is today, and that the world would be what it is today, I should have questioned his reason."[93]

In 1925, White wrote *Some Cycles of Cathay*, a work that fairly summarized much of the thinking and many of the fears of that remarkable group of men and women who had fought with their pens for progressive purposes for more than a generation. He claimed that his belief in democratic growth under the influence of the Christian philosophy as expressed in the teachings of Christ and the Golden Rule remained unshakable. It alone provided a framework that dignified "individual humanity." That had been his message all along.[94]

White and his contemporaries remained convinced that there was a "moral purpose behind man's destiny." People still needed to learn that central fact. The cycle in which people now lived had sadly shown that "men will not take truth except through force and at a terrible cost." However, eventually they had to be made to see that the only hope for the human community was in recognizing "the destiny God has given us." That destiny had to continue to be made known to them by writers of the new generation. It was a destiny in which all people could progress "together" or not at all, for they could live "by faith" which would sustain a "larger vision" or they would succumb to the "chaos" around them.[95]

White's hope, and the hope of his fellow foot soldiers, was that social justice would become a permanent part of economic and political institutions as people came to develop the "Christ" that was in them. This belief was a complex of many ideas, most central of which were the writers' own evangelical upbringings, the impact of Darwinian evolution and the higher criticism of that belief, and their lifelong struggle to integrate their faith with the social problems their generation encountered. What makes their work all the more remarkable was that it sprang from the crucible of the writers' own spiritual and intellectual struggles, yet became translated into a social program designed to solve the fundamental injustices of their era.

The paradox of the progressive program the muckrakers espoused was that many of them wondered whether it could really be made to work. These men and women who earnestly tried to teach other men and women to be their brother's keeper remained lifelong pupils themselves. Their lives were experiments in man's personal struggle with God and his social relationship to other men.

NOTES

1. Ray Stannard Baker, Notebook "K," (1908), 131. Library of Congress, Washington, D.C.

2. Ella Winter and Granville Hicks, eds., *The Letters of Lincoln Steffens*, 2 vols. (1938; reprint, Westport, Conn.: Greenwood Press, 1974), 2:928. Copy of letter from Steffens to Upton Sinclair, dated September 25, 1932.

3. See Harry H. Stein, "American Muckrakers and Muckraking: The 50-Year Scholarship," *Journalism Quarterly* 56 (1979): 9–17, for a summary of the literature. Major works that describe the development of thinking on the muckrakers include H. U. Faulkner, *The Quest for Social Justice, 1898–1914* (New York: Macmillan, 1931); C. C. Regier, *The Era of the Muckrakers* (Chapel Hill; University of North Carolina Press, 1932), and Louis Filler, *Crusaders for American Liberalism* (University Park Pa.: University of Pennsylvania Press, 1976). Compare to postwar works by Richard Hofstadter, *Age of Reform: From Bryan to F.D.R.* (New York: Vintage Books, 1955); Eric Goldman, *Rendezvous with Destiny/A History of Modern American Reform* (New York: Vintage, 1959); Henry F. May, *The End of American Innocence: A Study of the First Years of Our Time* (New York: Oxford University Press, 1959); Judson Grenier, "Muckraking and Muckrakers: An Historical Definition," *Journalism Quarterly* (1963); John E. Semonche, "Teddy Roosevelt's Muck-rake Speech: A Reassessment," *Mid-America* (April 1964); Stanley K. Schultz, "The Mo-

rality of Politics: The Muckraker's Vision of Democracy," *Journal of American History* (December 1965); John G. Cawelti, *Apostles of the Self-Made Man* (Chicago: University of Chicago Press, 1965); Harold Wilson, *McClure's Magazine and the Muckrakers* (Princeton, N.J.: Princeton University Press, 1970); Robert M. Crunden, *The Superfluous Men: Conservative Critics of American Culture, 1900–1945* (Austin: University of Texas Press, 1977); Richard L. McCormick, "My Discovery That Business Corrupts: A Reappraisal of the Origins of Progressivism," *American Historical Review* 86 (April 1981); Robert M. Crunden, *Ministers of Reform: The Progressive Achievement in American Civilization, 1889–1920* (New York: Basic Books, 1982); and Sheila Reaves, "How Radical Were the Muckrakers? Socialist Press Views, 1902–1906," *Journalism Quarterly* 61 (winter 1984).

4. See William David Sloan, "American Muckrakers, 1901–1917: Conservative Defenders or Liberal Reformers?" Paper given at the Association for Education in Journalism and Mass Communication Southeastern Regional Colloquium, March 29–30, 1985.

5. Wilson, *McClure's Magazine*, 265–289; Hofstadter, *Age of Reform*, 173–212.

6. Hofstadter, *Age of Reform*, 210. Samuel P. Hays, *Conservation and the Gospel of Efficiency: The Progressive Conservation Movement, 1890–1920* (Cambridge, Mass.: Harvard University Press, 1968). Robert H. Wiebe, *Businessmen and Reform: A Study of the Progressive Movement* (Cambridge, Mass.: Harvard University Press, 1962). See also, George E. Mowry, *The Era of Theodore Roosevelt, 1900–1912* (New York: Harper and Row, 1958); John Braeman, "Seven Progressives," *Business History Review* 35 (1961); and Gabriel Kolko, *The Triumph of Conservatism: A Reinterpretation of American History, 1910–1916* (Glencoe, Ill.: The Free Press, 1963).

7. Wilson, *McClure's Magazine*, 285–289.

8. Ibid., ch. 19.

9. S. S. McClure, *My Autobiography* (New York: F. Ungar, 1963), 18, 59 and 62.

10. McClure mss. Writings, n.d. Knox College class papers. Lilly Library, Indiana University, Bloomington, Indiana.

11. Ibid.

12. McClure mss. Correspondence. Box 3. Folder 4. April 12, 1894. S. S. McClure to Hattie McClure.

13. *McClure's Magazine*, May 1894, 8–9.

14. *McClure's Magazine*, December 1894, 3. Also, *McClure's Magazine*, July 1895, 16.

15. McClure mss. Correspondence. Box 3. Folder 7. Elyatt (Elizabeth) Simpson to S. S. McClure. September 2, 1895.

16. *McClure's Magazine*, October 1895, 480.

17. McClure mss. Correspondence. Box 3. Folder 10. Letter from S. S. McClure to Hattie McClure. September 2, 1895.

18. *McClure's Magazine*, January 1896, 206. Also, McClure mss. Correspondence. January 1896. Box 3. Folder 12.

19. McClure mss. Writings, n.d. "The Greatness of Knox College" (1894).

20. McClure mss. Correspondence. Box 3. Folder 12. Letter from S. S. McClure to John Phillips. February 10, 1896.

21. McClure mss. Correspondence. Box 3. Folder 13. Letters from S. S. McClure to Harriet McClure, dated May 4, 10, 11 and 16, 1896. On the 16th he added, "I

realize more and more the miracle of Christ's life. His words and deeds seem more and more wonderful."

22. McClure mss. Box 3. Folder 15. Letter from S. S. McClure to Harriet McClure. August 9, 1896.

23. *McClure's Magazine*, December 1896, p. 192, and October 1897, 1101.

24. McClure mss. Box 3. Folder 21. The letters were exchanged on June 2, 1899.

25. *McClure's Magazine*, October 1902. Also, McClure mss. Box 4. Folder 3. From S. S. McClure to Harriet McClure. April 24, 1902.

26. McClure mss. Box 4. Folder 6. Undated. Letter from S. S. McClure to Harriet McClure. Also, Box 4. Folder 8. Letter from S. S. McClure to Harriet McClure. March 22, 1903.

27. McClure mss. Box 4. Folder 12. Address to the Twentieth Century Club. Brooklyn, N.Y. January 30, 1904.

28. McClure mss. Box 6. Folder 6. Address to members of the 57th Street branch of the YMCA. April 10, 1911.

29. McClure mss. S. S. McClure to Ida Tarbell. October 1, 1937. See also McClure mss. Box 4. Folder 17. Letter from S. S. McClure to Harriet McClure. August 27, 1904.

30. Ida M. Tarbell, *All in a Day's Work* (New York: Macmillan, 1939), 15–16.

31. Kathleen Brady, *Ida M. Tarbell* (New York: Macmillan, 1984), 31 and 61.

32. Ida M. Tarbell, "My Religion," 1–2. Lawrence Lee Pelletier Library. Allegheny College. Meadville, Pennsylvania.

33. Ibid., 3–7.

34. Tarbell, *All in a Day's Work*, 407.

35. Ibid., 16, 27–29 and 407. Also, Tarbell, *History of Standard Oil* (New York: McClure, Phillips & Co., 1904), 268 and 287–289.

36. Tarbell, "My Religion," 7–8. Also, Mary E. Tomkins, *Ida M. Tarbell* (New York: Twayne, 1974), 158.

37. Tarbell, "My Religion," 7–8.

38. Ray Stannard Baker, *American Chronicle: The Autobiography of Ray Stannard Baker* (New York: C. Scribner's Sons, 1945), 2, 58.

39. Robert C. Bannister, *Ray Stannard Baker: The Mind and Thought of a Progressive* (New Haven: Yale University Press, 1966), 3, 12, and 13.

40. Ibid., 14.

41. Baker, *American Chronicle*, 17.

42. Ibid., 57–58.

43. William T. Stead, *If Christ Came to Chicago* (Chicago: Laird and Lee 1894). See also, Stead, *The Americanization of the World* (New York: H. Markley, 1901).

44. Baker, *American Chronicle*, 30–32. Also, Bannister, *Ray Stannard Baker*, 34.

45. Ray Stannard Baker, *The Spiritual Unrest* (New York: Frederick A. Stokes, 1910), chs. 1 and 2, particularly 87–100.

46. Ibid., 142, 230. Also, Baker, Notebook "7," p. 116. Library of Congress.

47. Baker, *The Spiritual Unrest*, 272–281.

48. Baker, *American Chronicle*, 182–184. Also, Baker, Notebook "I," 104 and Notebook "L," 20.

49. Ray Stannard Baker, *Woodrow Wilson and World Settlement*, vol. I (Garden City, N.Y.: Doubleday, Page & Co., 1972), 1-Z 13–14, 21. Also, Baker, *American Chronicle*, 60, 92–93 and 176–178.

50. Baker, Notebook VII, 149–153. Also, Notebook "L," 20. Also, Bannister, *Ray Stannard Baker*, 119.

51. Joseph Lincoln Steffens, *Autobiography of Lincoln Steffens* (New York: Harcourt, Brace and Co., 1931), 523–526.

52. Ibid., 525.

53. Ibid., 72. Also, Justin Kaplan, *Lincoln Steffens: A Biography* (New York: Simon and Schuster, 1974), 22.

54. Winter and Hicks, *Letters of Lincoln Steffens*, 11. Copy of letter from Lincoln Steffens to Lou Steffens. Aug. 25, 1889. Also, 49. Copy of letter from Lincoln Steffens to Joseph Steffens, July 18, 1890.

55. Joseph Lincoln Steffens, *Lincoln Steffens Speaking* (New York: Harcourt, Brace & Co., 1936), ix. Also, Steffens, *Autobiography*, 375.

56. Steffens, *Autobiography*, 375.

57. Winter and Hicks, *Letters of Lincoln Steffens*, 234–235. Copy of letter from Lincoln Steffens to Mrs. Joseph Steffens. December 21, 1909.

58. There is an excellent summary of the impact of the McNamara case on Steffens in Russell M. Horton's *Lincoln Steffens* (New York: Twayne, 1974), 83–86. See also, Steffens, *Autobiography*, 670–675, and Winter and Hicks, *Letters of Lincoln Steffens*, 286–288.

59. Winter and Hicks, *Letters of Lincoln Steffens*, 243. Copy of letter from Lincoln Steffens to William Kent. April 19, 1910.

60. Winter and Hicks, *Letters of Lincoln Steffens*, 243. Copy of letter from Lincoln Steffens to Laura Steffens. November 1911. Also, 286. Copy of letter from Lincoln Steffens to Lou and Allen Suggett. December 24, 1911.

61. Steffens, *Autobiography*, 688. Also, Horton, *Lincoln Steffens*, 85.

62. Kaplan, *Lincoln Steffens*, 118.

63. Steffens, *Autobiography*, 434–435.

64. Upton Sinclair, *My Lifetime in Letters* (Columbia: University of Missouri Press, 1960), 52. Copy of letter from Lincoln Steffens to Upton Sinclair. October 15, 1915.

65. Steffens, *Autobiography*, 434–435.

66. Upton Sinclair mss. Biographical Data Correspondence. 1814–1916. Box 1. Folder 1. Lilly Library, Indiana University. Bloomington, Indiana.

67. Upton Sinclair, *Cup of Fury* (Great Neck, N.Y.: Channel Press, 1956), 12 and 13. Also, Upton Sinclair, *The Autobiography of Upton Sinclair* (London: W. H. Allen, 1963), 27.

68. Sinclair, *Cup of Fury*, 20–21.

69. Ibid., 14–15.

70. Sinclair mss. Box 1. Folder 5. Copy of letter from Upton Sinclair to Priscilla Sinclair (1894–18).

71. Sinclair mss. Box 1. Folder 2. "Little Known Facts About Well-Known People," an article by Dale Carnegie. Also, Sinclair, *Autobiography*, 31. Also, Leon Harris, *Upton Sinclair: American Rebel* (New York: Crowell, 1971), 11–14.

72. Sinclair, *Autobiography*, 112. Also Harris, *Upton Sinclair*, 171.

73. Sinclair, *Autobiography*, 55. Also, Sinclair, *Cup of Fury*, 16. Harris, *Upton Sinclair*, 168.

74. Sinclair, *Letters*, 96. Letter from Edwin Markham to Upton Sinclair, May 26, 1910.

75. Louis Filler, *The Unknown Edwin Markham* (Yellow Springs, Ohio: Antioch Press, 1966), ch. 5. Also, William L. Stidger, *Edwin Markham* (New York: The Abingdon Press, 1933), ch. 6.

76. Edwin Markham, *The Man with the Hoe* (New York: Doxey's, 1899), 19.

77. Ibid., 23.

78. Ibid., 32, 37–39, and 45–47.

79. Ibid., 47.

80. Edwin Markham, *Lincoln and Other Poems* (New York: McClure, Phillips & Co., 1901). Also, Edwin Markham, *The Shoes of Happiness and Other Poems* (1913; reprint, Garden City, N.Y.: Doubleday, Doran & Co., 1932). Also, Edwin Markham, *Gates of Paradise and Other Poems* (Garden City, N.Y.: Doubleday, Doran & Co., 1920).

81. Edwin Markham Scrapbook. "The Markham Book." January 1894. Box 3455. Library of Congress. Washington, D.C. Also, an article he wrote for the *New York Times*, Oct. 21, 1899, and an interview with the *San Francisco Bulletin*, appearing Dec. 30, 1900, in Box 3455.

82. William Allen White, *The Autobiography of William Allen White* (New York: Macmillan, 1946), 300. Also, William Allen White, Letterbook. Sept. 20, 1913. A letter from William Allen White to Fred D. Warren. Container B29, pt. 2. Library of Congress.

83. William Allen White, *A Theory of Spiritual Progress* (Emporia, Kans.: The Gazette Press, 1910), 3, 13, 15, 24 and 36.

84. William Allen White, Letterbook. June 3, 1914. A letter from William Allen White to Rev. Clifford Cole. Container B29, pt. 2. Library of Congress.

85. Sally Griffith, *Home Town News* (New York: Oxford University Press, 1989), ch. 1, particularly p. 28, and ch. 4, particularly 169–179.

86. White, *Autobiography*, 6–7.

87. Ibid., 38.

88. Ibid., 108.

89. John DeWitt McKee, *William Allen White: Maverick on Main Street* (Westport, Conn.: Greenwood Press, 1988), 199–200.

90. William Allen White, Letterbook. November 23, 1914. A letter from William Allen White to Eugene Bryan. Library of Congress.

91. William Allen White, *The Old Order Changeth* (New York: Macmillan, 1910), 251 and 263.

92. Walter Johnson, ed., *Selected Letters of William Allen White: 1899–1943* (New York: H. Holt & Co., 1947), 34 and 97. Also, White, *The Old Order Changeth*, 34 and 229–238. Also, McKee, *William Allen White*, 198–203.

93. Johnson, *Selected Letters*, 213. Copy of letter from William Allen White to Ray Stannard Baker. December 8, 1920.

94. William Allen White, *Some Cycles of Cathay* (Chapel Hill: University of North Carolina Press, 1925), preface and 16–23.

95. Ibid., 23, 60 and 87–88.

2

Anatomy of a Crusade: The *Buffalo News'* Campaign for Immigrants

Michael Dillon

The Gilded Age was a time when new American fortunes were peaking, when the steady drumbeat of commercialism had created a class of industrialists whose excesses were just coming into the public's view. It was also a time of crushing poverty; a time when thousands of immigrants had flooded American cities providing a cheap labor source, but also drawing the wrath of workers who feared for their jobs. The result was tension in cities that were already wrought with anxiety from an economy that fluctuated wildly. As the 1880s dawned, America was a land of contrasts, for sure. Amidst all the head-spinning social upheaval, came a newspaper industry that was also changing rapidly, moving from a personal and often partisan journalism to one that was seeking to capture the new immigrants as well as the urban holdovers who represented a very different America. In Buffalo, a city in western New York that had attracted Polish immigrants, E. H. Butler's *Buffalo News* tackled this dual task by sending reporters into the immigrant tenements where they found sordid living conditions for the newcomers. The *News* proceeded to crusade for reform, mixing editorial opinion and reporting in ways that have been generally credited to Joseph Pulitzer and his "new journalism." Butler demanded that both the government and residents of Buffalo find ways to help the new arrivals. In essence, Michael Dillon finds, Butler's *News* was redefining who belonged in the new urban community as well as the role journalism needed to play in a rapidly changing industrial democracy.

Buffalo readers who glanced at the front page of the *Evening News* on June 15, 1881, were treated to the penny paper's usual smorgasbord of domestic dramas, sensational crimes and commercial schemes. A young girl was missing in nearby Black Rock, and the neighborhood's citizens had formed a search party.[1] One Chauncey B. Williams of North Division Street awoke to the sting of acid in his face, thrown by a "dastardly" unknown assailant.[2] A "wild-eyed Celtic truckman" was stalking an edgy local schoolmaster who was "getting gray fast."[3] An advertisement recommended to readers that they try "Burdick's Blood Bitters" for any ailment ranging from impotence to consumption.

A brief story in the third column, however, struck quite a different tone. The story detailed the death of a young Polish immigrant and took readers on a tour of the city's south-side tenements. The writing was poignant and realistic; the scene was wrenching: "In the same house at this moment 40 persons exist, and six children are lying at the point of death and close beside them a woman, with scarcely enough clothes to cover her, tosses about on the floor in a high fever." The story bore the headline "The City's Disgrace."[4]

Short though it was, the story signaled the beginning of a summer-long crusade for the city's Polish immigrants. By August, more than a dozen immigrants—mostly small children—would be dead from scarlet fever, diphtheria, small pox and malnutrition. Many of the survivors, however, would be living in sanitary housing built by the city and by local entrepreneurs, housing that was built largely because the *Buffalo News* insisted it be built. Fighting against a tide of political indifference and public prejudice, the *Buffalo News* used its power to right a wrong and, in the process, conducted one of the first modern newspaper crusades.

Two decades later, the muckrakers writing in mass-circulation magazines would conduct a searing examination of the major institutions of American life—the rapacious monopoly, the kept Senate, the graft rings that ran major cities.[5] But the muckrakers' grand efforts grew out of the more narrowly focused investigative stories of the reform-minded "New Journalists" of the 1870s and 1880s.[6] Historian Arthur Schlesinger has commented that the reformers of this period created the template for all reform movements that followed. "So thoroughly did these crusaders work out the pattern of reform organization and propaganda a hundred years ago that later generations found little to add beyond taking advantage of new communications devices."[7]

GENESIS OF THE CRUSADING "NEW JOURNALISM"

Popular newspapers in the post–Civil War era performed a difficult balancing act. On the one hand, the cheap, lively, inclusive dailies that came to form the critical mass of the "New Journalism" did their utmost to make themselves indispensable to readers and attractive to advertisers.[8] They did so by offering up sensationalism, "spicy" up-to-date news, and lively writing.[9] In short, they thrived on the chaos of the age and in so doing invented the modern form of news.[10] But at the same time as they boomed the beneficent progress of the machine age,[11] the best of these new journals simultaneously became social inquisitors, rooting out corruption in civic and commercial institutions. Their efforts were largely aimed at empowering the lower and emergent middle classes that constituted the bulk of their readership.

The vehicle of inquisition came to be known as the crusade—and rightly so, for early investigative reporting came in a frame of almost biblical morality and fury. The crusades served many roles: First, they reflected a sincere desire on the part of largely middle-class idealists to improve the conditions of society. Second, in some measure, they reflected fear of the rapidity and brutality of industrial progress.[12] Third, crusades were exciting, dramatic, suspenseful and marvelously literary.

The fact that readers were engaged and, in many ways, entertained by these inquiries into social dysfunction does not at all diminish the important political victories the crusaders won. Indeed, reform-minded popular writers carried "conviction where the professional agitator batters against stone walls. They also reach readers who would be bored by political or sociological disquisitions."[13]

Crusading, the evolutionary forerunner of muckraking, has roots in the penny press of the 1830s, when James Gordon Bennett proved that with energetic inquiries, creative writing and a cheap paper, a publisher had the power to turn a prostitute's murder into an episodic sensation.[14] Crusading, however, flowered as a pervasive journalistic genre only after the Civil War. In the wake of Appomatox, the destiny of the nation was up for grabs, and visionaries and fools alike wanted a part in reshaping the United States.

During the 1870s and 1880s, a diverse group of publishers was exploring the tremendous social power of the "new journalism." The American newspaper—born into the role of propagandist during Revolutionary times—had always filled the role of critic. But with big readerships, big revenues and political autonomy, late nineteenth-century publishers were discovering they could also shape policies, exert the pressure of public outrage to bring about change and even mediate conflicts between their diverse constituencies.

While many publishers declared their political independence after the Civil War, their objective was to remove themselves from under the thumb of political parties, not to disengage from politics. While some historians and critics have argued that politics was deemphasized in the commercial press of the nineteenth century,[15] it would be more accurate to say that independent journalism opened politics to a wider audience. Crusades on behalf of the impoverished, for instance, might not have resembled the impassioned discourses on governmental policies found in the partisan press, but they were no less political. Given that the new journalism increased coverage of social life—crime, courts, labor disputes—it actually provided readers with broader social and political contexts for their lives. By conceiving of news as an omnibus of human experience, the new journalism recognized that the activities of daily life were by nature political.[16]

Astute publishers realized that the power of a mayor, congressman or senator was trifling compared to a newspaper publisher with a readership in the hundreds of thousands or even millions. Joseph Pulitzer clearly saw the political possibilities of the new activist journalism he was helping to create—and it did not entail being a mere cipher of "the people." Pulitzer knew that the education he provided his immigrant readers was also a form of political indoctrination. "You may write the most sublime philosophy," Pulitzer wrote, "but if nobody reads it, where are you? You must go for your million circulation, and, when you have got it, turn the minds and the votes of your readers one way or the other at critical moments."[17]

THE MAKING OF A NEW JOURNALIST

Perhaps because it is so often written by former scribes, journalism history is too often predicated on scoops, firsts and personalities. Thus we "know" that Pulitzer invented the new journalism single-handedly[18] in the pages of his *New York World* and brought the crusade fully formed into the world.[19] Alas, the truth is more complex. New York, then as now, was America's least typical city. In other cities, a diverse group of publishers was also discovering the power of popular journalism and trying to use it to bring about social change. New journalism may indeed have reached its zenith and fullest expression in the *World*, but other publishers were employing the techniques of new journalism before either the *Post-Dispatch* or the *World* appeared on the scene—notably Joseph McCullough, from whose *St. Louis Globe-Democrat* Pulitzer learned much about new journalism.[20]

Edward H. Butler brought the new brand of journalism to Buffalo. The son of an itinerant minister, Butler was born into genial, small-town poverty in 1850. When his father died suddenly, the family's fortunes plunged and Butler and his siblings went to work. Edward began his journalistic career as a printer's devil in rural Leroy, New York.[21] Before he was 20, he served as an apprentice on the political papers of the hardscrabble Pennsylvania anthracite coal region.[22]

In 1872, Butler entered Buffalo with near-empty pockets and discovered a newspaper field crowded with commercial and political journals that catered to a small elite.[23] They could scarcely be said to offer news at all—at least not according to the modern notions of news invented by Bennett and Benjamin Day in the 1830s and refined by men like Butler, Pulitzer, E. W. Scripps, Melville Stone, Joseph Medill and Charles Dana, during the Gilded Age.

The disorganized front pages of Buffalo's little journals overflowed with announcements and advertising. The *real* action was in the editorial columns, where partisan scribes held forth on the glories of their parties and attacked rivals. These papers, like partisan papers everywhere, defined news narrowly as the official acts of politicians or the political opinions of editors. As Robert Park observed, the old-time partisan editor "was inclined to a contempt for news. News for him was simply material upon which to base an editorial."[24]

The early penny press and, later, the new journalism attracted wide readership by greatly broadening the subject of news. Instead of a litany of political speeches and rumors, these papers reflected and projected a kaleidoscope of social life. Anyone or anything might be worthy of a few sticks of newsprint, provided their stories contained at least some of the modern elements of news (timeliness, unusualness, prominence, consequence) first established by Day and Bennett.

With little capital, Butler could not compete with the half-dozen dailies that dominated Buffalo and so he staked out the vacant Sunday field instead. The *Buffalo Sunday Morning News* debuted in December 1873—five years before the *Post and Dispatch*—and within two years had a circulation equal to all of the other journals in Buffalo combined.[25] The paper outstripped its competition, snaring a mass readership with up-to-date news reports on crime, foreign affairs, politics and commerce.

In building a loyal readership—a constituency, really—Butler attacked the institutions that had long held sway over Buffalo's social and political life, especially the political parties and the papers that served as their mouthpieces. In 1877, when the Great Strike enveloped Buffalo, Butler's *News* was the only paper to rally with the workers against the city's politicians and industrialists.[26]

As his paper grew in size and popularity, Butler struggled during the 1870s to find a suitable means to wield power and to achieve objectives he deemed good for readers and the city. He vowed his paper would follow a "policy of strict independence. It is the organ of no party. We are the slaves of no party leaders."[27] The paper lambasted and ridiculed inept politicians, referring to entrenched party bosses and rival partisan editors as "old fogies"[28] and "low scums" interested only in personal or partisan gain.[29] It successfully put across a bipartisan election ticket to ensure that neither party machine could dominate city politics.[30] The *News* exposed quack doctors and warned them to get out of town (and then boasted that they had).[31] It also published lurid tales of conditions at the pauper's graveyard.[32]

In each instance, the newspaper approached a civic problem as a manifestation of political ineptitude or moral laxness and then proceeded to the pulpit to denounce those responsible for the crisis. Many of these early civic campaigns shared a common theme: beneath the specific critiques of failed community institutions lay an attack on partisan politics, whose primary goal was the maintenance of party, not necessarily the betterment of the community at large. The *News* insisted that the solutions to Buffalo's problems must come from a broader, more popular style of government.

These early crusades differed greatly in style from the sophisticated inquisitions the newspaper would conduct in the 1880s. By then, the *News*, which went daily in 1880, had sufficient capital to truly investigate and expose significant facts. The crusades of the 1870s alluded to the facts upon which the newspaper's exhortations were founded, but the facts themselves stayed in the background. Names were rare and specific figures or dates were rarely proffered.

Thomas Leonard has pointed out that one of the first great "exposés"— the toppling of Tammany Hall in the 1870s—was more a symbolic exorcism than a true crusade. The *New York Times* and *Harper's Weekly*, which led the attack on Tammany, did so largely through cartoons and aspersions and made no larger point about the meaning of the Tammany scandals. "The *Times* and *Harper's Weekly* were far better at getting citizens moving than at telling them where they were going. Neither publication was really curious about the way Tammany worked, nor did either encourage readers to think very hard about the city they lived in."[33]

The attacks the *Buffalo News* leveled at political and social targets during the 1870s were similarly ambiguous. They lacked detailed reporting, in part, because tradition dictated that the editorial was the primary weapon in a publisher's arsenal, and, in part, because during its first few years the paper lacked the revenue to finance an adequate reporting staff. These first attempts by the paper to assert its civic leadership, however, were part of an evolution that culminated in one of the first sophisticated, factual, literary crusades in American journalism: The *News'* 1881 crusade to alleviate the suffering of impoverished Polish immigrants.

The crusade reflected the tensions of the time. Between 1870 and 1880, the population of the United States increased by nearly a third[34] and the chaos one would expect to follow such a radical upheaval manifested itself quickly. In Buffalo, the nation's thirteenth largest city,[35] the population boom was even more dramatic. Fueled by immigration, the city nearly doubled its population to 155,000 between 1873 and 1880.[36] By the mid-1880s, there were 10 million foreign-born people in the United States; New York State was home to a quarter of them.[37]

The pace of city life picked up as immigrants poured in. Thanks to improved lighting, factories chugged around the clock. Extensive rail and telegraph networks opened up provincial regions to the wider world and all facets of life—economic, social, political—became increasingly interdependent. The rhythm of American life was quickening, and more and more its beat emanated from the city rather than the countryside.[38]

Buffalo was an important economic center, a locus of both Great Lakes shipping and northeastern rail traffic. Grain elevators, rubber factories and steel mills together formed a smoke-shrouded barrier on the shores of Lake Erie. Amid simmering class tensions and ethnic prejudices, industries demanded more workers who would come from the ranks of the lower classes and immigrants. The Polish crisis, apart from its literal details, served as an intersection of the tensions that bedeviled many industrial cities in the late nineteenth century.

By the summer of 1881, the newcomers were living—barely—and dying—frequently—in dilapidated shanties on the city's south side. The Poles had arrived in droves in cities all along the rail lines in the 1870s and 1880s, seeking work that had been promised to them by the steamship companies that booked their passage to America. Instead, they found poverty, squalor and discrimination.[39]

The *News'* crusade on their behalf reached its full pitch during the early summer of 1881. As the crusade wound down in August, several lessons were clear. The most obvious was that through factual reporting and gripping narrative, a newspaper could arouse and sustain popular indignation, and then use that indignation as a weapon to combat social problems. More than that, progressive modern papers were among the first institutions in American life to redefine class conflict and upheavals of immigration as social problems, rather than as mere civic inconveniences.

Because partisan ties were weakening during this period, politicians, shorn of the weapon of party discipline, could be intimidated by both the reality *and* the perception of popular outrage. The *News* also demonstrated that in a burgeoning city of conflicting class, ethnic and economic interests, a newspaper might act as conciliator and mediator in community disputes. Finally, the *News* learned that no matter how just its cause and how gripping its coverage, a newspaper could get only so far ahead of public sentiment before losing some of its moral authority.

IMMIGRANTS ARRIVE IN "SWARMS THICKER THAN LOCUSTS"

The first mention of the plight of the Polish immigrants appeared two months before the real onset of the crusade.[40] A brief story reported on the hardships of the newcomers, urging the city council to allocate relief funds, which it did, approving $500 to build temporary barracks. However, the money was not spent, the barracks were not built and Poles continued to flood into the city—"in swarms thicker than locusts," according to one city official.[41]

By June, the *News*, which had made brief editorial queries about the status of the barracks, had grown exasperated with the city government's dawdling. When two months had passed without action, Butler decided that the *News* would provide leadership in what it construed to be a moral, political and health crisis.

"The City's Disgrace," which appeared on June 15, foreshadowed both the literary and moral tone that would characterize the crusade through the balance of the summer. A comparison of this first real crusade story with the June 15 edition's top story—the disappearance of a young Black Rock girl, the child of an established city family—yields insights into the relative position of the immigrants in the Buffalo community.

The *News* reporters who covered the search for little Dora Higgins gave a detailed account of how the child had wandered away, describing her parents as "plunged in the deepest grief" as a search party looked for her.[42] The crusade story also centered on a child, an infant immigrant girl, who had died of malnutrition in an Alabama Street tenement. Unlike the missing Black Rock girl, however, the young Polish child was not named, and there was little personal information about her or her family. Whether or not her parents were "plunged in the deepest grief" was left to the imagination of the reader.

Though she was unnamed and unmourned in the *News* account, the child would be the first of many immigrants to die that summer, and her death provided Buffalo's citizens with the first glimpse of the conditions in which the despised newcomers lived. By the next day, June 16, the lost little Black Rock girl was found unharmed and her story forgotten. By the next day, the plight of the nameless immigrant girl and her countrymen had moved to the top of the page. On June 16, the day after it reported the death of the immigrant child, *News* reporters interviewed city Health Physician A. H. Briggs, who blamed the appalling conditions on Alabama Street and other sections of the south side on an indifferent city government.[43] Dr. Briggs' pleas to the paper for help showed that he understood that this relatively new player—the popular newspaper—might more quickly lubricate the wheels of civic action than any partisan on the council. "On the press we rely chiefly for support," he told the paper.[44] Without fast action, the doctor warned, the situation would rapidly grow worse: "If these poor victims are allowed to remain here much longer, there will be no occasion for their removal. Grim death will relieve them of all their sufferings, and all that the board of health will be required to do will be to remove the bodies and fumigate the premises."[45]

The doctor's impassioned and eloquent quote seems almost a bit too epigrammatic, raising the possibility that perhaps the reporter took some dramatic license to add to the story's emotional and literary impact. Made up or not, the quote served its narrative purpose as a segué to a stinging rebuke of the Board of Health, which—along with the City Council—the *News* reporter charged, was "meeting with severe condemnation on all sides."[46]

Actually, in the early days of the crusade, the only condemnation officials faced was from the *News* itself. Buffalo's other newspapers ignored the conditions in the Polish slums and only began to publish stories about them after the *News* had generated so much noise about the tenement issue that continued silence became impractical. When Buffalo's other papers did begin covering slum conditions, they castigated the immigrants and proposed that they simply be removed from the city en masse.

Thus, for the *News*, the crusade was a lonely business. Its rivals treated the crusade with complete contempt. The *Commercial Advertiser*, for instance, admonished the *News* for printing stories about the Poles and referred to the immigrants as a kind of civic infection. "The presence of a large and growing colony of Poles in this city means . . . the planting of new germs of pauperism and pestilence in our limits. The Polish settlement is a breeding ground for disease and paupers. What are we going to do about it?"[47] The paper urged that no immigrant be given aid without being made to perform work and that all of the Poles be forcibly put on trains and moved west no matter the condition of their health.

The *Express* was even harsher in its view of the Poles. "They are of the lowest class, who seem to delight in crowding themselves into as small a living space as possible with absolutely no idea of cleanliness."[48] None of Buffalo's other papers sent reporters to the tenements or reported the facts about conditions there, conditions that the Express said "delighted" the victims. Their stories on the Poles were short, mean, and derisive. Despite the reluctance of politicians, the fear of readers and the vitriol of competitors, however, the *News* continued to confront the city with the humanity of the victims: "In these dark cellars, human beings are living and dying," the *News* admonished its critics.[49]

The June 16 edition illustrated the intensified tone of the crusade. The story was headlined "BUFFALO'S SHAME"—a significant appellation because once again the paper chose to underscore the moral dimensions of the crisis. (The headline also foreshadowed the moralistic zeal of later muckrakers such as Lincoln Steffens, who penned the "The Shame of the Cities.") The story was not content to merely describe the problem and assign blame. Instead, the *News* concluded by urging citizens of the Third Ward, where the tenements were located, to aid the Poles.

Starting with the June 16 edition, the *News* hammered at city officials to act on the Polish situation. With a single exception,[50] lengthy crusade stories ran on the front page every day until July 2, when President Garfield was shot in Washington. Even then, the paper did not let up. Through July and August, the *News* made withering attacks on public officials in both its news and editorial columns. It also did its best to prod the consciences of Buffalo's citizens.

Editorials buttressed the wrenching news stories. The problem of the Poles, the paper charged editorially, went beyond a failure of civic leadership; that citizens would do nothing while strangers died in their midst, demonstrated both collective and individual moral failure. Helping the unfortunate immigrants would not only relieve their suffering, it would redeem the larger community.

Unlike the oratory-driven crusades of a decade earlier, the Polish crusade stories were built of hard facts and literary realism. The change in tack illustrated how, during the Gilded Age, the traditional practice of passing judgment on the editorial page was displaced by the act of bearing witness in the news columns.[51] Rather than try to persuade readers with reason and conclusions, the new style of journalism made them confront the details of civic rot for themselves; only then, would the editorial writer attempt to marshal public sentiment toward a particular solution.

The subheadline over the June 16 story read, "A Visit to the House of Death." The reporter who wrote it—unnamed—and the *News* itself played prominent roles. The story's imagery was harrowing, and its tone full of indignation.

A *News* reporter visited the house this morning, and upon entering was nearly stifled by the foul air that pervaded the place. In a dark room, he found a sight that was terrible to behold, and which ought to shame the many "noble and philanthropic" charity societies in our midst . . . In one corner lay a dirty babe upon the floor with a pillow for a bed. Its thin arms were thrown languidly and wearily across its breast.[52]

The story criticized "disgraceful official neglect" and explained in great detail—just in case appeals to conscience failed—that the conditions in the Polish slums constituted a city-wide health menace. The prospect of an epidemic was not unfounded. As cities grew denser and residents left traditional neighborhoods to work and shop, the fragile interdependence of all citizens—rich, poor, native-born, immigrant—grew. Cities like Chicago and Pittsburgh were virtually wiped out by great fires in the nineteenth century as wind-swept flames consumed wooden buildings and even streaked across gunpowder-dry bridges.[53]

It would be inaccurate to conclude that traditional civic institutions failed to fulfill their duties as growth and population raced out of control. Like massive fires and epidemics, the waves of immigration such as those that broke over Buffalo and other cities in the late 1800s were without precedent; there simply was no mechanism in place to manage such rapid change. As Esmond Wright notes, "In an age of laissez faire, there was very little planning in urban growth. City development lay largely in the hands of real estate men who did as they pleased."[54]

In any case, the established political rings did not find much incentive to adopt policies to manage change, even as the consequences of that change became clear. Reformers like Butler attacked the partisan rings largely out of a sense of alarm that they could not possibly react effectively to the massive changes in American life. "The growth of the cities," Wright comments, "presented at least two major problems to those who were honestly concerned with the public welfare. In the first place, it was necessary to curb dishonesty in city governments so that the people's money would not be stolen from them. In the second place, the urgent need for protecting the large urban populations from fire, disease, and crime required increased governmental regulation of private enterprise."[55]

A singular theme emerged as the *News'* crusade continued: Since the city had failed in its duty to resolve the Polish crisis, which it should have anticipated months earlier when the *News* first brought the matter to public attention, the *News* would assert its moral and civic authority to step forward and lead. As the *News* hectored city officials to react to the crisis, it also warned citizens that they, too, had an obligation to act charitably in order to escape the taint of "shame."

Throughout the crusade, public reaction became a prominent part of the coverage. A crusade is always a self-fulfilling event; once the story gets going its progress becomes a *part* of the story. This was true in the sensational series of stories Bennett published about the murder of Ellen Jewett in the 1830s.[56] It was also true of the more sophisticated news products Joseph Pulitzer manufactured in the 1880s and 1890s (such as Nellie Bly's race to beat the fictional Phileas Fogg's record for circling the globe).[57]

It is difficult, however, to gauge how much actual civic outrage exposés inspired, and how much outrage was embellished by newspapers hyping their own campaigns. Government and corporate officials under attack from the crusaders often acted on the presumption that spontaneous public outrage might lead to the destruction of individual careers, the reduction of profits or the implementation of government reforms.

The *News'* relentless investigation into the Polish crisis provided much more than a chronicle of the Poles' hard times. It provided a lens through which readers could see their city and themselves from new perspectives made necessary by explosive growth, mechanization and increasing social, class and ethnic divisions.

Over the course of the crusade, moreover, one can see a newspaper finding a sense of itself, a newspaper not content to merely comment or report, but intent on inserting itself into the management of the city itself—as conscience, reformer, planner and prognosticator.

THE NEWSPAPER AS CULTURAL AND SOCIAL INTERSECTION

In a nation where face-to-face politics had become increasingly impractical, the modern newspaper served as a cultural and social intersection, a public forum where civic issues could be engaged and debated, and perhaps even resolved. Jurgen Habermas has noted that in the mid-1800s, the "public sphere"—once quite literally the market square—was transformed from a sphere of discourse to one of consumption.[58] The colonization of this public sphere by mass-circulation newspapers, Habermas argues, diminished citizens' roles as political participants.[59]

The market square politics made unworkable and ineffective by growth and urbanization was, in effect, reconstituted in an abstract space by the newspaper.[60] Control of this new forum brought to the newspaper new power that it could, and did, wield to change conditions in the city. The Polish Crusade was an important expression of this new power.[61]

Unlike New York City, a long-time destination for European immigrants, western cities like Buffalo were unprepared and ill-equipped to absorb a tide of impoverished immigrants. As the Poles poured into Buffalo, the city was forced to redefine its values and, ultimately, its responsibilities for conditions that brought misery to the Poles and fear of chaos, or even plague, to the city.

In the nineteenth century, services for the poor or afflicted were not considered to be the responsibilities of the city or state, except in cases of indigence. Churches, private charities and philanthropic societies were considered the proper sources of aid; city-run institutions—which also depended partially on private benevolence—included the insane asylum, the orphanage, the workhouse and the jail. In Buffalo, as elsewhere, these institutions were the private fiefdoms of the political parties. As the crisis in the Polish tenements worsened and private charity organizations proved indifferent or unequal to the task of helping the Poles, the city Health and Sanitation Departments began to assess the situation, but they were slow to act.

The Buffalo City Council took the position that the Polish crisis was the responsibility of Health Inspector Briggs. But he told the *News* that he could do little to help the immigrants because the council would not free up relief funds for new housing for the Poles. In any case, he added, "Charity moves slowly, you know"[62]—a flippant remark that began a transformation of Briggs from hero to villain in the drama.[63]

Without the crusade, it is doubtful there would have been a groundswell of concern and support for the suffering immigrants. To the provincial eyes of most Buffalonians, the Poles were unkempt, unintelligible and undesirable. The position of one reader, voiced in a letter to the editor, was typical of many others written by Buffalo's citizens. The writer insisted that "these Poles prefer charity to work. . . . A good plan would be to care for the sick, send the children to school and their lazy parents to the workhouse."[64]

Even older, skilled Poles who had earlier settled in the city shunned the newcomers. Health officials took half-hearted actions to help contain disease, but were little inclined to help the Poles themselves. Even as the magnitude of the crisis in the Polish tenements was made apparent, only one physician was appointed to oversee 300 cases of illness.[65] Some of the immigrants had been reduced to subsisting on rotten apples—a situation the paper called "the most pitiable scene of all."[66] Lucky immigrants received prescription medicines but their inability to understand English led them to administer the medicine improperly.[67]

The *News* urged the construction of suitable housing in the city's Fifth

Ward and even published a crude sketch of what such housing might look like. Officials quickly vowed to build the structures and others like it, if need be. The *News* had spurred action, but would not be satisfied until officials followed through.

The city's rather informal web of charitable institutions simply was not up to the task of aiding the Poles; these institutions showed no indication they would add any vigor to the meager efforts they had made so far. If the problem were to be solved, the *News* argued in an editorial, Buffalo's progressives would have to take charge.

What has become of Buffalo's boasted charity that poor immigrants are permitted to starve in our midst without being made to alleviate their suffering? Is this right, just or human? We put this question to every man in Buffalo that has a heart. This is grave work and it can only be corrected by intelligent work. It will not do for gentlemen to meet and tickle each other's vanity, for this will do no good; but there must be relief for the poor and helpless.[68]

"WHERE DEATH IS BUSY!"

On Friday, June 17, the *News* reported that the City Council committee in charge of administering aid to the immigrants "woke up last night and made some progress, halting and inadequate, but still encouraging."[69] The paper made sure its readers knew that the *News* had spurred the progress. While the newspaper was not ham-handed in taking credit for producing action by the city government, stories were peppered with references and reminders of the paper's extensive coverage of the crisis.

The committee decided upon a new site for sanitary housing for residents of the tenements. At the same time, however, the paper reported the discovery of still more tenements whose pitiful residents were also in need of aid. The problem was growing, thwarting the hopes of city politicians that it could be expediently solved with as little bother—and money—as possible. The *News* made clear it would not let the matter rest until *all* of the Poles had been accounted for. The story also reported a seventh death at the original Alabama Street "den"—another child.[70] The *News* urged health officials to send more doctors into the tenements more often.

The next day, Saturday, June 18, the *News* devoted two columns to another narrative tour of the tenements "where death is busy." Valerian Kuzyans, three-years-old, and Michael Bagasinski, a child whose age was not reported, succumbed during the night. The *News* reporter described the scene in spare, chilling prose: "Three children and one grown person slept in the room with the corpses. A *News* reporter found Poormaster Kraft at the house, surrounded by crying women with bare feet and dirty faces. 'My God! It is dreadful,' said Mr. Kraft, 'that such scenes are allowed to exist in a civilized community.' "[71]

On O'Brien Street, meanwhile, the reporter discovered another "human hive" where immigrants were crowded into cellars whose floors were covered with putrid water. The children in this terrible house, the *News* warned, "sucked up the seeds of death, which, if not checked, will spread to every portion of the city, carrying ruin and desolation."[72] Despite the extensive and sympathetic coverage of the immigrants' travails, some public health officials and politicians quoted in the story spoke of the Poles as nuisances or even as subhuman. An alderman named Benzinger, the *News* reported, rejected the construction of housing in his ward because "there were enough pig pens in that ward and [he] didn't care to see anymore."[73] The story did, however, trumpet that city officials were "moving at last . . . urged doubtless by the expression of popular indignation at their tardiness."[74]

Happily, construction of temporary quarters had started in the Fifth Ward. By the end of the next week, it seemed, the Poles would begin their exodus from the tenements. Despite the progress, though, the Polish crisis was not to be easily resolved.

To established working-class residents, the immigrants, who had been identified as the potential source of plague and who were supposedly willing to work for pennies, represented both health and economic threats. Because the *News* circulated among all classes and groups, it found itself challenged to balance its roles as a voice of reason, as an advocate for the immigrants and as a friend to both businessman and laborer.

Despite the *News'* balancing act, however, its readers were not blindly following the paper's exhortations for mercy and tolerance. On Monday, June 20, the *News* reported that Fifth Ward residents had, the previous night, destroyed the partially completed barracks, scattering lumber and shingles throughout the neighborhood and causing $100 in damage—20 percent of the funds set aside for Polish relief.[75] Even though the *News* had championed the construction of the barracks in the Fifth Ward, it reacted with restraint, letting ward residents and leaders air their complaints against the relocation of the Poles, while gently counseling tolerance.[76]

The pastor of the neighborhood's Catholic church defended the raid, while a city official endorsed the mob and expressed the popular position on the Poles: "If they come here without money and what they earn they send to bring others here, they should be sent to the workhouse to earn their living."[77]

Without rebuking the official, the priest or the mob, the *News'* story attempted to defuse their fears by patiently explaining what had drawn the Poles to Buffalo in the first place. Rather than speaking for the Poles, the *News* let them speak for themselves. The *News* interviewed Sarah Schnardowski who was part of the established Polish community in Buffalo and had been acting as an interpreter for city officials and reporters in the tenement districts. Schnardowski explained how the steamship companies and railroads circulated fliers touting American opportunities among Polish peasants and then abandoned them when they arrived in America.

"All they care is to sell their passage tickets, and when they get them here and all their money is gone they dump them out of the cars like cattle," Schnardowski explained. "We don't live in such places because we like to, but we have to live somewhere."[78]

Indeed, the young woman explained, some of the very merchants and officials who opposed aiding the Poles had enticed the immigrants to Buffalo in the hope of lowering wages in the city. Schnardowski interpreted the story of one recent immigrant, who explained how one local employer had brought Poles over to replace higher-paid workers and then set the Poles into competition with each other. "He brought a shipload of Polacks here to work for him, and after he got them here he paid them 60 and 70 cents a day. The railroads do the same. That's the way we are kept poor all the time."[79] Asked why he did not move his family west, the immigrant explained that relatives in western cities reported the same conditions.[80]

An editorial in the same edition argued that the railroads and large employers were to blame for the plight of the Poles;[81] later editorials would call for the federal government to curtail spurious recruitment campaigns of peasants.[82] Butler's newspaper then turned its gaze upon culprits closer to home, namely the landlords who charged high rents for the "foul and filthy" tenements in which the immigrants lived and died.[83] The paper criticized landlords for charging not by the size of the dwelling, but by the size of the family that occupied it—thus, those who lived under the most crowded conditions paid the most.

The *News* was not content to scrutinize or castigate agencies charged with solving the Polish crisis. Leaders of the city government were ultimately responsible for the problems of the city, even if they had, as in the case of the Poles, distanced themselves from a crisis that on the surface affected an unpopular, poor, disenfranchised—and therefore politically useless—social group.

The *News*, founded upon the notion that partisan politics was anachronistic and damaging to a progressive social order, took the issue to the top of city government. If city leaders would not step forward and lead, the *News* would make them justify their inaction. If leaders chose to stay silent, the *News* would upbraid them for their indifference.

The lead story on June 22 detailed an unsuccessful attempt to elicit comment and action from Buffalo's mayor, Alexander Brush. Headlined, "TOO BUSY—Mayor Brush Hasn't Time to Attend to Polacks," the story ridiculed Brush and his fatuous excuses for avoiding the problem.[84] It is worth noting that not once during the series did the *News* identify public officials by party affiliation; nor did it try to reduce the crisis to simple causes. Instead, the paper methodically examined all of the causes of the problem and showed how they were interrelated.

Each day brought new revelations of filthy tenements in the city. As the scope of the crisis grew, and as the *News* urged social agencies to act, the paper supplied a steady stream of heart-wrenching stories of the immigrants' despair. Butler, aware of his readers' prejudices, kept the Poles' stories of suffering and degradation constantly before them. Also in the June 22 edition, amid stories explaining the issues and political maneuvering around the crisis, stories headlined, "A Broken Sewer" and "A Human Cell" appeared.[85] One story revealed:

Before the door under the stairway was a pool of dirty stagnant water. The floor of the room was five feet below ground. The walls were cracked and huge holes were visible in the ceiling. Only one window gave light into this dark, damp human cell. Martin Pocorski and wife and children have lived in this apartment one month. There were three filthy beds, and when it rains the water rushes into the doorway and inundates the place. Everything in the room bespeaks poverty and distress.[86]

HAVES AND HAVE-NOTS

In advocating for the immigrants and investigating the causes of the crisis, the newspaper was trying to fill an ever-widening breach between the haves and have-nots of both a changing Buffalo and an emerging urban America. The upstart independent newspapers of the late nineteenth century at once undermined partisanship and offered themselves as a more honest and effective public "meeting place."[87]

It would be a mistake, however, to consider the *News* radical. For at the same time the *News* was trying to establish an independent political identity, it was also trying to establish a sound economic base grounded in a diverse readership. Unlike the established party papers, the *Buffalo News* cost but a penny—and that, as much as its populist non-partisanship, spurred its high circulation among diverse city groups. Simply railing at the "system" or the city would have alienated readers and advertisers alike. Instead, like other nascent reformers, Butler championed stability and order, not equality—and certainly not socialism.

The Polish crusade fit neatly into a pattern evident since the founding of the *Buffalo News* in 1873 and continuing through the mid-1880s, when a wealthy and often absent Butler took a somewhat reactionary turn: Responsible elites had an obligation to oversee the integration of the lower classes into the political and economic life of the city. Once integrated, however, the lower classes were expected to know their place. Unless one could seize the opportunity to become a "self-made man"—the ultimate achievement in a free-labor system—one would be expected to accept his lower status as natural and destined.

The *Buffalo News'* strategy in moving the crusade forward hinged on more than emotional descriptions of tenement life or editorial ripostes at official apathy, indifference or incompetence. The crusade showed clearly that Butler understood that the coming of the Eastern European immigrants held consequences for everyone in the community. But partisan politics and partisan journalism, which acknowledged only their own constituencies and points of view, were too shortsighted to see the causes and effects of the rapid change befalling Buffalo and other cities. In a growing and increasingly fragmented and contentious metropolis, the *News* provided a platform where factions could see and hear one another, even if ultimately they could not come together in a harmonious hierarchy, as reformers such as Butler might have wished.

The Polish crusade was not merely a matter of improving government; reform demanded consensus and decisions made in the city needed to be weighed according to the ramifications they held for each faction and class. The influx of the Poles and other immigrants had long-term implications that went far beyond health and sanitation concerns. The appearance of half-starved immigrants willing to work for any wage upset the balance of power in the industrial community. If a lasting accommodation was to be found, it would have to reflect everyone's interests.

As self-appointed architect of that accommodation, the *News* took pains to ensure that all factions and classes had their say in the columns in the newspaper. Rather than simply offering up the letters to the editor page, Butler sent reporters out to attend the meetings of various civic groups and to interview their leaders.

The trade unions were especially nervous about the Polish situation, but were torn between empathy (most union members, after all, were not so far removed from the immigrant experience) and suspicion towards this group of potential wage-breakers in the city. During one trade union meeting, several members spoke out against the Poles, but the union ultimately adopted a series of resolutions expressing solidarity with the unfortunates and endorsing city aid to alleviate their suffering.

One union official assured the membership that the Poles would not work for less than prevailing rates and encouraged his brothers to actively take the side of the immigrants. "I rejoice in the emigration of people from lands of oppression and serfdom, and as long as our liberty gates are open, I say let them come, and we will do the best we can for them," the *News* quoted him as saying.[88]

The systematic inclusion of all groups in the community with a stake in the Polish crisis—workers, entrepreneurs, older immigrants, and the impoverished Poles themselves—illustrates how the *News* succeeded in making itself a vital, open meeting ground where the splintering metropolis might be bound up again. Groups that did not ordinarily meet came to know each other in the pages of the *News*.

On June 23, the *News* announced that a new site had been found for the Polish "barracks."[89] The Poles' new home was slated to be built in a different part of the Fifth Ward, on the east side, home to a small settlement of established Poles who had come to the city at least a decade before. There, it was presumed, there would likely be less antipathy and violence. With the political question of where to house the Poles seemingly settled, construction began at once.

While the *News'* sympathy for the Poles was hardly waning now that action on their behalf appeared imminent, the *News* began to demand that the immigrants keep their half of the implicit reform bargain: obedience to the social order—as defined by reformers such as Butler. Despite tension between older and newer immigrants, the *News* counseled the established Poles to take care of their own. The paper admonished the newcomers to learn from the earlier immigrants.[90]

Politicians in the established Polish enclave in the Fifth Ward welcomed the "invasion" of the new immigrants. "They will make good citizens," opined one, "and good voters,"[91] added another. At a meeting of Fifth Ward residents, immigrants who had come to Buffalo broke and then prospered through hard work were quoted approvingly by the *News*.

Other naturalized Poles—skilled, sophisticated workers from Polish cities—wanted no part of the bargain. It was unfair, they argued, to taint hardworking, integrated Poles with the contempt the community at large felt toward the newcomers. A *News* reporter described the tension between the two groups: "Everywhere the newcomers were denounced by the old settlers as lazy and filthy interlopers."[92]

One of the established Poles described the newcomers as " 'vags' or gypsies of the lower class of Russian Poles who will not work in their own country and immigrated to this country to become mendicants."[93] Their animosity reflected a prejudice the older, skilled, urban-rooted Poles carried over from the old country, as well as the general antipathy of skilled immigrants for the newly arrived unskilled immigrants. No matter; construction continued on the east side.

As new barracks were built and the Poles were moved from their old tenements, the *News* continued to monitor the progress of the city government in resolving the crisis. Alas, the *News* discovered that without constant scrutiny, construction lagged and officials turned their attention to politically expedient matters.

Butler and his *News* were therefore delighted to discover that city entrepreneurs had seized the opportunity created by the condemned slums to start a "building boom" to house the Polish immigrants. Individual enterprise on the part of "practical men" was an ideal solution.[94] The new dwellings appeared to the *News* to offer satisfactory sanitary conditions and fair rents.

The children of this world are wiser than the children of light. While the charity people are deserving of big tenements in the future, practical businessmen have come to the front, and are providing means to relieve the overcrowded dwellings and give the Poles decent quarters. Men of capital in the fifth ward have caught the idea of erecting small and comfortable quarters for the Polacks.[95]

But while the *News* gloated over the fact that men of action had outstripped the city government, the paper made it clear that politicians and bureaucrats must assume responsibility for the supervision of the city's infrastructure and long-term civic planning—tasks beyond the purview of individual businessmen. The city council was chastised for moving too slowly in providing sewers and drainage near the new dwellings.

As the Poles began to move into the new barracks, the *News* found its attention absorbed by the July 2 shooting of President Garfield and the long, drawn-out death drama that followed.[96] But the immigrants' story was not forgotten for long.

In early July, the newspaper's tone turned to frustration. Despite its best efforts—and reluctant action on the part of city officials—new tenement disasters kept surfacing. On July 11, the paper reported finding another "Nest of Destitute Poles," on Broadway. The tenement held twenty-three people, some of whom were "living in a horse stall and eating cast-off food"; down the street a case of typhoid fever had been reported.[97]

The next day, June 12, the newspaper vented its wrath at city health officials. Headlined, "All For Want of Nerve," the story retraced the Polish crisis and castigated the Health Department for procrastinating on the construction of new barracks and failing to identify existing habitable apartments for impoverished Poles. Uncharacteristically, the newspaper, which had thus far urged civic action and mercy for the immigrants, suggested that if the Poles were simply evicted from their filthy tenements, they would have to find cleaner apartments nearby. The story also reported that a sick Polish man given a quarter to buy milk had bought whiskey instead.[98] Meanwhile, "men under the influence of liquor" were lounging near the new barracks and occasionally throwing stones at the immigrants who lived there.[99]

Despite its rather callous lapse in sympathy for the immigrants, by July 21, the *News* was again aiming its barbs at the real culprits in the tenement saga. When a reporter discovered that Dr. Briggs was refusing to send sickly Poles to the hospital because "it costs me $5 every time I do out of my own pocket,"[100] the newspaper responded the next day with a front-page story headlined simply, "Dr. Briggs is Mad."

Briggs probably should have ducked the paper after his faux pas, but instead granted another interview to a *News* reporter. At the onset of the crusade he had declared that the Polish problem could not be solved without the support of the newspaper, but one month later he had had enough of the *News*. The problem, he explained, was that the paper's emotional stories had made citizens *too* interested in conditions in the tenements.

Describing his encounter with an earnest volunteer who wanted to help a sick immigrant she had read about in the paper, Briggs complained that, "The lady who called upon me is one of those people with [an] idea of revolutionizing the world in five minutes. Why she hadn't been in this country[101] more than three hours before her eye lit on the *News*, and she caught the statement of the man's condition and came to me."[102] He urged the paper to cease its sympathetic stories of the immigrants and asserted that if the Poles did not find work to support themselves they deserved to perish.[103]

Briggs' seeming contempt of the Poles and his unwillingness to act vigorously on their behalf slowed the exodus of the Poles from the tenements to sanitary housing. Meanwhile, more immigrants were arriving every day. The *News* continued to criticize the city for overfilling new dwellings and lamented that while improvement had been made, "in other respects the Poles are as badly off as ever, and are just as certain to gather filth and disease as before."[104]

By summer's end, the newspaper reported that the city's death rate that summer had been extraordinarily high, due largely to diseases that had incubated in the tenement districts. Buffalo had tried—grudgingly—to help the immigrants, but the city and its government were incapable of completely resolving the crisis. The result was, as the paper put it, "Death's Harvest Time."[105]

"PLAIN STARK FEAR"

The *News* did not accomplish all it set out to with its crusade on behalf of the Polish immigrants. One progressive newspaper, even one with a large circulation, could not change public opinion or policy overnight. But the *News* had demonstrated the power of a popular paper to influence civic events, a power that would grow with the years.

The paper was not shy about making sure readers knew it was responsible for leading the city towards practical and moral solutions to the Polish crisis. "Weeks ago, the *NEWS* urged that definite measures be taken to vacate the most crowded tenements on the East Side, and some slow progress has been made in that direction," one story boasted.[106] An editorial headlined, "A Good Work Commenced" also boomed the paper's role in clearing the tenements. "After a long fight in favor of health and cleanliness, the Evening News has succeeded in prompting the health officers of the city to do their duty, and the result is, some of the tenement houses which would be a disgrace to the scums [*sic*] of New York or London have been cleared."[107]

As a vehicle of reform, the *Buffalo News* asserted the right and the power to explore civic problems and lead the way in solving them. Unlike the stories that would appear in later muckraking magazines, the *News* crusade for the Poles did not serve as an allegory for an overall social critique aimed at overthrowing or altering existing institutions.

The forces that motivated Butler to crusade for the Poles were diverse and complex. As a struggling publisher not so far removed from poverty himself, he surely felt kinship with the city's workers and others fighting to survive on the margins. His religious upbringing had given him a strong sense of right and wrong. In addition, the continued expansion of his newspaper depended on ever-increasing circulation, and new readership was to be found primarily among the burgeoning lower classes.

Butler's advocacy for the Poles was the highlight of his career as a reformer. He had first promised readers in the *Sunday Morning News* in the 1870s that his would be "The Firm Friend and Acknowledged Organ of the People," and "The Newspaper Which Dares Call a Liar a Liar and Villain a Villain."[108] The crusades and editorials that appeared in his paper through the mid-1880s bore witness to his sincerity. Ironically, however, advocating for the working classes brought Butler great wealth, and by the 1890s he had become a rather arrogant patrician.[109] The man who had stood alone in defense of workers during the great strike of 1877 led the call for the National Guard to put down strikers by force in a similar strike in 1892.[110]

Social conditions and ideology also drove Butler and other reformers. Nell Irvin Painter and others have argued convincingly that fear was ultimately at the root of the outwardly optimistic reform movement:

Plain, stark fear lay at the core of much of the reform on the part of the middle and upper classes. Fear of revolution appeared repeatedly in explanations of why this or that social evil needed to be eliminated. Fear of working class violence explains much of what has been called progressive reform.[111]

Certainly a sense of foreboding is present in the *Buffalo News'* crusade on behalf of the Poles, but the specter that threatened Buffalo was disease, not revolution. Still, the *News'* stance toward the problem of massive immigration seemed to be that unless the impoverished underclass was shown a modicum of decency now and invited to assimilate, it might one day rise up and turn on the established interests of the city.

Butler and the *Buffalo News* made clear that once rescued from the filth of the tenements, assimilated Poles could join an orderly working class. At no time did the *News* suggest that the Poles—with limited education and skills—could become anything more than constituents in a Buffalo led by Anglo reformers.

But "plain, stark fear" does not adequately describe the crusade for the Poles. The *News* balanced appeals to fear of plague with impassioned pleas for Buffalonians of all classes and political persuasions to act on their sense of justice and humanity. Given the public resistance he faced, the crusade was a courageous act on the part of Butler, who as a boy had learned right from wrong at the knee of his minister father.

The emotional narrative style of the stories was aimed more at evoking pathos and empathy than fear. When residents rose up to destroy the first new barracks for the Poles, the *News* chastised them and urged that the barracks be built no matter what public sentiments prevailed—a risky stand for a popular newspaper.

In a community that, under the pressure of rapid growth, industrialization, and increasing heterogeneity, was losing its center—once held firm by the political parties—Butler tried to make the *Buffalo News* the substitute for that center. While Butler was genuinely driven by a sense of moral obligation in his crusades against injustice, he had other motives, too. A newspaper that considered the interests of all groups in the community would also be bought and read by the members of those groups, reaping for its owner profits and an enviable political base.

By the end of the crusade, living conditions had improved for Buffalo's Polish immigrants. The crusade had proved that a newspaper could and should insert itself into community affairs as an independent advocate for all citizens. Party papers atomized or excluded Buffalo's civic factions. The cheap, broad-based *News* of E. H. Butler bound them up.

A newspaper alone, however, could not reconstitute the personal and intimate market-square politics destroyed by urbanism and industrialization. However, as familiar institutions waned, it could offer an effective, if temporary, surrogate for that market square by reflecting and instilling popular beliefs, representing and directing citizens and revealing and attempting to heal potentially serious rifts in the volatile metropolis. The slum crusade became increasingly popular in the 1880s; Jacob Riis investigated the tenements of the New York's Lower East Side and, in 1890, published a terrifying book with text, photographs and sketches detailing the misery he found there.[112]

The crusading journalism exemplified by the *Buffalo News* and other American reform newspapers of the late nineteenth century offered a first step toward political, social and cultural adjustment to a rapidly changing society and a comprehensive and detailed examination of its changing people and institutions. The next step would come with the muckraking magazines that began to appear in the next decade.

NOTES

1. "A Missing Girl: Dora Higgins, a Pupil in School 6, Mysteriously Disappears," *Buffalo Evening News*, June 15, 1881, 1. Hereinafter referred to as *Evening News*.

2. "Vitriol Throwing. A Dastardly Attempt to Blind or Disfigure a Sleeping Man," *Evening News*, June 15, 1881, 1.

3. "With Blood in His Eye," *Evening News*, June 15, 1881, 1.

4. "The City's Disgrace," *Evening News*, June 15, 1881, 1.

5. See Ida Tarbell, *The History of Standard Oil* (New York: McClure, Phillips & Co., 1904) on monopoly. The U.S. Senate is the target of David Graham Phillips' *The Treason of the Senate* (Chicago: Quadrangle Books, 1964). Urban corruption is documented in Lincoln Steffens' *The Shame of the Cities* (New York: McClure, Phillips & Co., 1904).

6. One major difference between newspaper and magazine crusading is that magazine writers worked for months to investigate their subjects and prepare their

articles, taking time to think through implications and connections; newspaper investigators, by contrast, flew by the seat of their pants, working on daily deadlines and reacting to events as they unfolded.

7. Arthur M. Schlesinger, *The American as Reformer* (Cambridge, Mass.: Harvard University Press, 1968), 52.

8. The "New Journalism" of the post–Civil War period was predicated on aggressive news coverage, a strong social agenda, and large profits that arose from a broad conception of news. "Partisan editors viewed their readers as voters and geared their content to such an audience," writes Gerald Baldasty. But by century's end, "publishers saw their readers not only as voters but as consumers and produced content that went far beyond politics and voting." Baldasty, *The Commercialization of the Press in the 19th Century* (Madison: University of Wisconsin Press, 1993), 5.

9. Michael Shudson also points to the effects of commercialization of the press. Professionalism and sophistication among reporters led to several stylistic innovations in journalism that distinguished new journalism from its predecessors; interviews, a focus on brevity, and summary leads made the news more immediate and compelling. Schudson, *The Good Citizen* (New York: The Free Press, 1998), 176–180.

10. Although many of the modern criteria of news—drama, human interest, factuality, consequence—can be found in the penny press of the 1830s, this style of news did not come to *dominate* American journalism until the decades after the Civil War. As Marion Marzolf writes, "today's standards and values were mainly shaped around the turn of the century when a 'new journalism' challenged an old journalism that was rooted in the partisan political tradition. In modified form, the new journalism is still today's journalism." Marzolf, *Civilizing Voices: American Press Criticism 1880–1950* (New York: Longman, 1991), 3.

11. A true progressive, Edward Butler was a leader in introducing new technologies to Buffalo, and to the news business there. A direct telegraph line was installed at the *News* in 1880. When he erected a new building after the successful debut of the *Evening News*, Butler had it wired and installed a huge electric light that, not coincidentally, brought crowds to the newspaper office. Michael Dillon, "A Smart Live Journal: E. H. Butler's *Buffalo News* and the Rise and Decline of an Open Public Forum, 1873–1914," Ph.D. diss., Pennsylvania State University, 1995, 115–131.

12. Robert H. Wiebe, *The Search for Order, 1877–1920* (New York: Hill and Wang, 1967), 56; Nell Irvin Painter, *Standing at Armageddon: The United States, 1877–1919* (New York: Norton & Co., 1987), xii.

13. Schlesinger, *American as Reformer*, 51.

14. In 1836, James Gordon Bennett's epic series on the murder of prostitute Ellen Jewett caused a sensation. Bennett took his readers on a tour of New York's brothels and turned Jewett into a symbol of every feminine myth of the age. The stories about Jewett first appeared in the *Herald* in April 1836. The series is documented in Andie Tucher, *Froth and Scum: Truth, Beauty, Goodness and the Ax Murder in America's First Mass Medium* (Chapel Hill: University of North Carolina Press, 1994).

15. For instance, Michael McGerr argues that the appearance of cheap, popular newspapers defused political energy by transforming politics into a topic for coverage rather than an activity in which citizens vigorously participated. McGerr, *The Decline*

of Popular Politics: The American North, 1865–1928 (New York: Oxford University Press, 1986).

16. As Schudson points out, "One might say that, for the first time, the newspaper reflected not just commerce or politics, but social life." Schudson, *Discovering the News* (New York: Basic Books, 1978).

17. Quoted in W.A. Swanberg, *Pulitzer* (New York: Charles Scribners and Sons, 1967), 61.

18. Historian Frank Luther Mott proposed that Pulitzer "invented" new journalism and his observations have been cited endlessly. According to Mott, "No wonder newspaper publishers elsewhere studied the *World* and imitated its policies until a new journalism grew out of them." Mott, *American Journalism: A History* (New York: Macmillan, 1962), 436.

19. Standard histories of journalism, such as Emery and Emery, fix the widespread appearance of "muckraking" in the early 1890s and credit Pulitzer with the creation of crusading journalism. Michael Emery and Edwin Emery, *The Press and America: An Interpretive History of the Mass Media* (Englewood Cliffs, N.J., Prentice Hall 1988), 203–207. In addition, a Pulitzer biographer points out that Pulitzer's crusades with his *St. Louis Post and Dispatch* were primarily on behalf of the middle class. Not until he opened the *World* in 1883—two years after the *Buffalo Evening News* Polish crusade—did Pulitzer consistently take up the causes of the impoverished Julian S. Rammelkamp, *Pulitzer's Post and Dispatch, 1878–1883* (Princeton, N.J.: Princeton University Press, 1967), 67.

20. Rammelkamp, *Pulitzer's Post and Dispatch*, 34–35.

21. Butler got his start on the tiny *Leroy Gazette*, where, even as a teen, he dreamed about one day opening a paper "along the lines of" James Gordon Bennett's *Herald*. Butler chronicled his childhood in Leroy and his early days in Buffalo in a series of reminiscences, some of which were published in the *News* and elsewhere. His original drafts are collected with Butler's other papers in the Butler Library at the State University College at Buffalo.

22. Butler rose to managing editor of the *Scranton Tribune*. When he and three partners decided they could start a new paper in Scranton, it was decided that it would only pay enough to support two partners. The four men held a coin toss and the losers—Butler and one J. B. Adams—decamped for Buffalo to start a Sunday sheet. Adams left the partnership shortly afterward. Butler Papers, State University College at Buffalo.

23. Antebellum Buffalo was dominated by Norman Mack's Republican *Morning Express*, and William J. Conners' Democratic *Courier*. The two publishers were prominent in both city and state politics. Conners, who held sway over the city's vast lakefront workforce, had much to lose by the appearance of a popular journal aimed at the working class. Shortly after the debut of the Buffalo *Evening News* in 1880, the Scripps brothers opened the *Evening Telegraph* in Buffalo. It quickly failed in competition with the *News*, and when it folded Butler bought its lists. See Dillon, "Smart Live Journal."

24. Robert Park, "The Natural History of the Newspaper," *The American Journal of Sociology* (November 1923): 284.

25. According to an audit by George P. Rowell & Co., the *Buffalo Sunday Morning News* actually surpassed its combined city rivals within two years of its introduction, when it reached 16,000 readers. "The Buffalo Press," *Buffalo Sunday*

Morning News, June 13, 1875. (At the time of the crusade, Sunday readership had grown still more, and the daily's circulation had reached 17,000. By the mid-1880s, circulation had grown to 40,000 and at the turn of the century the *News* sold 100,000 papers in a city of 350,000.)

26. Dillon, "From Patriarch to Patrician: Edward H. Butler's Buffalo News and the Crisis of Labor, 1877–1892," *American Journalism* (winter 1999): 41–58.

27. Editorial, *Buffalo Sunday Morning News,* June 14, 1874, 1.

28. Editorial *Buffalo Sunday Morning News,* July 31, 1875, 1.

29. Editorial, *Buffalo Sunday Morning News,* May 10, 1874, 1.

30. In October 1874, Butler recast his 10,000 *Sunday Morning News* readers into "10,000 Honest Voters," and proposed a bipartisan People's Ticket that would prevent either political party from gaining a monopoly on city government; only one of the ticket's candidates lost.

31. "Are They Quacks? Medical Vultures Who Prey Upon the Vitals of Humanity," *Buffalo Sunday Morning News,* October 10, 1875, 1.

32. "Horrible! The Pauper Dead!" *Buffalo Sunday Morning News,* June 7, 1874, 1.

33. Thomas C. Leonard, *Power of the Press: The Birth of American Political Reporting* (New York: Oxford University Press, 1986), 97–123.

34. Historical United States Census Date Browser, statistics culled from "Historical Demographic, Economic and Social Data: The United States, 1790–1970" ⟨http://fisher.lib.virginia.edu/census/⟩.

35. Buffalo Industrial Census, 1880.

36. The Poles made up a large percentage of the immigrants who arrived in Buffalo during this period. The city went from having a modest Polish district in the 1870s to having the third largest Polish population in the United States by early 1880s, trailing only Milwaukee and Chicago. John Theodore Horton, *History of Northwestern New York* (New York: Lewis Historical Publishing Company Inc., 1947), 319.

37. Maldwyn Allen Jones, *American Immigration* (Chicago: University of Chicago Press, 1993), 178.

38. In 1860, fewer than 20 percent of Americans lived in cities; by 1900, that figure had jumped to 40 percent. Esmond Wright, *The American Dream—From Reconstruction to Reagan* (Cambridge, Mass.: Blackwell Publishers, 1996), 97.

39. Low wages, high taxes and land shortages drove many Poles from their homeland. By most standards, no matter how bad things were in America, they were even worse at home. Paul Fox, *The Poles in America* (New York: Arno Press, 1970), 59.

40. "Buffalo's Shame," *Evening News,* June 16, 1881, 1.

41. "They Come to Buffalo in 'Swarms Thicker than Locusts' " (editorial), *Evening News,* April 29, 1881, 2.

42. "A Missing Girl," *Evening News,* June 15, 1881, 1.

43. "Buffalo's Shame," *Evening News,* June 16, 1881, 1.

44. Ibid.

45. Ibid.

46. Ibid.

47. Editorial, *Buffalo Commercial Advertiser,* June 21, 1881, 3.

48. Editorial, *Buffalo Express,* June 20, 1881, 3.

49. "People Living in Dark Cellars—Pestilence-Breeding Filth," *Evening News*, June 19, 1881, 1.

50. The June 27 edition carried no stories about the Poles, but it did contain a brief editorial on the continuing crisis.

51. During this period in American journalism, "the form of newswriting began to change. The paper became less the editor's scrapbook to be shared with like minded readers, and more an organization's product." Schudson, *The Good Citizen*, 179.

52. "A Visit to the House of Death," *Evening News*, June 16, 1881, 1.

53. In the small metropolis of the early eighteenth century, neighborhoods were small and connected enough so that residents could collectively manage their own affairs. The tremendous growth in size and population of America's cities, however, made such collective action unworkable. "Pell-mell expansion destroyed the groups and neighborhoods that sustained social action. The thousands recently arrived, the thousands more moving about, concentrated narrowly on their own security." Wiebe, *Search for Order*, 13.

54. Wright, *American Dream*, 98.

55. Ibid., 91–92.

56. After roiling the New York public with an almost erotic description of the murdered prostitute's corpse the day before, Bennett observed in the next edition that "news was received from Texas highly disastrous to the colonists, but the private tragedy of Ellen Jewett absorbed almost all attention." "The Recent Tragedy," *New York Herald*, April 23, 1.

57. James Gordon Bennett—who sent Stanley to search for Livingston—and Joseph Pulitzer were among the first publishers to discover that a newspaper needn't run on the world's schedule at all. By creating "events" and then covering them, Pulitzer's *World* routinely set its own schedule of breaking stories and sensations. Both would be surpassed in this field, of course, by yellow journalist William Randolph Hearst.

58. Jurgen Habermas, *The Structural Transformation of the Public Sphere* (Cambridge, Mass.: MIT Press, 1989), 164–169.

59. Ibid.

60. Robert Park asserted that, "the motive . . . of the writers and the press in all this is to reproduce, as far as possible, in the city conditions of life in the village." Park, "The Natural History of the Newspaper," 277.

61. On a practical level, "As the cities grew in size and population it became increasingly difficult, if not impossible, for the average citizen to know what was going on." Wright *The American Dream*, 84.

62. Briggs' comments appeared in a news story on June 16 and then were excerpted sarcastically in a brief standing column of mostly inane quotes by city officials called, "Some Professional People," *Evening News*, June 17, 1.

63. When Briggs later vaguely explained that he could not move more quickly because his hands were tied, the *News* did not let him off the hook and responded with a stinging editorial. "Who has tied the hands of Dr. Briggs, the Health Physician? Let the doctor speak, so that the blame may fall where it belongs." Editorial Notes, *Evening News*, June 17, 1881, 2.

64. "Will the Poles Work?" (letter to the editor), *Evening News*, June 23, 1881, 1.

65. "One Cause of the Mortality," *Evening News*, June 17, 1881, 1.

66. "Seventeen in One Room. Families Living on Rotten Apples—The Most Pitiable Scene of All," *Evening News*, June 18, 1881, 1.

67. "One Cause of the Mortality," *Evening News*, June 17, 1.

68. Editorial, *Evening News*, June 16, 1881, 2.

69. "Moving at Last. The Council Committee Providing for a Few of the Polanders," *Evening News*, June 17, 1881, 1.

70. "Another Death in the Alabama Street Den," *Evening News*, June 17, 1881, 1.

71. "Scenes in the Tenements," *Evening News*, June 18, 1881, 1.

72. "Another Death at 479 Alabama Street," *Evening News*, June 17, 1881, 1.

73. "A Midnight Raid. Residents of the Fifth Ward Tear Down Polish Barracks," *Evening News*, June 20, 1881, 1.

74. Ibid.

75. Ibid.

76. Tolerance was slow in coming. There were several attacks on Polish immigrants who moved into sanitary apartments in neighborhoods where they were not welcome. On June 24, as they held vigil for their dead 18-month-old son, a family of relocated Poles was attacked by youngsters throwing rocks. "Young Rioters. A Polack House in the First Ward Stoned By Boys," *Evening News*, June 24, 1881, 1.

77. "A Midnight Raid," *Evening News*, June 20, 1881, 1.

78. Why the Polacks Come. Deceived by the Representatives of the Railroad Agents," *Evening News*, June 20, 1881, 1.

79. Ibid.

80. Ibid.

81. Editorial, *Evening News*, June 22, 1881, 2.

82. Although many cities—including Buffalo—responded to the influx of immigrants by petitioning the State Department to protest unsavory recruitment of immigrants in Europe, the truth is that most European nations already had strict laws prohibiting such recruitment; most immigrants came to America unbidden because it offered the possibility of a new beginning. Jones, *American Immigration*, 57.

83. "Foul and Filthy"—How Landlords Get Big Rents From Poor Tenants," *Evening News*, June 21, 1881, 1.

84. "Too Busy—Mayor Brush Hasn't Time to Attend to Polacks," *Evening News*, June 22, 1881, 1.

85. "A Broken Sewer" and "A Human Cell," *Evening News*, June 22, 1881, 1.

86. "A Human Cell," ibid.

87. Patricia Dooley writes, "to acquire jurisdiction over political communication work, the members of the group (the press) had to convince the public that such work undertaken on its behalf was of supreme importance to the republic." Dooley, *Taking Their Political Place: Journalists and the Making of an Occupation* (Westport, Conn.: Greenwood Press, 1997), 179.

88. "What the Workingmen Say," *Evening News*, June 23, 1881, 1.

89. "A Change of Base," *Evening News*, June 23, 1881, 1.

90. "Old and New Poles. A Visit to the Settlement at East Buffalo—Habits of the People," *Evening News*, June 23, 1881, 1.

91. "Aldermen and Fifth Warders in Executive Session—Poles and Politics," *Evening News*, June 24, 1881, 1.

92. "Old and New Poles. A Visit to the Settlement at East Buffalo—Habits of the People," *Evening News*, June 23, 1881, 1.

93. Ibid.

94. "A Building Boom. Practical Men Find Way to Solve Polish Problem," *Evening News*, June 24, 1881, 1.

95. Ibid.

96. Garfield was shot by a disgruntled office seeker on July 2, 1881, and lingered with mortal wounds through the summer. It was a rare day that at least half of the front page was not devoted to the many twists and turns in his convalescence or to the journey through the courts and eventual murder of his assassin.

97. "Sick and Destitute. A Nest of Destitute Poles," *Evening News*, July 11, 1881, 1.

98. "All For Want of Nerve. Why the Polish Tenements Threaten the City's Health," *Evening News*, July 12, 1881, 1.

99. Ibid.

100. "Out of His Own Pocket—Pity Poor Dr. Briggs," *Evening News*, July 21, 1881, 1.

101. The doctor meant by this, in all probability, not that the woman was a newly arrived immigrant, but was a newcomer to the city.

102. "Dr. Briggs is Mad," *Evening News*, July 22, 1881, 1.

103. Ibid.

104. "Hiving the Polacks," *Evening News*, July 7, 1881, 1.

105. "Death's Harvest Time," *Evening News*, August 11, 1881, 1.

106. "Action at Last," *Evening News*, July 6, 1881, 1.

107. "A Good Work Commenced" (editorial), *Evening News*, July 7, 1881, 2.

108. *The Sunday Morning News*, October 24, 1875, 1.

109. Butler died in 1914. The *News*, which passed out of the hands of his heirs in 1977, is Buffalo's only remaining newspaper.

110. Dillon, "From Populist to Patrician."

111. Painter, *Standing at Armageddon*, xii.

112. Jacob Riis, *How the Other Half Lives: Studies Among the Tenements of New York* (New York: Charles Scribner's Sons, 1902).

3

Muckraking the World's Richest Church

Robert Miraldi

The most well-known muckraking crusades against what Progressives called the "interests" are Ida Tarbell's history and exposé of John D. Rockefeller's giant oil monopoly and Samuel Hopkins Adams' tale of medicinal fraud and dangerous over-the-counter drugs. Less well known and remembered is Charles Edward Russell's angry series of articles in 1908 and 1909 on America's wealthiest religious institution—Trinity Church of Manhattan, which also happened to be the biggest slum land- lord in New York City. Historian Vernon Parrington rightly points out that the muckrakers left few social justice causes untouched. From child labor to working conditions to racial injustice, the muckrakers sought out problems that were ripe for exposure. If it smelled bad, their noses twitched, Parrington said. But the church had gone unscathed—until Russell, the grandson of a minister, introduced a national audience to the Trinity scandal in articles in *Hampton's* and *Everybody's* magazines. Russell (1860–1941) was associated in various ways with all of America's major reform movements from the Civil War to World War I. Of the major muckraking writers, he was the most prolific, wrote on the widest range of topics, and muckraked for the longest period of time. Lincoln Steffens described Russell as the most wounded of the muckraking tribe. His passion and anger can be seen clearly in his attack on the slums that were owned by the world's richest church. One of Russell's articles on Trinity is reprinted in *The Muckrakers*, edited by Arthur and Lila Wein- berg (New York: Simon and Schuster, 1961), 311–320.

When Charles Edward Russell arrived in New York City in 1886, unable to find work after editing three midwestern newspapers, he discovered what it was like to be broke and hungry. He spent his first months, he said, "walking the streets and nearly starving." But over the next decade, as he made his way around Manhattan as a newspaper reporter for the *Commercial Advertiser* and the *Herald* and as an editor for the *World* and the *Journal*, sending reporters to cover the poorest regions of the growing metropolis, he learned what poverty really was.

In his time as a police reporter for the *Herald*, working during a period when Jacob Riis was startling New York City with stories of how the "other half" was living, Russell discovered "the stinking rear tenements" and slum housing of Manhattan. He called it "one of the most unsightly spots on earth." As a huddling spot for hordes of immigrants, the Lower East Side region had become more densely populated than Calcutta.[1] "I climbed the rickety and ill-smelling stairway of many a rear tenement," Russell recalled of the twenty-two years that he observed squalor unlike anything in the agrarian Midwest where he had grown up. At times, Russell thought he had "crossed a frontier into a foreign land." In many ways, of course, New York resembled a foreign enclave. As the city's population soared from 1.5 million in 1870 to 5 million by 1915, thousands of immigrants—Germans, Italians, Jews—had swarmed into overpriced, unlit, waterless and litter-filled tenements that made for horrible places to live but often brought a handsome profit for their owners. Coming from his comfortable upbringing in Davenport, Iowa, Russell was shocked that "poverty and insufficiency are so common"; that poverty "may be said to be the rule, and sufficiency the exception." No Iowa farmer, Russell noted, "would house hogs in the way 100,000 people are housed in New York City."[2]

Russell's education about poverty and slum tenements on the Lower East Side was an inevitable product of the stories he wrote—and those he didn't. One Sunday he was assigned a tenement suicide. A tailor who couldn't find work had hanged himself. "I remember that even I, by this time fairly well accustomed to East Side squalor, was depressed with what I saw," Russell recalled. The scene made a strong impression on him.[3] As he approached the wooden two-story building where the death had occurred, he saw dirty wastewater pouring into a courtyard in which ragged children, gaunt and pasty-faced, played and slopped. Sanitation sheds, where garbage had been dumped, were gaping open and spilling into the courtyard. "One was puzzled to think how human beings could endure the gases that flowed out," Russell said. He climbed up stairs that threatened to break with each step to find the tailor—"his face twisted with toil"—hanging from a cord in the middle of the one room where he lived with his wife and child. Even though accounts of suicides were common enough in the newspapers of the Gilded Age, he knew there was no newspaper story in the tailor's death because, he had learned, "the suicides of persons with foreign names residing in tenement house regions of the East Side were classed as trivial and left to the copy boys." Nonetheless, the vivid images of the reality of New York stuck with Russell. He concluded: "This New York is a cruel place."[4]

The awful effects of poverty were further brought home to him in the winter of 1892 when he interviewed dozens of tenement dwellers to see how a rise in coal prices in the mines of Pennsylvania was affecting the slums of the world's most populated city. What he found were people huddling around stoves without enough coal to get them through a brutally cold winter. Worst of all, he found people freezing to death. One widow remained etched in his memory many years after he saw her. When he arrived at her apartment, the police showed him the body—lying on a cot, covered with snow that had fallen through a skylight into an unheated apartment. Unable to afford coal, the woman had given up and simply froze to death. "Not one in thousand [*sic*] of fortunate New Yorkers has the slightest conception of the amount of poverty in New York," Russell thought.[5]

The line from the poverty of the Lower East Side of New York City— from what Russell called "the crushing influence of the tenement house"— ran directly to what was his greatest achievement as a journalist and reformer. In 1908, Russell applied the final blow to a forty-year effort to expose, improve and eliminate the wretched tenements owned by one of the biggest slum landlords in New York City—Trinity Church, "the mother all churches." By writing three dramatic and controversial articles in two national magazines with large circulations, Russell forced the wealthiest church in America to tear down its slums in favor of model housing, to open its financial ledgers to the public and to radically alter its conception of the responsibilities of a Christian landlord.[6]

By 1908 the efforts of a group of magazine writers who had become increasingly known as "muckrakers" had been going strong for nearly six years, ever since Ida Tarbell and Lincoln Steffens had begun it all in *McClure's Magazine*. Thomas Lawson's exposé of business (1904), Samuel Hopkins Adams' wicked attack on the patent medicines (1905), Sinclair's meat exposé and David Graham Phillips' blistering indictment of the U.S. Senate (both 1906)—all had helped fire up the forces of reform and led directly to a famous counterattack by Theodore Roosevelt in April 1906. Fearful that these "muck-rakers"—Roosevelt was the first to use the word publicly—were building a revolutionary fervor in the nation, Roosevelt implored the writers and the nation to remember all that was good in capitalist America. Look at the sky, not at the muck, he urged, in what was a sly way of unleashing a torrent of criticism of exposé journalism.[7] Russell understood what Roosevelt was trying to accomplish. He explained: "Whenever a depraved reformer suggests any change in this holy and perfectly authenticated order, there is first laughter, then contempt, then alarm, then a rapid banding together of the forces of righteousness [until there results] a glorious victory for the right and the total defeat of the forces of unrest."

Russell feared Roosevelt's speech was succeeding. "Many of the magazine editors took fright at the presidential command and abandoned exposé stuff," he noted. Louis Filler, the preeminent historian of the muckraking movement, concurs with Russell. After Roosevelt's speech, "the legend was now developed that muckraking was dead . . . that the public was thoroughly 'tired' of muckraking, and that the few remaining muckrakers were mere outlaws with no following."[8] But Russell was one of the outlaws and, at 48 years old, he was just beginning to hit his stride—as a muckraker at least. Already he had worked at the pinnacle of daily journalism for nearly a decade. He was called one of the ten best reporters in America when he worked in New York City for the *Herald*. Then, Pulitzer lured him to his *World*, making him city editor for four years. Not to be outdone by his rival, William Randolph Hearst then stole Russell—along with many other Pulitzer stars—and made him the *Journal's* managing editor during the tumultuous "yellow journalism" years. As Hearst expanded his journalism empire, he sent Russell to start up and publish his third newspaper, the *American*, in Chicago where Russell perfected the crusading and muckraking techniques that he had practiced under Pulitzer and Hearst. But, when his health failed in 1902, he took leave from the hectic and crazed daily pace of Hearst's papers. He traveled, rested and recuperated—and then became antsy. Finally, in 1905, he jumped back into reporting, writing a multipart series of articles for *Everybody's* magazine on what he perceived as the greatest threat to the American economy: the beef trust, a coalition of meatpackers who, he insisted, controlled the lifeblood of the economy. This "greatest trust in the world" needed to be stopped, he wrote in articles that spurred a congressional investigation and came months before Upton Sinclair tackled what he called, in a note to Russell, "the monster." Needing an outlet for his increasingly angry exposés and attacks on the political economic establishment, Russell turned to Benjamin Hampton's *New Broadway Magazine*, which was a mediocre little magazine with 12,000 readers when Hampton bought it in 1904. By 1908, with persistent muckraking articles, circulation for *Hampton's* had soared to 480,000. Russell would have an audience.[9]

Russell had first heard about Trinity Church from his father. When the family arrived in America in the late 1840s, they were briefly housed in a ramshackle tenement. It was owned by Trinity. The experience led the family to get out of New York. Russell may have felt he had a score to settle with Trinity, not unlike the grudge Ida Tarbell may have harbored after her father was forced out of the Pennsylvania oil fields by John D. Rockefeller. Another factor was more important for Russell, however: Trinity was the wealthiest church in America and it made an attractive, if not sensational, symbolic target. The church towered over Wall Street; from its bronze front door one could see the chief offices of Rockefeller's Standard Oil Company, as well as the mightiest banks and insurance companies in America. An attack on Trinity, the church of J. Pierpont Morgan, the financier who headed the nation's "banking trust," was an attack on corporate America. Russell had worked long enough for Pulitzer and Hearst, the two great masters who had perfected sensationalism, to know a fabulous story when he saw one.

Newspapers, in fact, had for years attacked the church, pointing out the delicious and obvious irony: One of the great moral institutions in New York City owned a slew of awful tenement buildings. How could this pillar of the community, with one of the largest charitable outreaches in New York, reap a financial windfall from what Russell called "drunken, disreputable, decayed, topsy-turvy old houses"? Yet Trinity had withstood these assaults for years.

A more substantive issue at stake in this story made it so important to Russell: the Trinity saga involved both poverty and housing, issues that were dear to Progressives and Socialists alike. Although he wouldn't admit it, in 1908 Russell could still be counted as both. On the one hand, he was a reformer who knew that his exposé would exert public pressure on Trinity to clean up an environment that was ruining the lives of thousands of Americans. For many Progressive reformers who followed in the footsteps of tenement house champion Jane Addams, the slum cause was as important as the regulation of the trusts and the control of municipal corruption. Reformers placed great faith in the potency of a changed physical environment. "There is such a thing as a criminal mind," Russell once wrote, "but in every instance it can be traced back to environment and living conditions."[10] Urban problems stemmed from rotten housing, not rotten hearts.

Moreover, as a budding socialist, Russell saw Trinity as a wonderful example of systemic failure—capitalism had forced even a beneficent institution such as Trinity to "divide responsibility between church and Wall Street."[11] The "system" forced even the good men of Trinity into following bad policies. While reform and regulation might ease some of the tenement's worst excesses (Russell praised the work of tenement reformers), it would not go far enough to suit Russell's more radical beliefs. Thus, Russell's Trinity exposé could kill two birds with one stone: lend a hand to the forces of tenement reform that had been making slow progress in urban America in improving housing conditions and also condemn the institution of the profiteering that was—as Russell increasingly saw it—at the root of the problem.

"HORRIBLE THINGS . . . UNSPEAKABLE TERROR"

Trinity, a Presbyterian church founded in the 1700s, was a perfect example of concentrated wealth, the kind that muckrakers and Progressives had been decrying for two decades. Plutocracy, they believed, was a threat to true democracy. Wealthy monopolists threatened individualism and competition, they halted small businesses from entering the marketplace and they ruled politics by buying votes and owning legislators. Henry Demarest Lloyd, who Russell had read in his school days in Vermont, had attacked the great combinations decades earlier in his famous treatise, *Wealth Against Commonwealth*. Tarbell had documented these threats with her exposé of

Rockefeller's oil monopoly and, in September 1907, the federal government sued in court to break up Standard's domination. Lawson's revelations in 1904 showed that, even on Wall Street, the buccaneers used their corrupt practices on each other to make their fortunes. Russell's beef trust articles were all about concentrated and hidden monopoly power. The problem of monopoly power "came at times to overshadow everything else," Russell believed. "The national life was being sapped. The process must stop or we perish."[12]

Trinity Church represented another aspect—as yet unexposed—of the corrosive effect of wealth. Russell labeled the church's lust for profit "yellow wizardry . . . the spell of yellow enchantment." Although it operated admirable schools and shelters, Trinity Church was also the biggest slum landlord on Manhattan Island, the owner of "the worst tenements in New York," Russell charged. This, he declared, "was a disgrace to civilization and to the city of New York." Indignant and determined, Russell set out to expose the Trinity/slum connection and to pressure the church into revealing, for the first time since 1814, the extent of its wealth and income. This was no easy task. Reformers had been looking into Trinity's tenements on and off for nearly two decades and Trinity was the church of the establishment—wealthy, powerful, well connected. Its board of directors consisted of Wall Street financial types who ran New York City, part of the "invisible government" that muckraker Lincoln Steffens had written about four years earlier in his "Shame of the Cities."[13]

As Russell and two researchers began to dig into the Lower East Side's "pangs of poverty," finding "dirt, darkness and squalor," it was not Trinity rulers who motivated them. It was the victims—"respectable and industrious Americans," he called them—many of whom were to his surprise second- and third-generation Americans, victims he had seen for years but about whom he now had a reason to write. In November 1907, Russell visited dozens of the properties owned by Trinity and he found "horrible things." He knocked at a door and a silver-haired, 70-year-old woman answered. "She looked respectable and decent despite her surroundings, but the last vestige of the human spirit had long been crushed out of her," Russell found. Dressed in rags, gaunt and bent, with "unspeakable terror in her eyes," she cringed at Russell's questions. "The utter dreariness of her surroundings had shriveled away the soul of humanity," he wrote.[14]

And then there were the children—"chalk-faced" and "growing up in terrible places" owned by Trinity, Russell wrote. One little girl in particular struck him. Her family lived behind a tiny and scantily stocked store. The girl was sick, lying on a filthy old mattress in a wooden shed that was her bedroom. Russell wrote: "The floor was filthy, the walls were bare, the room was a cold, cheerless hole." The child lay against a wall, beyond which was a backyard, "reeking of things I must not speak about," Russell said. The child was dying, as were so many of the children who "had been stupefied by the crushing misery in which they lived."[15]

Russell speculated that the child suffered from tuberculosis. Thus, he argued in the three articles he wrote about Trinity Church, the public had a real reason and a vital self-interest in forcing a cleanup of the slums. When a reader complained that Russell had no right to attack a private church because it was "none of his business," Russell responded angrily. On the contrary, "Such tenements as Trinity maintains are a very grave and incessant menace to the public health," he wrote. They are the worst of all breeding places for tuberculosis. "Don't clean them up because your heart bleeds for the dying and suffering children," he observed with a note of sarcasm, clean them up because if you don't "the germs of the rag-picker's child" will be "communicated to our own children or to ourselves."[16]

Beyond the threat of disease was the matter of taxes. Since Trinity made few improvements on its properties, the area where its properties abounded—the Eighth Ward—lagged far behind all others in Manhattan in producing tax revenue. Self-interest, not humanity, was the issue. Arguing for change for practical, over humanitarian, reasons became a Russell theme. Russell was hoping that the pragmatic American business spirit was more likely to respond to appeals to self-interest. So, for example, in 1911 he implored businessmen to combat poverty and poor urban housing because if they did not, he argued they would have no market for their goods and no workers for their factories. "You cannot achieve national success with a race of tenement house scarecrows," Russell wrote. Simply put, Russell said, "to tolerate slums does not pay. It is not good for business."[17]

It is unlikely that Russell had all that much enthusiasm for his own self-interest arguments—or at least unlikely that public health and tax revenue were the real motivating factors for a man who was the grandson of a preacher. He was angry at the conditions of Trinity's tenements and his heart bled at the sight of suffering children. "Every protest against them [the tenements] is a service to our children," he wrote. When his articles were attacked by Trinity's defenders, Russell said he had no objection to the criticism or to being called a muckraker. "I am glad to be called 'a muckraker,' " he said. "The only thing I object to is living in a world full of needless horrors and suffering without uttering one word of protest, however feeble and unheard."[18] Russell's articles did not go unheard, however.

All through the winter and spring of 1908, Russell and two assistants visited scores of Trinity properties in Lower Manhattan—138 on Hudson Street alone; 66 on Varick Street; 26 on Charlton Street; another 26 on Canal Street; and a dozen on Clarkson Street. The research is impressive, even by modern-day investigative reporting standards. "Wherever you walk in this dreadful region, you find something that Trinity owns," Russell said. Usually, he added with a sneer, it is a simple matter to discover Trinity's tenements. "To be sure," Russell wrote, "all tenement houses are bad, I know that." But "whenever I saw a house that looked as if it were about to fall down, one that looked in every way rotten and weary and dirty and disreputable, I found that it was owned by Trinity."[19] Beyond pounding the pavements and looking at buildings, Russell scoured whatever documents he could find, although he got little help from Trinity officials. Slowly, he pieced together the history, the finances and tenement records of the church.

Trinity's growth into the most powerful church in America was closely intertwined with the growth of New York City. The church built its first chapel in 1696 when the Dutch and British controlled New York. Then, in 1704, England's Queen Anne gave Trinity possession of two large farms. As the city's population soared, the church parceled out its land for the building of houses. But the church did not build; it simply leased the land, while others built housing, a pattern it stuck to up until Russell wrote his exposé. When leases on property expired, Trinity would often take control of the buildings; in this way it inherited buildings but was never saddled with the cost of construction—or the burden of maintaining the property. Trinity soon became a wealthy landlord, receiving, as Russell wrote, "a steadily waxing tide of gold," profits that "made the church rich."

The church became richer in 1814 when New York State passed legislation—for reasons that were never understood—that allowed Trinity to take possession of all the property in New York City that had previously been held by a number of Presbyterian churches. The parishioners of these churches objected strenuously and New York's governor refused to sign the new legislation, even though it became law without the governor's veto. The 1814 law marked a significant turning point for Trinity Church: First, it was the beginning of many years of public criticism that dogged the church up until Russell's articles. "From 1814 to this day the history of Trinity has been a story of conflict," Russell concluded, with Trinity "accused of almost every conceivable offense."[20]

Second, the 1814 law relieved Trinity of any obligation of reporting to the public or its parishioners anything about its finances. "From this time on," Russell found, "it has never been possible for any person outside of the [church's] vestry to gather any information as to the business of Trinity." "Impenetrable secrecy; rule of absolute silence; more secret than any mystic order; an unlifted curtain; an appendage to medievalism" were the phrases that Russell applied to Trinity which he took to calling a "Church of Mystery," a phrase that particularly galled the church's top officials who publicly rebuked the press for invoking this damning slogan. For ninety-three years, Russell declared, no one "has been able to learn the simplest facts" about Trinity Church. How does it spend its money? How much money does it have? How much property does it own? Those were the questions Russell asked. He found "very able lawyers, skilled cross examiners, [and] famous ferrets of the bar, have taken in hand the task of discovering at least the form and shape and extent of the Mystery: universally they have failed to discover anything."[21]

By working in much the same way as a modern investigative reporter, however, Russell discovered more about the church than most had. He utilized at least one secret source, combed every available public document—from records compiled by state investigators to the church's annual reports to New York City tax records—interviewed many residents of Trinity's properties, and spoke with church officials in a fruitless effort to get the church to respond to the allegations he was about to make. His best hope for information was the Reverend Morgan Dix, who at 81 years of age had been rector of Trinity for forty-six years. Although suffering from asthma, Dix was still firmly in charge of the church's operations, preaching in slow, measured cadences each Sunday to his wealthy congregation. For years he had defended Trinity against criticism of its tenements but, much like a skillful attorney, he was always careful not to reveal too much. Instead, he took the public relations tack of attacking the "organs of public opinion" which "go beyond their proper province."

When Russell came to visit—with a considerable reputation of his own as a powerful New York City newsman—Dix had to at least grant him an interview, but, as usual, he didn't have much to say. He told Russell that souls were his concern, not profits, and that he did not know much about the business of the Trinity Corporation. What he did know was that the leaders of the church, all prominent businessmen, names well known in New York City—Chauncey and Delafield, Fish and Parsons, Schermerhorn and Swords—had been unfairly accused. "The high standing of these gentlemen is a sufficient refutation of any such innuendoes," said Dr. Dix. Russell agreed, but added, tongue in cheek, "I cannot help a lingering wish that some of them were of standing not so high and had ways of life that did not lead so straight to Wall Street, where the great money hunger is."[22]

When Dix proved little help, Russell turned to Trinity's chief financial officer, its comptroller Henry Cammann, a 50-year-old, bearded, gray-haired, soft-spoken man, "a good man of integrity and ability," Russell concluded. Like Dix, he had little to say. Russell told Cammann that his research indicated that Trinity had spent $152,139 in 1906 but that $401,157 was unaccounted for.

"Your figures for the parish are not correct," Camman replied.

"What are the correct figures," Russell asked.

"It does not seem best to the vestry to take the public into our confidence concerning that matter," Cammann answered.

"Not," Russell responded, "when there has been so much controversy about this very point, so many bitter attacks against Trinity have been based upon it, and a word from you would make everything clear, putting an end to misrepresentation that must be both painful and harmful to the church?"

"No," Cammann told Russell, "not even on those grounds. We have found that everything we make public only invites further criticism, and it seems best, therefore, to say nothing."

"But you have made nothing public since 1814, have you?"

"No, not since 1814," Cammann replied.[23]

And so, Russell was left to speculate on the wealth of Trinity Church. His series began in April 1908 with the lead article in *Hampton's New Broadway Magazine*, "Trinity: Church of Mystery." The article was accompanied by photographs of the church's towering spire overlooking Broadway at the foot of Wall Street. "This is not a muck-raking article," Hampton declared in an editor's note before the article began, an odd statement since, sentences later, he said that Russell was about to "lift the veil" behind which Trinity had hidden for so many years. Despite Hampton's statement, what followed *was* classic muckraking, an effective combination of rhetorical flourishes, a dramatic narrative, and facts. "I have no quarrel with Trinity," Russell wrote in his first article. This too was disingenuous since all Russell did for the next four months was quarrel with a church that was hiding, he wrote with some hyperbole, "the most remarkable business secret in the country."[24]

Russell's first attack on Trinity was part moral tale, part sermon and much history. Relying heavily on documents compiled by a New York State Senate investigation of the church's finances, Russell wrote as much about what couldn't be found—details of the church's finances—as what could. His concluding point: This church has done "things impossible to reconcile with Christian character." A month later Russell lifted the curtain a bit more on the mystery, using statistics printed in various New York newspapers over nearly a decade, to speculate on the church's income and expenses. Then, in July, Russell climaxed his exposé with the most biting of his articles by guiding a group of "inquiring and well-fed tourists"—and the readers of *Everybody's* magazine, which published the third article—on a tour of Trinity's tenements. "Come inside and see how you like it," Russell implored. What the tourists found were flimsy, ramshackle buildings with no light, no ventilation, and one water tap on each floor in the common hallway. "A prolific breeding ground for the germs of tuberculosis," Russell called them. "It is of a nature that one might expect to see in Chinese cities, but never in the foremost city of America." How could Trinity Church draw an income from such places? "You would want to have the money disinfected before it touched your hand, would you not?" he asked.[25]

A MUCKRAKING TRIUMPH

Despite years of agitation against Trinity's secrecy and its ownership of slum tenements, nothing struck such a responsive chord with the public, as did Russell's articles. Ray Stannard Baker, a famous muckraking contemporary of Russell who had written important articles on America's railroads, was investigating and writing about religion in America when Russell's exposé appeared. "I have talked with many of the people connected with Trinity in various capacities," Baker said soon after Russell's articles appeared. "I found them all disturbed—indeed, astonished, perplexed, and unable to account for the extent and violence of the public agitation." To make matters worse, after Russell's first two articles appeared Rev. Dix died on April 30 after an asthma attack; some blamed the pressure from Russell's articles for Dix's death. "It was poignantly suggested that grief and chagrin over the attacks upon his corporation had caused his death," Russell recalled. "Muck-raking had become murder." Meanwhile, newspapers throughout the nation—from Seattle to Boston—published summaries of Russell's allegations. The Socialist *New York Call* labeled Trinity "hell's chief recruiting station" and called her tenements "the worst in the world." Hearst's *New York Journal* ran a full-page cartoon showing Trinity's pulpit hovering over slum tenements.[26]

Other publications came to the church's defense, however, echoing sentiments expressed by Baker who was a bit perplexed that this "most notable church in America" was "curiously under attack during recent months." Baker agreed with Russell that Trinity had a long and somewhat disreputable history, that its finances had remained closed to the public for too long, that even churches needed to be accountable to the citizenry, and that it was good that "democracy stands knocking at last at the closed doors of Old Trinity." But his investigative reporting found different facts about Trinity's tenements, which, he wrote, "are not as bad as I expected to find."[27] Baker, surprisingly, repeated the arguments Trinity made in its defense: its buildings were no worse than others in the area; its rents were very low; none of the properties supported saloons or prostitution; and the church did not own many of the buildings, just the land, and thus had no control over their condition. These were the exact arguments that could be found in the church-related publications that apologized also for Trinity's behavior—and criticized Russell for his attack. "Some of the buildings may be old. Their condition may be run down," church comptroller Cammann told one New York newspaper, "but it all depends upon the vigilance of the authorities. The city and the lessees are responsible; not the Trinity Corporation."[28] To Russell, however, those weren't excuses for misery. He held the church responsible for the properties from which it profited.

Aside from reaching different conclusions about Trinity, the differences between the journalism styles and ideologies of Russell and Baker are evident in their approaches to Trinity. Those differences mirror a split that was developing in the muckraking movement and in journalism. Baker, who was known for his fastidious reporting, was a devotee of factuality and balance. His reporting mirrored a growing concern about objectivity in journalism—

about fairness, balance, and neutrality. The *American* magazine, where Baker and Tarbell and Steffens had gone after leaving *McClure's Magazine,* was engaged at this very time in a debate about the direction of journalism. Steffens wanted reporters to offer solutions; Tarbell and Baker insisted that more facts were needed. Russell agreed with Steffens. He was working more in the crusading tradition that he had learned working under Pulitzer and Hearst. Facts were important, but they needed to point to a solution. The cautious Baker wanted balance. For example, he not only gave Trinity's defense of its tenement holdings, but he documented its missionary and philanthropic activities. His writing was also far less rhetorical and sarcastic than Russell's. "I shall here set down the facts," Baker wrote. And while he, too, indicted Trinity—"The plain fact is that Trinity did not care for the people"—he did so in a tone of moderation, writing caustically but cautiously. Baker was professorial, more in the "information" mode typified by the *New York Times*; Russell was an evangelical, a fire and brimstone preacher, more of an outraged advocate than an educator. While Baker was bent on educating people about the problem, Russell was campaigning for a solution. "The price of a battle-ship would build sanitary, airy, and spacious homes for 20,000 persons; such assets as the great insurance companies possess would turn all the slums of New York into civilized habitations," Russell wrote. Baker would never make such connections, which were more typical of an editorial than a news report.[29]

In the end, who was correct on the condition of Trinity's tenements? Were they as bad as Russell depicted or were they typical of what existed in New York but no worse than many others were, as Baker indicated? Facts might seem to support Ray Stannard Baker, but results supported Charles Edward Russell. One of the results of Russell's exposé was that Trinity Church hired Emily Wayland Dinwiddie, who had been an inspector with New York's Tenement House Department in 1904, to investigate Trinity housing. Dinwiddie was supervised by a respected former city official and the investigation was independent of church officials, conducted by a private organization. No one questioned either its integrity or independence. "No effort has been spared to get at the real conditions," Dinwiddie said when her research was completed.[30]

Dinwiddie gave Trinity virtually a clean bill of health, but one must read her report carefully to learn the reasons why. After a house-to-house inspection, she concluded that "sensationally bad conditions were not found in the tenements and smaller dwelling houses owned and controlled by Trinity Church." In fact, 96 percent of the 810 apartments and 334 buildings were in relatively good condition. Only twelve buildings were in bad condition. Dinwiddie saw little overcrowding, with two families per house, which was better than the average for the rest of the city. Sanitation was a problem in only 2 percent of the buildings while 85 percent of the families had their own water supply and 60 percent had their own toilets. The Trinity buildings, Dinwiddie found, were in "marked contrast" to others in the area. "Whether the result of contentment or of apathy, the length of residence common among the tenants does not indicate active dissatisfaction," she wrote.[31]

Dinwiddie's report was flawed and problematic, however. The problems were threefold. First, she constantly compared Trinity's buildings to others in the region. Lower Manhattan was notorious at the turn of the century for its horrid tenement conditions. It was hardly comforting to know that Trinity's buildings were better than the awful ones surrounding them. Second, it is difficult to know what standards Dinwiddie was using to measure cleanliness and safety. If the standards were those allowed by the laws of 1909, then her high marks for Trinity might be understandable. Those standards left much to be desired and, even if met, they would still make for conditions that were wholly inadequate. Even Rev. William T. Manning, who took over when Rev. Dix died, conceded that "there is some of the property the condition of which is far from being what it ought to be."[32]

But the third and most serious flaw in Dinwiddie's report was in what she didn't discuss—the tenements that Trinity did not own but which sat on its property. Dinwiddie said she wanted to include these properties (there may have been as many as 300) but that the owners refused to allow her access to make an inspection, saying that Trinity had no legal control over them. What this meant, of course, was that the worst of Trinity's buildings—albeit ones they didn't own—were left out of Dinwiddie's report. While Trinity's defense—that it could not force changes over property it did not control—was technically valid, everyone knew that it had for years done little to gain control over the buildings; that it had simply sat back, ignored the horrible conditions, and collected rents. Its position was legally defensible but morally indefensible. These were the buildings that Russell had focused on, not unfairly, and they were the ones that desperately needed attention. Russell knew it, Baker knew it and Trinity's bosses knew it also.

One other fact made Dinwiddie's investigation especially suspect. Soon after she completed her investigation, she was hired by the church to supervise the improvement of Trinity's properties. Did her favorable findings get her the job with Trinity? Did she alter any findings in order to please the powerful and rich Trinity administrators? Although it is common enough today for regulators to take jobs with those they regulate, certainly questions are raised by her joining forces with Trinity so soon after her "independent" investigation.

Trinity Church had warded off attacks on its character and properties for nearly one hundred years. However, the combination of the surging tide of reform and Progressivism; an unrelated action by the church to disassociate itself from one of its nearby parish churches; and the appointment of a new rector, Reverend Manning, made change in response to Russell's articles inevitable.

Three months after Russell's last article, Trinity announced plans to close St. John's Chapel, one of the ten churches it controlled, and consolidate its operation with the nearby St. Luke's Church. The church cited financial concerns, and, moreover, asserted that the two churches had overlapping congregations; efficiency of operation made the change necessary. Whatever the reason, the announcement caused a furor, just what a church already under fire didn't need. "The floodgates of criticism opened wide," one historian asserted. And the critics' easiest point of attack was the slum tenements owned by the church. Reverend Manning had responded privately to the Russell articles by appointing a committee to make a personal study of the church's holdings. "I say unhesitatingly," Manning declared, "that as property owners . . . we are bound to do everything in our power" to improve conditions. "We ought to set not only a high standard, but the very highest. Far better, if necessary, that all our charities should be given up . . . than that we should maintain any of them by revenue derived from properties in an unsanitary or questionable condition."[33]

Manning knew also that, aside from tackling the tenement issue, he needed to rid the church of its air of mystery. Thus, the church began the new year 1909 by slipping into the pews of its parishioners one Sunday morning a detailed financial statement for the Trinity Corporation—the first since 1814. The *New York Times* put the story on page one, and as far west as St. Louis, newspapers applauded the action, declaring "a tremendous victory for publicity . . . a recognition of the people's right to know what a big corporation does with the money it handles." Russell had estimated that Trinity had assets totaling $39 million, but the church said its assets were only $14 million. This still made it the wealthiest church in the world. The church said it made only $732,741 on rents from its properties. "This property is not, as has been often asserted, a source of large revenue to the parish. It is quite the reverse," the report asserted.[34] Furthermore, the report said that the properties were not in the terrible condition that some had charged but, nonetheless, the church was planning large-scale improvements to many properties.

The extent of those changes became clear a month later when the church—to everyone's shock—announced that: First, it would no longer continue as a landlord and, second, that it would sell all of its real estate, except for that which housed its churches and offices. As long as the church has any tenements, an unnamed source told the *Times*, it would be criticized. The source then repeated what had become Trinity's frequent refrain: our properties are not as bad as has been charged. Citing Russell's articles on Trinity's tenements, the church said the pictures accompanying the text were of buildings not owned by the church—but, of course, the church did own the land.[35] Despite moving forward to change the practices that had drawn criticism, the church was also carefully plotting a public relations defense strategy: hit back at the critics who were overstepping their journalistic limits; emphasize the positive by citing the church's charitable work; and obfuscate and confuse the issues by reiterating how its hands were tied on properties it did not own.

In April, Reverend Manning spoke publicly for the first time in defense of the church he had headed for nearly a year. "The air has been full of the most astonishing statements . . . which no serious person could have been expected to believe," Manning said. "Honest difference of judgment" is one thing, Manning said, "but the recent discussion can hardly be said to have been conducted in the spirit of generous and helpful criticism." Manning then responded to Russell. Since we have opened our books to the public— an act, he said, that had been planned before the criticism—"it can never be said again that Trinity pursues a policy of secrecy or of mystery." As to the conditions of Trinity's tenements, the charges are "grossly untrue." Years later, still stinging from Manning's denial, Russell said he always asked one question of his critics: "You say these tenement houses are not really bad. Would you like to live in one of them? Take the best of them all. Would you like to live in it?"[36]

The answer from Manning was no, he would not. While he still offered the standard Trinity arguments about low rents and good conditions, he added the new church position: we will do whatever it takes to clean up all our tenements, both those we own and those that sit on our property. Such a decision did not come easily because, inside the church, many opposed Manning's decision to spend considerable sums to make improvements. By 1910, however, 225 tenements had been taken down by the church as not worth reconditioning. By 1916, 367 houses owned by Trinity were in good condition and a credit to the parish. The city's newspapers began to feature stories about Trinity's model tenements.[37]

Charles Edward Russell and the forces of tenement house reform that had been building in New York City for two decades had forced America's wealthiest church to do the right thing—finally. Many years after the victory, Russell was exultant, recalling how his family had been forced to live in a terrible Trinity tenement. He commented, "The grandson of the émigré of that day had the pleasure of seeing that old rookery destroyed as a result of a campaign he had instigated." Unfortunately, he added, "It was a work of grace sixty years delayed."[38]

NOTES

1. His comment on his first months in New York is found in, "Autobiography of an Author. Chas. E. Russell Tells About Himself," Doubleday, Page & Co.'s *Notes on Books and Authors*, no date, Russell Papers, Library of Congress. Charles Edward

Russell, *Why I Am A Socialist* (New York: George H. Doran, 1910), 69, and "The Cry of the Slums," *Everybody's*, December 1907, 61, photographs of the slums by Bessie March and a short essay by Russell. Accounts of life in lower Manhattan can be found in Moses Rischin, *The Promised City: New York's Jews, 1870–1914* (Cambridge, Mass.: Harvard University Press, 1962), and Irving Howe, *World of Our Fathers* (New York: Harcourt, Brace, Jovanovich, 1976).

2. Russell, *Why I Am A Socialist*, 3, 140, and "The Slum as a National Asset," *Everybody's Magazine*, February 1909, 172, 170.

3. Russell, *Why I Am A Socialist*, 3, 70.

4. Russell, *These Shifting Scenes* (New York: George Doran Co., 1914), 71.

5. Russell, *Why I Am A Socialist*, 3, 140.

6. Russell's three articles are "Trinity: Church of Mystery," *The New Broadway Magazine*, April 1908, 1–12, subsequently referred to as "Mystery"; "Trinity Corporation: A Riddle of Riches," *The New Broadway Magazine*, May 1908, 187–195, referred to as "Trinity"; and "Tenements of Trinity Church," *Everybody's*, July 1908, 47–57, referred to as "Tenements." For a history of the church, see Clifford P. Morehouse, *Trinity: Mother of Churches; An Informal History of Trinity Parish in the City of New York* (New York: Seabury Press, 1973).

7. Roosevelt's speech is reprinted verbatim in *Bookman* 33 (March 1911), 12, and in David Graham Phillips, *The Treason of the Senate*, ed. George Mowry and Judson A. Grenier (Chicago: Quadrangle, 1964), 216–225. A good discussion of the speech's development is in Grenier, "Muckrakers and Muckraking: An Historical Definition," *Journalism Quarterly* 37 (autumn 1960).

8. Russell, *Bare Hands and Stone Walls* (New York: Scribner's Sons, 1933), 144, 146. Louis Filler, *Crusaders for American Liberalism* (New York: Harcourt, Brace & Co., 1939), 260. On the reasons why muckraking faded, see Miraldi, "Muckrakers are Chased Away," *Muckraking and Objectivity: Journalism's Colliding Traditions* (Westport, Conn.: Greenwood Press, 1991), 57–80.

9. The magazine was originally called *Hampton's* but changed its name a number of times, mostly because of financial problems that beset Benjamin Hampton. The problems of the muckraking magazines are traced adequately in Peter Barry, "The Decline of Muckraking: A View from the Magazines," Ph.D. diss., Wayne State University, 1973.

10. Russell, "Tenements," 47; Russell, *Bare Hands*, 94. Discussion of Progressive attitudes toward housing and poverty are in Roy Lubove, *The Progressives and the Slums: Tenement House Reform in New York City 1890–1917* (Westport, Conn.: Greenwood Press, 1962), and Robert Bremner, *From the Depths: The Discovery of Poverty in the United States* (New York: New York University Press, 1956).

11. Russell, "Trinity," 195.

12. Henry Demarest Lloyd, *Wealth Against Commonwealth* (New York: Harper, 1894); Ida Tarbell, *History of Standard Oil* (New York: McClure, Phillips & Co, 1904); and Thomas Lawson, *Frenzied Finance: The Story of Amalgamated* (New York: Ridgeway-Thayer, 1904). Russell, *Bare Hands*, 240.

13. Russell, "Tenements," 48. Attempts to improve housing in New York, not just that of Trinity, had been taking place since the 1880s when, under the leadership of Richard Watson Gilder, various groups and city commissions investigated conditions and proposed legislation. Russell noted Gilder's work in a letter to the *New York Times*, "Tenement Reform," May 8, 1909, 6. And Gilder summarized Trinity's

housing record in a letter to the *New York Evening Post*, "Trinity and the Tenements," Dec. 28, 1908. On the evolution of tenement reform, see Richard Plunz, *A History of Housing in New York City* (New York: Columbia University Press, 1990), and James Ford, *Slums and Housing* (Westport, Conn.: Negro Universities Press, 1936). Lincoln Steffens' "Shame of the Cities" appeared originally in *McClure's* beginning in October 1902.

14. Russell, "Tenements," 52.

15. Ibid., 56–57.

16. Russell, "Trinity's Tenements—The Public's Business," *Everybody's*, February 1909, 279.

17. Russell, *Business: The Heart of the Nation* (New York: John Lane Co., 1911), 177, 197.

18. Letter to the *New York Times*, see note 13. Russell, "Trinity's Tenements," 279.

19. Russell, "Tenements," 54.

20. Russell, "Mystery," 5. Various histories discuss Trinity. See Morehouse, *Trinity*; John C. Goodbody, *One Peppercorn: A Popular History of the Parish at Trinity Church* (New York: Parish of Trinity Church, 1982); Morgan Dix, ed., *A History of the Parish of Trinity Church in the City of New York* (New York: Putnam, 1898).

21. Russell, "Mystery," 5, 6.

22. Dix attacked the press in a long letter to the *Churchman* magazine, Dec. 22, 1894, 834–35. He defended the church leaders and Russell's responses are in "Trinity," 194.

23. Ibid., 190–91.

24. Russell, "Trinity," 1, 8.

25. Ibid.,11; Russell, "Tenements," 49.

26. Baker, "The Case Against Trinity," *American*, May 1909, p. 15. The article became part of Baker's book on religion, *The Spiritual Unrest* (New York: Frederick A. Stokes, 1910), 1–48. On Dix's death, *New York Times*, April 30, 1908, p. 1, and Russell, *Bare Hands and Stone Walls* (New York: Scribner's, 1933), 147. *Call*, June 26, 1908. Satirical cartoons about Trinity appeared also in the *Evening New York World*, Jan. 6, 1909, and the *New York Evening Mail*, Jan. 20, 1909. Summaries and reactions to the article appeared in the *Houston Post, Columbus Journal, Seattle Times, Arkansas Gazette*, and *Springfield Republican*, among others.

27. Baker, "Case Against Trinity," 3.

28. Cammann made this statement to the *New York Evening Post*; reprinted in *The Churchman*, Aug. 15, 1908, 10.

29. A discussion of the various approaches to writing by the muckrakers can be found in Miraldi, *Muckraking and Objectivity*, 23–56. The quotation from Baker, "The Case Against Trinity," 15. Baker's life and work is chronicled in two biographies, John Semonche, *Ray Stannard Baker: A Quest for Democracy in Modern America, 1870–1918* (Chapel Hill: University of North Carolina Press, 1969) and Robert C. Bannister Jr., *Ray Stannard Baker: The Mind and Thought of a Progressive* (New Haven: Yale University Press, 1966). A discussion of the "information" mode is in Michael Schudson, *Discovering the News* (New York: Basic Books, 1978). Russell, "The Slum As A National Asset," *Everybody's*, February 1909, 180.

30. "Trinity's Tenements," a report compiled and published by Trinity, written by Dinwiddie, 2. A copy of the report was supplied to the author by the church. A

slightly different version of the report was reprinted as "The Truth About Trinity's Tenements," *Survey* 23, Feb. 26, 1910. Dinwiddie's comment is not in that version.

31. Ibid., 15.

32. "To Have Charge of Trinity Tenements," *The Common Welfare*, 1912, 145–146. "Manning Hits Back at Trinity Critics," *New York Times*, April 19, 1909, 9.

33. Charles T. Bridgeman, *A History of the Parish of Trinity Church in the City of New York* (New York: Trinity Church, 1962), 119. Bridgeman discusses the St. John's controversy, 77–101. Manning's comments are in the *New York Times*, ibid.

34. "Trinity Explains How It Uses Funds," *New York Times*, Jan. 2, 1909, 1, 5. Bridgeman, *History of the Parrish*, discusses the church's finances, 128–31. The *St. Louis Mirror* wrote an editorial on Trinity; quoted in "A Notable Victory for Publicity," *Printers' Ink*, Jan. 27, 1909, 36. Based on correspondence with the former librarian of Trinity's archives, the author believes that the church has copies of not only the original reports made on the 1908 controversy, but a number of internal memos that discuss the church's actions. In 1992, the church temporarily closed its archives, however, and church officials refused to respond to numerous written and telephone requests for access to the documents.

35. "Trinity Will Sell All Its Real Estate," *New York Times*, February 7, 1909, 1.

36. "Manning Hits Back at Trinity Critics," *New York Times*, April 19, 1909, 9. Russell, *Bare Hands*, 146.

37. Bridgeman, *History of the Parish*, describes the improvements made by the church in its properties and the favorable response of the New York media, 125–26.

38. This comment came in a profile of Russell's father, *A Pioneer Editor in Early Iowa* (Washington, D.C.: Ransdell, 1941), 8.

4

Women and Exposé: Reform and Housekeeping

Agnes Hooper Gottlieb

When discussions of muckraking occur, inevitably, only one woman is mentioned—and that is Ida Tarbell. She is famous, of course, for her 1902–1903 articles in *McClure's Magazine* that showed how John D. Rockefeller created—as both genius and buccaneer—his Standard Oil corporation and his vast personal fortune. Tarbell's life has been recalled in various biographies. But, despite the myth, Tarbell was far from alone as a woman seeking to expose evils and change the ways of Progressive Era America. As this chapter shows, various women and publications were straddling the line between exposé and advocacy well before and after Tarbell did her work. Gottlieb not only documents the women writers who were spearheading a "municipal housekeeping" movement, she jumps into the long-running and lively debate about how to define muckraking. Her chapter mirrors and underscores what Harry H. Stein wrote twenty years ago: "A half-century of scholarship has sown a near wilderness of facts, notions, surmises, unknowns, instances and gener-alizations about muckraking in the United States," but no consensus on definition has yet emerged "American Muckrakers and Muckraking: The 50-Year Scholarship," *Journalism Quarterly* 56 [Spring 1979]: 9–17). What is clear, however, is that women have been underemphasized and neglected in accounts of the role and power of journalism to help trans-form America at the turn of the century.

A few years ago, the "Divine Miss M," singer and actress Bette Midler, founded the New York Restoration Project to clean up the city where she lived. The project was responsible for carting away 8,000 tons of garbage from New York City's parks, purchasing community gardens in poor neighborhoods and involving inner-city kids in a boat-building program. "In a funny way, I'm just a big housekeeper," Midler told the *Ladies' Home Journal*. "Martha Stewart has it to a much worse degree, but it's definitely a compulsion."[1]

How apropos that Midler, interviewed at the end of the twentieth century, invoked the domestic imagery that was so popular in women's magazines 100 years ago when, for example, *Good Housekeeping* told women to concern themselves with "street, the neighborhood, the community—the larger home."[2] Indeed, the use of the "housekeeping" metaphor to explain American women's involvement in civic projects can be found in the writing of women as far back as the 1890s. Dr. Sarah Hackett Stevenson, president of a Chicago women's club, told a national gathering of club women in 1898 that the women she knew "intend to demonstrate that housekeeping does not begin at the front and end at the back door, but rather begins in the street, includes the back alley and all the vacant lots around."[3] The trend itself—which allowed women to involve themselves in municipal reform activities—began even earlier than that. In fact, half a century earlier, one author suggested that although women "cannot reform the world in a moment, we can begin the work by reforming ourselves and our households—it is woman's mission. Let her not look away from her own little family circle for the means of producing moral and social reforms, but begin at home."[4]

The roots of domestic metaphor can be traced to a desire by nineteenth-century women to explain why it was important, and indeed necessary, to involve themselves in "municipal housekeeping." The prevailing sentiment for middle-class white women for more than three-quarters of the century was that theirs was a private sphere and that their influence was over their homes. The rough-and-tumble public sphere—which included the political and industrial—belonged to their husbands.

But women were not to be deterred from establishing and nurturing their influence over their communities. Yes, they said, a woman's place is in the home, but the home is larger than the four walls that shelter us. The home is our community, the women said, and therefore it is our right and our duty to protect our homes from outside dangers that threaten us. Anything that threatens our house, our children or our husbands is our concern. Consequently, armies of American women worked tirelessly to clean and beautify their towns, improve school systems, eliminate juvenile delinquency, and ameliorate the public health. Anything that threatened the quality of life of a community's women and children eventually captured the interest of the municipal housekeepers. Many worked under the aegis of their women's clubs, which proliferated in the last quarter of the nineteenth century and often included involvement in civic projects. America's libraries, parks and kindergartens are in large part the outgrowth of tireless club women.

American women's participation in public events, as fund-raisers and volunteers, effectively served to expand their sphere of activity to include their towns. And as women pushed the limits of their sphere to include previously unheard of activities, women journalists were there to chronicle and encourage the movement. Just as newspapers and magazines earlier in the nineteenth century fostered the confining ideal that women belonged at home, they also promoted municipal housekeeping projects at the turn of the century as appropriate extensions of woman's appropriate sphere. By appealing to women's traditional and conservative duties to their home, articles in newspapers and magazines helped make the concept of a wider sphere for women palatable to those who might otherwise have rejected a public role.

Although the term "municipal housekeeping" was in vogue at the dawn of the twentieth century—kept there by both suffragists and club women who believed it served their own different purposes—the references to it were popularized in newspapers and women's magazines around the country. Just as mass media welcomed and sometimes derided the arrival of the "New Woman," who wore her hair in the upturned fashion of a "Gibson Girl" and earned her own way, magazines and newspapers also created images of municipal reformers as housekeepers on a grand scale. And the images were embraced by both club women and suffragists.

An 1894 article in the *North American Review* about "the woman question" concluded that women should "sweep" out the "dark corners" of society. "It is for us to set the human household in order, to see to it that all is clean and sweet and comfortable for the men who are fit to help us to make a home in it," author Sarah Grand argued. Grand was evoking an example of the domestic imagery that became increasingly popular a decade later.[5]

More specifically, numerous references to "municipal housekeeping" can be found in articles about women's role in society. One early reference to municipal housekeeping was in an 1895 article by Jane Cunningham Croly in her magazine for club women. Croly, a journalist and founder of the national women's club movement, stated in an article in the *New Cycle* that "the first practical steps toward improved municipal housekeeping have in so many instances been taken by women." Croly asserted that this was part of a "universal movement" by women to study "the problem of good housekeeping for towns and cities as they have studied it for ages in the houses."[6]

In 1902, an article in the *Arena* forecast that the club movement would succeed in "enlarging woman's sphere." Author Winnifred Harper Cooley stated that it was only natural that women should involve themselves in city problems. "City government is only housekeeping upon a large scale," she wrote. "Women have the training of the ages back of them in domestic economics: what class is better fitted to undertake the problems of our cities?"[7] Cooley then linked the reform work to suffrage, arguing that women could "never work with absolute effectiveness" until they had the vote.[8]

This suffrage argument can be found in newspapers, magazines and books of the day. In 1904, the *New York Evening Post* quoted one activist as saying that club women wanted to be the nation's housekeepers and argued that even the most conservative people believed that housekeeping was women's work—housekeeping on a grander scale. "Man never did enjoy housecleaning, so it is the women's duty to show their patriotism by cleaning up."[9]

In 1906, Hull House founder Jane Addams stated in the woman's section of the same paper: "Women have always kept house, and should now be allowed their share in the larger task."[10] A 1909 article in the *Journal of Home Economics* argued that by lobbying for healthy milk and clean streets housekeepers created "an environment which is similar to the old-fashioned home."[11] That same year, Ida Husted Harper wrote an article titled "Woman's Broom in Municipal Housekeeping" in the woman's magazine the *Delineator*. Subtitled "The Man with His Vote Seems to Need a Woman With Her Broom to Clean Up After Him," it relied on domestic imagery to show how women became attracted to the duties of municipal housekeeping:

And then the woman said, "The broom shall be my emblem; too long have I used it only to sweep around my own hearthstone; henceforth it shall do service for the whole community; as once I and my neighbors conferred with each other in the interest only of our homes and children, so now we will counsel together for the highest good of all homes and children." And thus women began their municipal housekeeping.[12]

Harper claimed this social housekeeping was easier in states where women had the vote and argued emphatically that there was no reason why women should not have the municipal franchise throughout the United States. "Under modern conditions, housekeeping and rearing of children are no longer private matters—they are public functions, and in their performance the woman of today finds herself brought into contact with every problem of municipal life."[13]

The term municipal housekeeping often was linked to women's work in clubs like the Woman's Municipal League and the Council of Mothers. A 1912 magazine article, by the president of the Women's Municipal League of Boston, outlined "Woman's Home-Making Function Applied to the Municipality." The author also issued this challenge: "Women must now learn to make of their cities great community homes for all people."[14]

While writers and club women invoked the housekeeping metaphor to promote a wider sphere for women, the National American Woman Suffrage Association (NAWSA) used domestic imagery and domestic responsibility to attract club women and reform workers to its cause. Throughout the first two decades of the twentieth century, the NAWSA issued pamphlets, articles and flyers that invoked the cause of municipal housekeeping and linked it to the fight for suffrage. A 1900 pamphlet argued that women were "by nature and training, housekeepers, let them have a hand in the city's housekeeping"[15] This municipal housekeeping/suffrage campaign discussed municipal housekeeping as a natural duty for women but rarely mentioned outright the cause of suffrage. Instead, pamphlets underscored that the existing political structure hampered reform efforts by women.

Addams was one of the suffragists who used the housekeeping argument to recruit tradition-bound women to the ranks of the suffragists. In a NAWSA pamphlet on "Women and Public Housekeeping," Addams said city housekeeping was failing because women were not consulted, even though domestic issues were within their traditional sphere of influence.[16] Addams also wrote "Why Women Should Vote," a tiny twenty-page pamphlet arguing that mothers couldn't possibly "preserve the home" without exercising civic influence. Addams stated that women did not want to be radical, but sought "an opportunity to do their own work and to take care of those affairs which naturally and historically belong to women."[17]

Another NAWSA pamphlet on "Woman's Place" argued that women knew their homes were "the entire city—the State—the country—perhaps the whole world."[18] "Municipal housekeeping is not so very different from family housekeeping," the pamphlet asserted. A 1913 NAWSA pamphlet on "Business versus the Home," argued that some businesses harmed the public health and, therefore, the home. The author then protested that the city's housekeepers had "no voice in the matter." Other essays explained "Why the Housekeeper Needs the Vote," "The Political Duty of Mothers," and "Votes and Babies."

These suffrage pamphlets were meant to appeal to traditional women but turned that argument to use for their cause. "If women are to look after their children, they must grapple with forces far wider than four walls," stated one suffragist.[19]

While most of the municipal housekeeping imagery appeared after 1900, Croly promoted the idea of municipal housekeeping long before the new century dawned. She suggested in the 1870s that the reform of social ills affecting women and children was an appropriate avenue for women who wanted public involvement. Croly and other writers also conjured up the image of the "new woman," who by the turn of the century epitomized the activism of the club women.

The typical municipal housekeeper was a volunteer or club woman. But, as historian Alice Kessler-Harris points out, some were members of the "helping professions," who used their positions to clean up the cities. During the Progressive Era, paying positions as social workers, doctors, sociologists and journalists became more accessible to women. Because women were asked to "point the way to a more moral and rational society" their work in these professions "in a rough kind of way . . . fell within the province of the social housekeeper."[20] Thus, in this way, then, women journalists became involved in the municipal housekeeping movement.

The women's magazines, which grew in circulation and influence throughout the century, were able to reach women with a twofold message: their rightful sphere was the home, and the home included their community. While women today tend to speak less frequently of themselves as the natural housekeepers of municipalities, that image is so potent that it endures even as women have infiltrated the messiest of political debates and controversies over urban reform.

Was the municipal housekeeping journalism that emerged just another form of muckraking? Although women were involved in and wrote about social problems long before the term "municipal housekeeping" was coined in the 1890s, the trend certainly exploded in newspapers and magazines at the same time as did muckraking, which is predominant during the first fifteen years of the century. However, this preoccupation by women writers with municipal problems and reforms, was more than just a journalism of exposure that so characterized the muckrakers. Muckraking focused primarily on political and economic ills; municipal housekeeping journalism exposed social ills. Moreover, municipal housekeeping articles often went beyond exposure and proposed viable solutions to the problems, solutions that often included civic involvement of America's club women. Journalism historian Kathleen Endres has argued, however, that instead of opening up a new line of inquiry into the work of the municipal housekeepers, scholars should expand the narrow definition of the term "muckraking" to include articles written by women that appeared in mass circulation women's magazines.[21] I disagree. Municipal housekeeping was a movement of women that was inseparable from and bolstered by the increasingly popular women's clubs at the turn of the century. To lump it in with muckraking undermines the work and efforts of the legions of women who were involved in it. "The investigative journalism—the muckraking—of the women's magazines differed substantially in content, reporters, advocacy," Endres observed.[22] Therefore, it seems to me, it needs to be treated differently. Indeed, Endres is correct when she observes that the reform writing in women's magazines and by women for newspapers often has been overlooked. Muckraking is remembered instead as the articles by an elite few in a few elite journals during the Progressive Era.[23]

In fact, municipal housekeeping journalism had three specific outcomes. First, it encouraged women to involve themselves in reforms that had been previously considered outside of their sphere of influence. Second, it provided publicity for social ills that were often ignored or overlooked by mainstream newspapers. And, third, it gave women reporters strong, powerful stories, a welcome alternative to the fluff that they often were assigned to cover as part of their jobs.

When *Good Housekeeping* magazine began publishing a series of articles that exposed the deplorable conditions at schools around the country in 1909, mothers who were readers knew that it was their duty to go to their children's schools and look for fire hazards and structural weaknesses. When the *Baltimore American* exposed the plight of young street children convicted of petty offenses who were sent to adult prisons, club women there believed it was their responsibility to lobby for a juvenile court.[24]

BYLINES, CELEBRITY, CLOUT

The tradition of women writing about municipal concerns, social problems and the plight of women and children can be traced back to the 1840s and the pioneer work of Margaret Fuller, one of the very first of the century's woman journalists. Writing for Horace Greeley's *New York Tribune,* Fuller traveled to the city's Blackwell's Island, a snake pit for the insane, and exposed the plight of the patients there. Fuller actually had been hired by Greeley as a literary critic, but she turned away from literature and turned toward social problems. Through the 1840s she wrote about prostitution, mental illness and prisons. She exposed problems and proposed solutions. Although she never suggested that it was woman's duty to rectify these social ills—that was half a century away—Fuller's impact was enormous. She established for the women journalists who came after her an extremely wide breadth for story topics.

In fact, after Fuller, newspaper and magazine editors recognized the importance of the woman's perspective because women were increasingly becoming the family's consumers. If women were the ones who were making the family purchases, then women readers were the ones who needed to be delivered to advertisers. What better way, the reasoning went, to woo women readers than to provide articles that were written by women and for women. Thus, editors from about 1850 onward began hiring women for writing jobs that had previously been closed to them. And, although many newspapers exhibited an unspoken quota of one woman on staff, the newspaper office was no longer absolutely off limits to women. By 1900, most newspapers had formalized their effort to attract women readers by providing a weekly or daily section called "The Woman's Page." Prior to the all-out section approach, however, beginning in the 1850s, women began to voice their ideas and opinions within the pages of newspapers. Ideas about women's sphere and women's duties to community found a forum.

Bowing to the social taboo that a woman's name appeared in print only when she married or died, writers of the period chose alliterative and floral pen names. Men writing at the same time period had no need for such subterfuge because bylines in general were rare before the twentieth century. But women's work was always identified, a practice dating back as far as Fuller, whose copy was marked with an asterisk. The practice of giving by-lines to women served a double purpose: editors were able to trumpet the fact that they had a woman writing for them, while at the same time dis-tancing themselves from anything that the woman might assert. Just as male readers throughout this century knew that the women's pages were not for them, so too the male readers a century ago knew that the articles by "Jennie June," "Fanny Fern," "Grace Greenwood" and others were not for them.

The practice obviously marginalized the women writers on staff, but also had another unforeseen side effect—the bylines gave them celebrity. Women journalists numbered among the most prominent women of the day—many of their biographies appeared in *Who's Who*, and biographical dictionaries, including Frances Willard's two-volume 1897 book, *American Women*. In fact, male reporters were unsettled by their female colleagues' newfound notoriety. Turn-of-the-century Boston journalist Helen M. Winslow recalled how her editor insisted she sign her name to her articles for her woman's section. She agreed, but then was upset because copy editors in the city department were "mutilating" her page. The managing editor conceded that the editors were upset because "you are getting a great deal of glory out of it and some of the men upstairs, who do good work but are not allowed to sign it, are jealous."[25] The unspoken rule that women's articles were signed makes it easier today to identify women who were writing for newspapers and the topics they wrote about.

Another important factor in the argument that women were involved in and promoted reform writing is an understanding that women often were left to their own devices to choose the focus of their articles. Historian Marian Marzolf has described the state of "benign neglect" by male editors toward their newspaper's women's pages. Editors interfered rarely; and ba-sically let the women write about whatever they chose.[26] In fact, the trend did not begin with the 1890s women's pages, but was evidenced in the groundbreaking work of Fuller, who told her brother that she was her own assignment editor: "I do just as I please and as much or little as I please, and the Editors express themselves perfectly satisfied . . ."[27]

Thus, the women reporters often were given great leeway to seek out interesting assignments and write about issues that were important to them. Some of this story brainstorming occurred within the warm embrace of women's press clubs, which also flourished at the turn of the century. The Woman's Press Club of New York City, for example, often invited guest speakers to discuss such topics as city sweatshops, the sorry state of public education and other municipal housekeeping concerns. Those in attendance were then encouraged to use their editorial influence in their newspapers to rectify the ills. At the May 1899 meeting, for example, the press club heard a speech by the New York superintendent of public vacation schools (vocational schools that were held during the summer months especially to keep city children busy and out of trouble). The superintendent implored the women to join the cause.[28] The Press Club's education chair, identified in the club minutes only as Mrs. Clarence Burns, repeatedly encouraged the women journalists to "excite public interest" about public education and its problems. The club ultimately adopted a resolution that members would "use their influence through the press, irrespective of party, in favor of the recommendations of our chairman on education."[29] Throughout the years the clubs flourished, municipal housekeeping projects were presented to the members as possible topics for stories that they wrote. The importance of this evidence is that it underscores the interest of women journalists in municipal housekeeping affairs and it demonstrates that the press women were inspired, in part, by the clubs to write about these reforms.

Perhaps the best way to explore municipal housekeeping journalism by women writers is to look at specific examples that demonstrate how the trend developed momentum over time and how it continued long after muckraking faded from fashion about 1914. If we define municipal housekeeping as simply the belief that women's sphere included involvement in the social ills of their towns and cities, it is easy to see that most women writers after Margaret Fuller at least dabbled in this area.

Consider, for example, the tirades of Jane Swisshelm in the 1860s against the filthy streets in Washington, D.C., where streets were littered "with dead horses, dead dogs, cats, rats, rubbish and refuse of all kinds."[30] Another Washington correspondent, Mary Clemmer Ames, supported women's work for the federal government, while Sara Clarke Lippincott (who used the pen name Grace Greenwood) writing in the *New York Times* also promoted women's involvement in municipal affairs.

One of the most prominent municipal housekeepers was Helen Campbell, who wrote a series of articles on the slums of New York in 1886 for the *New York Tribune*. Reporter Jacob Riis is today remembered for exposing the plight of the impoverished in New York's slums in his 1890 book, *How the Other Half Lives*, which was based on his reports for the *New York Tribune* and the *New York Evening Sun*. But Campbell's series on the "Prisoners of Poverty" focused on the experience of women and children in New York's tenements four years earlier. When Campbell's series appeared, however, the *Tribune*'s editors pursued an unusual tactic by publishing a disclaimer, stating that they disagreed with her conclusions. She had been hired to write the series because she was an established professional who had written extensively about the slums in both fiction and nonfiction settings, but when she proposed broad, sweeping reforms that bordered on socialism, the editors stated: "It is in no way a disparagement of the reporter's ability to say that she has been more successful in describing the actual conditions which call for reform than in proposing remedies."[31] When Campbell also co-authored a book in 1891 about New York's seedier side, the publisher explained why she had been chosen: "Who but a woman could describe to women the scenes of sin, sorrow and suffering among this people that have presented themselves to her womanly eye and heart?"[32]

Shortly after Campbell's journalistic adventures in New York, stunt journalism came into vogue. Although journalism historians tend to use stunt journalism as evidence of the sensationalistic nature of newspapers in the 1890s, it is also possible to argue that stunt journalism actually encouraged municipal housekeeping reforms. It also put the writing of women reporters firmly on the front page, a section that previously had been off-limits to them. When Elizabeth Cochrane, the *New York World*'s Nellie Bly, feigned insanity and had herself committed to Blackwell's Island for the sake of a story, she certainly was more sensationalistic than Margaret Fuller, who had toured the facility nearly fifty years earlier. However, the results were the same. Exposure in the newspaper brought about legislative reforms. Annie Laurie (Winifred Black who worked for the *San Francisco Examiner*) exposed the horrific conditions at one of her city's hospitals by feigning illness and allowing herself to be carted to the hospital in a prison van. Her sensationalistic story, however, prompted public outcry. Many of the stunt stories contained elements of reform, and often focused on urban problems that fell into the municipal housekeeping venue.

While writers like Nellie Bly and Annie Laurie followed a more flamboyant approach to reform, other writers in the 1890s were using their forums to encourage members of women's clubs to involve themselves in municipal concerns. Foremost among these writers was Jane Cunningham Croly, who spent the decade editing magazines for club women and fostering the national club movement.

Croly, who used the pen name Jennie June, had long been a prominent figure in New York journalistic circles. She had begun writing for New York newspapers in the 1850s and then worked as columnist and editor for *Demorest's Magazine*, a woman's fashion magazine founded in the 1860s to promote and sell the dress patterns that the company manufactured. During her tenure there, Croly wrote a longstanding column, which displayed her belief that women should be involved in their communities.

Croly was so supportive of women's involvement beyond the home that she cooked up the idea of a "Woman's Parliament" and sponsored it in 1869. She envisioned a legislature and a president of women who would make vital decisions on the issues that affected women and children. Although today this might appear to be a more radical idea than simply giving women the right to vote, Croly believed this could be a more traditional route for women to follow. Although about seventy women heeded her call, which was publicized in her newspaper columns and in circulars, her idea was ahead of its time. By the 1890s, however, after decades of writing and speaking publicly on a more public role for women, Croly found satisfaction in the fact that thousands of American club women followed the civic reform agenda of her General Federation of Women's Clubs, the national umbrella organization she founded.

Croly, who was born in 1828, was both representative and atypical of women of her generation. She was tradition-bound, in that she never publicly supported suffrage and adhered closely to the belief that the best sphere for women was the private sphere of the home. But there the similarity ends. She publicly lobbied for women to involve themselves in reform and was one of the earliest writers to actually use the term municipal housekeeping to describe women's responsibilities to their communities. She was one of the founders of the women's club movement, which was considered a radical idea when it began in 1868. Croly founded the club Sorosis in New York that year because she was livid when she was denied entrance to a New York Press Club lecture that featured Charles Dickens as the guest speaker. She organized her friends, many of them also writers, and suggested the procedures for meetings and events. Newspapers mocked them publicly, but the club women were undeterred and the trend spread around the country.

In print, Croly was relentless. Throughout the 1890s, the last decade of her life, she was among the most vocal women writers to call upon other women to expand their sphere of activity outside their homes. Croly promoted women's involvement in municipal housekeeping in her magazines, the *Woman's Cycle*, the *Home-Maker* and the *New Cycle*. Prior to this, *Demorest*'s had provided Croly with a forum for a monthly column, "Talks with Women," which throughout the 1860s and 1870s reached a wide audience and revealed her thoughts about the role of women.

In her columns, Croly argued clearly for separate spheres for women and also advocated that women should take a more active role in the larger society. In a column devoted to woman's rights, Croly asserted her belief that the right to work, not the right to suffrage, should be the focus of women's activities. She stated: "The right that women most want in this country is the right to work, without feeling that it is a degradation, or that by doing so, they lose caste, and forfeit position in society."[33]

She believed women's roles as mothers especially equipped them to handle some public roles. Women were bored in their homes and needed a mission, she argued. As a founder of the nineteenth century's women's club movement, she believed that the club with its associated self-education and reform interests was the forum for many women to make the step into a public life. And she used her columns in *Demorest*'s and New York's newspapers to reinforce and spread that belief.

Throughout the 1860s, Croly continued to walk a middle ground in terms of women's roles. Just two months before the founding of the National Woman Suffrage Association, Croly helped found the less radical club movement in March 1868.[34] It, too, grew out of frustration with women's limited opportunities, but Croly and her club women sought a socially acceptable forum.

Croly's first club magazine, the *Woman's Cycle*, published on September 19, 1889, was designed to "represent the life, and particularly the associative life of the modern woman, its interests and working activities—literary, social, educational and industrial."[35] During the next seven years, Croly was involved in two additional ventures to promote club life and reform work to women. In that first issue of the *Woman's Cycle*, Croly issued a plea to all women "interested in an effort to represent the aim of thinking women" to cooperate with her venture and submit to her "their honest opinions and practical efforts on the lines of human advancement in morals and ideas."[36] In this same article, Croly outlined her belief that women needed a public role in society: "It is women who should be school commissioners and school trustees, it is women who should be prison inspectors and poor-law guardians."[37] Thus, years before the concept of active reform work and municipal housekeeping was suggested and popularized in articles in the 1890s, Croly had publicly stated her belief that this was women's proper sphere. In an essay on "Woman and her 'Sphere,' " Croly argued that women erred when they tried to "beat men upon their own ground, and with their own weapons."[38]

She suggested at a meeting of the General Federation of Women's Clubs that all clubs had an obligation to pursue increased civic involvement. In a speech that was later reprinted in the *Home-Maker*, Croly foresaw a wide role for women in the investigation of civic affairs and reforms "in the jails, in the schools, in the streets, in the planting of trees, in the disposition of refuse, and the provision for light."[39]

Croly herself believed that women's work in their clubs would help them earn the vote, and several unsigned articles, most likely written by her because she wrote the majority of the editorial matter, reflected this position. One article stated that women were slowly winning "this great concession" of suffrage not so much through protest, but "by the wisdom they have shown in dealing with education questions and minor public affairs."[40] Another unsigned article titled "The Question" predicted that "the enfranchisement of the sex is near at hand."[41] While the prediction was about twenty-five years premature, the article also stated that there were practically no arguments against municipal suffrage for women. Women should "take advantage of the opportunities which are already opened to them on school boards and other municipal matters."[42] Then, women's increased involvement in municipal affairs could be an entree into the larger political world.

While Croly did not publicly support suffrage, she provided a platform for prominent suffragists to argue their case. Croly's argument that "the tongue and the pen" were mightier than the ballot advanced a sort of "separate but equal" philosophy. She argued, for example, that women had an influence equal to the power of men because they had been "behind the throne."[43] Men needed the support and assistance of women, Croly argued.

However, she noted, most women actually preferred the shadows to the limelight.[44]

Croly lobbied for women's involvement in education and other municipal activities through her writing until she stepped down as editor of the *New Cycle* in 1896 to write a history of the club movement. When she retired, she handed over the responsibility of reaching club women through a magazine to her friend from Boston, Helen M. Winslow.

The *New Cycle* ceased, but it was replaced by the *Club Woman*, edited and published by Winslow, who had been writing for the *Boston Transcript*. The new monthly magazine was both edited and owned by Winslow, who had written for the *Home-Maker* and the *New Cycle* and had been Croly's associate editor for the last few issues of the *New Cycle*. The *Club Woman*, published in Boston, met with greater success in both advertising and circulation than Croly's publications. It continued her message to potential municipal housekeepers.

The *Club Woman* was for "an up-to-do and progressive club woman."[45] In the thirty-two–page magazine, Winslow promised readers that her magazine would provide guidance: "We shall tell what various clubs are doing for social reform, philanthropy, education progress and every other cause where earnest, well-directed effort counts."[46]

Winslow's early writing reflected concern for progressive reforms. She highlighted programs for the handicapped, advocated special industrial training in public schools and sympathized with striking factory workers. Women, she argued, had a job to do in the necessary social reforms of the day. She believed women needed to teach their families to have "broader and more humanitarian views of the rights of other men and women."[47] She also stated that women who had moved into public life needed to use their power "to make the world better for the masses of human beings yet to come."[48]

Winslow devoted many pages in the *Club Woman* to progressive causes. She published a regular feature, "What Some Clubs Are Doing," which featured the social reform activities of some of the most exemplary clubs. Winslow argued for women's increased involvement in municipal affairs, applauded the efforts of women who succeeded in this area and highlighted the work of professional women and those whose example could encourage others. Like Croly, she believed that once women succeeded on a municipal level, suffrage would follow.

Articles in the magazine advised on the formation of a club, charities for children, the creation of a summer kindergarten in Cambridge, Massachusetts, possible reform activities for clubs, ways to promote school hygiene and ways women's clubs could help the public school system, among other progressive topics. Repeatedly, the *Club Woman* published articles that suggested to its readers that they could employ womanly virtues for the betterment of society. An article on women's roles in the public schools suggested that a "noble work" for women's clubs would be to lobby within their communities to "demand that their noblest and ablest men and women be elected to their school boards, regardless of politics, party, race or religion."[49]

In addition to editing, Winslow also wrote a regular monthly feature, "The Mellowing of Occasion," for the *Club Woman*, arguing that women had the power to change the lives of others. In the January 1900 issue, Winslow suggested that women make an important New Year's resolution: "That we will enlarge our vision, that we will broaden our sphere, that we will deepen our love to humanity, that we will be true to our best selves."[50] Another column defended women's clubs against detractors who disparaged them. Winslow said the balance was in favor of the clubs "when we count up the libraries, the improved sanitary conditions of towns and cities, the increased educational advantages."[51] She said that the club movement was "one of the greatest factors in the world's progress."[52]

Seven years after Winslow established the *Club Woman*, she sold it because she said she was worn out and exhausted. She continued to express support for municipal housekeeping—this time, through her novels and a monthly column about clubs for the *Delineator*, which was published by a dress pattern company. There, Winslow publicized the importance of municipal housekeeping chores for club women, describing how women could agitate for changes in child labor laws and for pure food legislation and promoting club women's increased involvement in civic activities. She told readers that "organized effort" was the only effective way to promote reforms and that action needed to be based on knowledge of the facts.[53]

While Winslow never apparently worked publicly in support of woman's rights, she agreed with the goals of the suffragists. She asserted that club activities were preparing women for the day they could vote. "[T]he power of the ballot, when it comes to woman, will only be a power to such as have the best all-around education," she wrote.[54] Like the suffragists, Winslow linked the vote to a woman's moral obligation to better society. Thirteen years later, in an article about the club movement in *New England Magazine*, Winslow credited the clubs and the suffrage movements with generating a "general awakening" of women. Winslow said most club women initially "were not ready for anything so radical as asking for the ballot."[55] But, after thirty years of growth within the club movement, women accepted suffrage sufficiently so that it could be discussed "calmly and dispassionately" in the club forum.[56]

EXPOSÉ AND ADVOCACY AT *HAMPTON'S*

At the same time that Winslow was encouraging club women to join in municipal housekeeping affairs, journalist Rheta Childe Dorr began writing extensively on the club movement in America. She studied the plight of working women and the effects of poverty and inhumane working conditions. Her writing for the national magazine *Hampton's*, which also published Charles Edward Russell's crusade against Trinity Church, typified reform writing of the municipal housekeeper–journalists during the pre–World War I period. Her topics revolved around urban problems, women, children, health, education and poverty.

Born in Omaha, Nebraska in 1866, Dorr was committed to bettering the lives of the poorest and weakest members of society, especially women and children.[57] Like other women of her day, she married young and had a child, but there the similarities to typical Victorian women ended. Dorr abandoned her husband in 1898 and moved to New York with their young son. She joined the *New York Post* staff in 1902 to write for the women's section, then moved on after four years to the staff of *Hampton's Broadway Magazine*, where she found an audience for her own reform ideas and progressive beliefs. At *Hampton's*, "given unlimited opportunity to express my own ideas in my own fashion," she wrote a series of articles that promoted better working and living conditions for women and children.[58] *Hampton's*, which first was published in 1907 during the height of muckraking, underwent several name changes in subsequent years, but editorially it provided a consistent middle ground between investigative magazines like *McClure's* and popular literary periodicals.

The magazine also gave a forum to Dorr, who wrote articles about working conditions for women, the condition of children, the need for a juvenile court system, suffrage and education, areas that were representative of the municipal housekeeping tasks tackled by women journalists. In all, she wrote more than twenty articles—all relating to municipal housekeeping topics.

Journalism historian Frank Luther Mott argued that in this forum, Dorr had "a field all her own."[59] Louis Filler, the preeminent historian of muckraking, described her as a "woman's muckraker" because her writing exposed social ills that were of concern primarily to women.[60] Her subjects, however, actually were broader than only women's issues. Dorr's articles described in detail the plight of women and children, but also the urban, political and social ills that were at the root of their woes—and that had focused the attention of many of the muckraking writers.

"The Wreck of the Home," one of her earliest pieces at *Hampton's*, described women's double bind as wage earners and mothers. Another article, which focused on the need for pure milk for babies, suggested that women's clubs should promote the cause of clean milk and education for poor mothers who were ignorant about how to care for their children.[61] Dorr passionately believed that women's clubs were appropriate forums for municipal reforms. A series of articles for *Hampton's* focused on the reform responsibilities of the women's club movement. She claimed the women's club was the "parent" of civic reform, noting that one-tenth of the 8 million American women–800,000 women—belonged to active civic clubs.[62]

One article exposed the deadly dangers of fire by portraying the horror of the Triangle Shirtwaist fire in 1911. Dorr used the fire to illustrate the hazards facing factory workers. Dorr vividly described how "doomed creatures" trapped on the upper floors of what was believed to be a fireproof building shrieked and clawed at each other to escape.[63] The only viable solution, she contended, was to focus energy on fire prevention. Fireproof buildings were inadequate; death-proof buildings were needed.

Dorr's articles at *Hampton's* were extensively illustrated with touching photographs of working women, children in factories, unsafe factories and women carrying picket signs. Her writing style relied heavily on anecdotes. She also appealed to readers' altruistic tendencies by describing in detail organizations and societies that were working to improve the urban environments. Women's clubs, settlement houses and schools were highlighted in an effort to show readers that volunteer activities could make a difference. Dorr also suggested remedies for social ills by publicizing the work of women who dedicated their lives to settlement houses, schools and clinics to help unfortunate women and children.

Dorr used her writing to constantly push women readers to become increasingly involved in a host of urban activities. She literally preached to her readers and, when necessary, chastised them. When juvenile court systems, pushed through by club women, failed to solve juvenile delinquency, Dorr told her readers it was "because you have done an incomplete work."[64]

Dorr spent two and a half years writing for *Hampton's*, but her career there ended when the magazine fell upon hard financial times. She turned instead to the cause of suffrage because she believed the "suffragists and the feminists . . . were working towards a definite goal, constructive, progressive and sane."[65] Dorr moved on to the next stage of her career, which involved "waking women up to feminism."[66]

The writing of the women journalists described in this essay illustrates how the municipal housekeeping movement evolved and became more radical over time. While these writers generally believed in the concept of a separate sphere for women, they pushed the limits of that sphere.

By the time Dorr abandoned her municipal housekeeping writing because *Hampton's* folded, the spirit of reform that had captured America's interest had been pushed aside. The threat of war became a major preoccupation and the Progressive Era "turned sour" and then faded away.[67] Indeed, interest in municipal housekeeping lost its momentum, sidetracked by talks of war and suffrage. But unlike muckraking, municipal housekeeping never faded away. There are scores of other examples: Sophie Loeb who devoted her journalistic career at the *New York Evening World* from 1910 to 1929 to promoting the causes of women and children; activist Florence Kelley who used journalism as a tool to abolish sweatshops and promote protectionist legislation; Cara Reese, who wrote a series of articles for *Good House-keeping* in 1909 and 1910 to expose dangerous conditions in public schools. The list is extensive.

By the outbreak of World War I, society in general had accepted women's participation in municipal concerns. Women in many states had been granted municipal suffrage. Even more common, women had gained school suffrage, which permitted them to vote for school board members, recognition of women's role in raising children.[68] Beautification of the cities, improvement of prison conditions, concern for poor children and women and hygienic problems were accepted as women's issues. The home no longer was defined as a mere building, it *was* the community where women lived.

As the concept of women's role in society expanded to include these concerns, women naturally took a more public profile. Women, especially club women, became civic leaders. The most important byproduct of this was that more and more traditional women, including club members, naturally accepted the fact that they belonged in a public sphere. Logically, support for suffrage was an important extension of this view. Club women no longer wondered *if* they would earn the vote, but rather *when* the vote would be theirs. Even traditional women who considered themselves "ladies," no longer thought of the vote as a radical, outlandish idea.

The journalists involved in the municipal housekeeping movement played key roles in the push for a wider sphere for women by writing extensively about the need for women to help with social causes outside their homes. While distinct from, and different than, muckraking, the writing of these women exposed social problems and proposed solutions.

These women were among a bevy of women journalists who involved themselves in promoting a wider sphere for women by publicizing the idea of municipal housekeeping. Historian Karen Blair argued that the municipal housekeepers "rendered obsolete the notion that 'women's place is in the home.' "[69] Perhaps it is more precise to say that municipal housekeepers, including women journalists, redefined what the "home" was, thus making it the duty of "ladylike" women to expand their role in society. Municipal housekeepers did not challenge the idea that women had a special sphere of activity; they simply believed that anything that affected women and children, including education, public health, labor legislation and the courts, fell within that sphere. The journalists who promoted municipal housekeeping played an important, and heretofore unrecognized, role in providing middle-class, traditional women with the vision of an expanded role in society.

And although the writing of women journalists expanded throughout the century to eventually include the "male" domains of politics and war, the interest in municipal housekeeping has never really gone away. From the public activities of Eleanor Roosevelt on behalf of women and children to Ladybird Johnson's project to beautify America to Barbara Bush's literacy campaigns, newspapers and magazines have highlighted the "natural work" of women in their communities. Thus, Bette Midler made headlines when she attempted to clean up New York City's neighborhoods, but municipal housekeeping is not limited to the rich and the famous. The terminology has fallen out of vogue, but a survey of women's magazines in any month presents evidence that women journalists are still promoting domestic causes for their readers: from *Family Circle*'s feature on a one-woman campaign to reestablish playgrounds in Harlem,[70] to a *Good Housekeeping* cover story on "Sick Schools," which described the toxic buildings that school officials were ignoring. "Is your child safe?" the article asked.[71] Municipal housekeeping continues to be a concern of American women, in large part because newspapers and magazines subtly continue to keep women aware that they always have been—and continue to be—the housekeepers for the nation.

NOTES

1. "Best Bette," by Melina Gerosam, *Ladies' Home Journal*, 116, September 9, 1999, 176.
2. Clinton Roger Woodruff, "Woman and Her Larger Home," *Good Housekeeping*, January 1909, 4–5.
3. Jane Cunningham Croly, *History of the Women's Club Movement* (New York: H. G. Allen & Co., 1847), 117–118.
4. T. S. Arthur, *The Lady at Home: or, Leaves from the Every-Day Book of an American Woman* (Philadelphia: Lippincott, Grambo & Co., 1847), 177–178.
5. Sarah Grand, "The New Aspect of the Woman Question," *North American Review*, March 1894, 276.
6. J.C.C., "The Reason Why," *New Cycle*, April 1895, 722.
7. Winnifred Harper Cooley, "The Future of the Woman's Club," *Arena*, April 1902, 379.
8. Ibid.
9. "Women and Their Interests," *New York Evening Post*, May 14, 1904, 4S.
10. "Women and Their Interests," *New York Evening Post*, February 17, 1906, 4SS.
11. Caroline Hunt, "Women's Public Work for the Home an Ethical Substitute for Cooperative Housekeeping," *Journal of Home Economics* 1 (June 1909), 222.
12. Ida Husted Harper, "Women's Broom in Municipal Housekeeping," *Delineator* (February 1909): 213.
13. Ibid., 294.
14. Mrs. T. J. Bowlker, "Women's Home-Making Function Applied to the Municipality," *The American City* 6 (1912): 863.
15. Susan W. Fitzgerald, "Women in the Home," reprinted in Anne Firor Scott and Andrew M. Scott, *One Half the People: The Fight for Woman Suffrage* (Philadelphia: J. B. Lippincott, 1975), 114–115.
16. Jane Addams, "Women and Public Housekeeping," published by the National American Woman Suffrage Public Co., Inc. This and other pamphlets can be found in the NAWSA Collection, Sophia Smith Collection, Smith College, Northampton, Mass. Hereinafter cited as Smith collection.

17. Jane Addams, "Why Women Should Vote," NAWSA pamphlet, 18, Smith Collection.

18. Mary Alden Hopkins, "Woman's Place," undated NAWSA pamphlet, Smith Collection.

19. Prof. E. B. Pollard, "Women, Home and Government," National Woman Suffrage Publishing Co., undated, part of the NAWSA Collection, Smith Collection.

20. Alice Kessler-Harris, *Women Have Always Worked: A Historical Overview* (Old Westbury, N.Y.: The Feminist Press, 1981), 121.

21. Kathleen Endres, "Muckraking: A Term Worth Redefining," *American Journalism* 14, 3–4 (summer-fall 1997): 333–335.

22. Kathleen Endres, "Women and the 'Larger Household': The 'Big Six' and Muckraking," *American Journalism* 14, 3–4 (summer-fall 1997): 266.

23. For a more complete argument on the difference between muckraking and municipal housekeeping journalism, see Agnes Hooper Gottlieb, "Beyond Muckraking: Women and Municipal Housekeeping Journalism," *American Journalism* 14:3–4 (summer-fall 1997): 330–332.

24. For a full discussion of the municipal housekeeping movement in Baltimore see Agnes Hooper Gottlieb, "Malloy of the *American*: Baltimore's Pioneer Woman Journalist," *Maryland Historical Magazine* 91:1 (spring 1996): 28–46.

25. Helen M. Winslow, "The Confessions of a Newspaper Woman," *Atlantic*, February 1905, 208.

26. Marian Marzolf, *Up From the Footnote* (New York: Hastings House, 1977), 205–207.

27. Quoted in Mary Elain (Zunt) Trapp, "The Journalism of Margaret Fuller, 1844–1850," master's thesis, Kent State University, 1973, 25.

28. Minutes of the Women's Press Club of New York City (WPCNYC), 27 May 1899, Columbia University Manuscript Collection, Butler Library, New York.

29. WPCNYC Minutes, December 10, 1898.

30. As quoted in Arthur J. Larsen, ed., *Crusader and Feminist: Letters of Jane Grey Swisshelm, 1858–1865* (St. Paul: Minnesota Historical Society, 1934), 269. Letter appeared in the *St. Cloud Democrat*, September 24, 1863.

31. "Conclusion of Prisoners of Poverty," *New York Tribune*, March 13, 1887, 4, quoted in Susan Henry, "The Unsavory Researches of Helen Campbell: A 19th Century Journalist's Investigation of Urban Women's Poverty," unpublished paper presented to the annual meeting of the Association for Education in Journalism and Mass Communication, Portland, Oregon, August 1983, 16.

32. Helen Campbell, Thomas W. Knox and Thomas Byrnes, *Darkness and Daylight or, Lights and Shadows of New York Life* (Hartford, Conn.: A. D. Worthington, 1892), frontispiece.

33. Jennie June, "Talks with Women: Woman's Rights," *Demorest's Magazine*, August 1866, 204.

34. Croly's New York–based Sorosis was one of the earliest women's clubs and, along with the Boston-based New England Women's Club, vied for the honor of being the very first.

35. *Woman's Cycle*, September 19, 1899, 3.

36. Ibid.

37. Ibid.

38. Jenny June, "Our Little World: Women and her 'Sphere,' " *Home-Maker*, June 1891, 331.

39. "Cycle Department," *Home-Maker*, June 1891, 362.

40. *New Cycle*, January 1894, 135.

41. "The Question," *New Cycle*, July 1894, 1–2.

42. Ibid.

43. June, "Our Little World," 331.

44. Ibid.

45. *Club Woman*, June 1898, 67.

46. "Introduction," *The Club Woman*, October 1897, 3.

47. Helen M. Winslow, "Strikes and Their Causes," *New Cycle*, April 1895, 727.

48. Ibid., 728.

49. Ellen S. Morse, "What Can Women's Clubs Do For Public Schools?" *Club Woman*, February 1898, 136.

50. "The Mellowing of Occasion," *Club Woman*, January 1900, 144. While this column was not signed, an article in the October 1900 issue of the magazine noted that Winslow was the author of the monthly column.

51. "The Mellowing of Occasion," *Club Woman*, April 1898, 4.

52. Ibid.

53. See, for example, Winslow, "Club Programmes," *Delineator*, February 1906, 374.

54. Winslow, "Strikes and Their Causes," 728.

55. Helen M. Winslow, "The Story of the Woman's Club Movement," *New England Magazine*, July 1908, 554.

56. Ibid.

57. "Writers and their Work," *Hampton's Broadway Magazine*, June 1909, 863.

58. Rheta Childe Dorr, *A Woman of Fifty* (New York: Funk & Wagnalls, 1924), 203.

59. Frank Luther Mott, *A History of American Magazines*, Vol. 5 (Cambridge, Mass.: Belknap Press, 1968), 149.

60. Louis Filler, *The Muckrakers* (University Park: The Pennsylvania State University Press, 1968), 273.

61. Rheta Childe Dorr, "The Square Deal for the Babies," *Hampton's Broadway Magazine*, April 1909, 514.

62. Rheta Childe Dorr, "What Eight Million Women Want," *Hampton's Broadway Magazine*, August 1909, 175.

63. Rheta Childe Dorr, "Deathproof versus Fireproof," *Hampton's Magazine*, June 1911, 688.

64. Rheta Childe Dorr, "Another Chance for the Bad Boy," *Hampton's Magazine*, December 1910, 801.

65. Dorr, *A Woman of Fifty*, 219.

66. Ibid., 224.

67. Richard Hofstadter, *The Age of Reform: From Bryan to FDR* (New York: Vintage Books, 1955), 20.

68. Alice Stone Blackwell, "Gains in Equal Suffrage," NAWSA pamphlet, 1911, NAWSA archives, Smith Collection.

69. Karen Blair, *The Clubwoman as Feminist: True Womanhood Redefined, 1868–1914* (New York: Holmes & Meier, 1980), 119.

70. Caroline Brewer, "All Children Need a Safe Place to Play," *Family Circle*, August 3, 1999, 17.

71. Jean Davidson and Keith Mulvihill, "Sick Schools," *Good Housekeeping*, May 5, 1999, 124–127, 184, 187.

5

Lincoln Steffens: The Paradoxical Muckraker

Stephen Whitfield

The prototype of the muckraking journalist is Lincoln Steffens, around whom a minor industry of publication has been built. His anecdotal writing style in the "Shame of the Cities," which *McClure's Magazine* published in 1902 and 1903, is perhaps the most well known of the muckraking exposés. It continues to be cited in high school textbooks and is still invoked in contemporary journalism whenever some lingering American shame is revealed. The famous 1960 CBS television documentary, "Harvest of Shame," took its title from Steffens's work, for example. But Stephen Whitfield's chapter goes well beyond Steffens's probing of the cities' shames as he follows Steffens's contradictory and paradoxical impulses right through to his final years when his autobiography made him famous all over again. Steffens's politics, in the end, were pragmatic and confusing and, much like both the muckrakers and America, ranged from conservative to radical, capturing the ideological diversity that so enlivened the early years of the American century. This chapter is reprinted with the permission of the *Virginia Quarterly Review* where it first appeared in the winter of 1978.

So ferocious was the reputation of the warriors who swept out of the steppes in the thirteenth century that the appearance of a single Mongol horseman at the gates of a city might be enough to compel its surrender.

In the early twentieth century, a lone journalist could, by his presence, induce American cities to submit as well. Their leading inhabitants disclosed to him their clandestine mingling of business and political affairs, their techniques for corrupting the polling booth and courthouse and police station.

So awesome did the journalist's fame become that civic organizations begged him to document their shame, to publicize their failures of democracy. Then he went on to muckrake the states, and then to study the federal government, and then to witness revolutions in Mexico and Russia. In 1931, in *The Autobiography of Lincoln Steffens*, he muckraked himself and produced a classic of American letters.

In a republic whose Declaration of Independence had professed "a decent respect to the opinions of mankind," Steffens raised the sights of our journalism even as he dragged his rake. Walter Lippmann and John Reed were among his protégés, and William Randolph Hearst called him the best interviewer he had ever met. Herbert Bayard Swope of the *New York World* worshipped him as a "demi-god," and Max Eastman of the radical *Masses* praised the brilliance and audacity of his reporting. President Theodore Roosevelt even wrote a card addressed "To any, officer of or employee of the Government: Please tell Mr. Lincoln Steffens anything whatever about the running of the government that you know (not incompatible with the public interests) and provided only that you tell him the truth—no matter what it may be—I will see that you are not hurt."[1] In 1905, when reform candidates were elected throughout the country, a future chief justice, Harlan Fiske Stone, wrote the journalist: "You more than any other man may take credit for the result of the elections wherever 'boss or no boss' was the issue." His *Autobiography*, Granville Hicks recalled two decades after its publication, was "possibly the most influential book of the 1930s."[2] Another endorsement came from Edmund Wilson, who discerned in Steffens "a philosophical point of view which few newspapermen have."[3]

Indeed, he presented himself as more than a reporter. Steffens wished to be the journalist as thinker, propelling himself beyond the modest tradition that began with the testament of "Benjamin Franklin, printer" and that included the unpretentious newspaper days that marked H. L. Mencken's early recollections. The *Autobiography* records the hunches he stretched into hypotheses, the generalizations he tested and discarded, the attempts to delineate a system. To be sure, Steffens shared the trade's hunger for facts, yet he was not appeased by nothing-but-the-facts. He traced the pattern of events; building upon his initial exposure of municipal corruption, he sketched the interlocking relations between business and government and then plotted the grand coordinates of history. Conversing with the boss of Philadelphia's political machine, for example, Steffens provided Israel W. Durham with "a philosophic view, of politics, an objective look at himself and his business," as though a symposium had been conducted.[4] Though some of Steffens's acquaintances, like Sherwood Anderson, detected in him "a queer trickiness of thought,"[5] historians and biographers have generally taken him at his own evaluation, from Louis Filler's standard *Crusaders for American Liberalism* (1950) down to Justin Kaplan's highly informative *Lincoln Steffens* (1974). As a result, the political ideas that affected two generations of American liberals and radicals have rarely been placed between the cross hairs of critical analysis.

Steffens was an elusive figure to size up and too ambiguous a writer to pin down, for he came upon his contemporaries from odd and unexpected angles. Named after the sixteenth president the year after the assassination, he was born and died in California; he witnessed the passing of the frontier and reported on the formation of an urban nation. Though a supremely American figure, he looked like a Russian, according to William Bullitt, who accompanied him on a secret mission to Moscow in 1919. In the coarse ambiance of the New York press at the turn of the century, Steffens was a cultivated gentleman, a dude in British clothing who had studied at Berkeley, Heidelberg, Leipzig, and the Sorbonne. Backroom politicians were later surprised to be interviewed by a sort of bohemian, a self-proclaimed "artist." As a cub reporter in New York, he considered himself "almost a Jew," nailing a *mezuzah* on his office door, fasting and attending High Holy Day services in east side synagogues. Yet Steffens became a heterodox born-again Christian, re-reading the Gospels (this time as "news") and once adopting "Christian" as his pseudonymous byline.[6] Professionally committed to the "letting in of light and air,"[7] he hoped to keep secret his engagement to one woman (Gussie Burgess), his marriage to a second (Josephine Bonetcou) and his divorce from a third (Ella Winter, to whom his *Autobiography* is dedicated).

A BOURGEOIS COMMUNIST

Particularly bemusing was his radicalism, which flowed from a style of living that was hardly plebeian. The tips he picked up covering Wall Street served him very well as an investor of funds from several inheritances. Without breaking stride, Steffens went from Greenwich Village, where he imbibed radical egalitarianism from Wobblies, to his Greenwich, Connecticut country home and servants. And when he sold his house to the chairman of the board of General Electric, he moved to a villa on the Italian Riviera, complete with cook, maid, and gardener. Of course the canons of respectability then required a servant class; even Karl Marx, pleading for money from Friedrich Engels, had proved how desperately impoverished his household was by complaining that the two servants were reduced to eating a few potatoes.[8]

But the Bolshevik revolution had presumably raised the ante of radicalism, issuing a stern challenge to bourgeois comfort. It did not inspire confidence in Steffens's sincerity that his 1932 appeal to support the Communist ticket and platform came after intending to preenroll his son at Groton. Nowhere is it stipulated that radicals must be insolvent, but credibility of Communist sympathies is not enhanced by such attachment to privilege. He could exalt the patient dedication of a young Bolshevik militant like Whitaker Cham-

bers, writing him in 1933: "Whenever I hear people talking about prole-
tarian art and literature, I'm going to ask them to shut their minds and look
at you."[9] Steffens could foresee a future that excluded democratic capitalism. But he refused to live in the Soviet Union, though he seems to have
considered expatriation when the comrades—knowing their man—hinted
at first-class accommodations. Another ardent fellow-traveler, Lion Feuchtwanger, was once asked why he didn't move to the country—the workers'
paradise—he praised so regularly. The novelist replied, "Do you think I'm
crazy?"[10]

Steffens was no fool either, and it might be argued that he was not even
a hypocrite, for he felt his background in the old order disqualified him for
utopia. He was reminded of Moses, alert enough to see but too old (and
ill-prepared) to enter—the Promised Land. An uncritical supporter of Soviet
policy, Steffens could not bring himself to join the party that most unswerv-
ingly supported its aims. He thus pleaded guilty before the bar of history:
he could welcome the revolution but not help make it. However, confession
is always appreciated and can draw attention from more grievous faults, as
Steffens himself once cannily advised Theodore Roosevelt; and *The Autobiography of Lincoln Steffens* deserves a fresh reading with that cue in mind.
For its author is vulnerable to a different indictment: Steffens, for all the
ideas that teemed in his head, was incapable of clear and precise thought.
A devilishly smooth interviewing technique and a repertoire of ready paradoxes have disguised a flaccidity of mind most characteristically shown in
his desire to have things both—or all—ways. Indiscriminate in his suscep-
tibilities, Steffens cheerfully acknowledged that he liked to change his mind.
But his flexibility was not primarily a gift for adapting to altered circum-
stances, a receptivity to signals from the *Zeitgeist*, for his writings need not
be analyzed diachronically. On the contrary, his inconsistent ideas were espoused concurrently. His reputation for complexity should be seen as a mask
for confusion. Pretending to dissolve opposites, he avoided discriminations
and choices. To apply a phrase Steffens might have heard translated for him
on the east side, he wanted to dance at all the weddings.

The standard version of his career makes Steffens a journalistic paladin of
the Age of Reform, and it is not inaccurate. The Progressive mind was,
according to Richard Hofstadter, essentially journalistic, with reality veiled
behind the smoke of backrooms and likely to be more sordid and conspir-
atorial than democratic idealism might suggest. Politics was not what was
projected from rostrums but what went on behind keyholes; and it was the
obligation of reformers—"the best men"—to ventilate these smoke-filled
rooms, to widen popular knowledge and participation in civic affairs.[11] As a
muckraker, Steffens indeed admired Robert La Follette of Wisconsin and
Mayor Tom Johnson of Cleveland. He praised their administrative innovations and sophistication, their rectitude and energy, their promise to abro-
gate privilege, their devotion to the common weal, and their effort to

promote representative government. The favorable article Steffens wrote on La Follette in 1904 "was like the decision of a court of last resort," the triumphant governor told him.[12]

However, Steffens also admired the Progressives' enemies and wrote with genuine affection about the bosses—Durham of Philadelphia, Richard Croker of Tammany Hall, George Cox of Cincinnati, Abe Ruef of San Francisco, Martin Lomasney of Boston's Ninth Ward. He relished the companionship of the men who ran the big city machines, but that is not surprising; most of those who had dealings with these politicians could not help but like them. Steffens also trusted them, however: His reminiscences neither criticize the frauds they perpetrated nor trace how they dishonored the ideals of public service. One explanation is that they had power, for Steffens gravitated toward strength, toward "principals" rather than "heelers." He went into a city to meet its masters, and even his imprimatur of La Follette characterized him as "a dictator dictating democracy." His strategy was not only to shame the cities but also to name the rascals who ran them. They were practical, effective, and prepossessing; therefore, Steffens raised no principled objections to their rule. He would have appreciated the last of their breed, Richard J. Daley of Chicago, whom Adlai Stevenson III, running as a reformer for the Senate, labeled a "feudal chief." Later, after Stevenson worked amicably enough with the Cook County machine and was asked about his campaign charge, he denied ever calling Daley a *bad* feudal chief.[13] Steffens would have liked that disclaimer too.

A second reason for authorial admiration of the bosses is that they were candid about their corruption, untainted by the righteousness that afflicted reformers. So repellent did Steffens find the moralism of "the best men" that he exaggerated the attractiveness of immorality; the more corrupt the politicians the more lavish Steffens's affection. He told Boston reformers in 1915 that "the leading grafters themselves should be the leaders in this 'reform movement.' " Misreading history in a manner that was barely corrigible, he added that "good people and the best men had been tried all through the world's history, and especially in Boston; and they had failed . . . Let's give up the good men and try the strong men." He also recognized the claim of a resident of Folsom Prison that the most hardened criminals should be the first released, because their promise to keep parole could be trusted. This descent into the penology of the absurd suggests how eagerly Steffens wished to shock his readers by playing the Good Bad Boy. It is almost as though he intended his book to extend the American tradition of criminal confessions, which until the mid-nineteenth century were the most popular autobiographies except for religious narratives. Philadelphia's boss Durham especially endeared himself to Steffens by calling him "a born crook that's gone straight."[14] But the old pol's remark was hardly perceptive, since the cultured son of a wealthy businessman had no need for the security of status for which ex-cons proverbially long. Steffens wanted privilege while attacking respectability; reformers valued respectability while attacking privilege. He was sometimes with them but not much like them.

His opinion of the bosses was complicated but intelligible; his attitude toward businessmen was simply inconsistent. Steffens shared the Progressive presumption that whenever rich representatives of private interests courted public officials, it usually wasn't Dutch treat. But he blamed bribery on favor-seeking businessmen rather than on the grafters themselves; for Steffens it was more blessed to receive than to give. *The Shame of the Cities* (1904) is a corroborating document for the view of historians like Arthur Schlesinger Jr. who have interpreted the past as a combat zone between liberals and commerce, a struggle to tame those who wielded and abused corporate power. "Moved typically by personal and class, rarely by public, considerations," Schlesinger wrote in 1944, "the business community has invariably brought national affairs to a state of crisis and exasperated the rest of society into dissatisfaction bordering on revolt."[15] Steffens took a similar stance: "The typical business man is a bad citizen." *The Shame of the Cities* denounces the capitalist ethos as "the spirit of profit, not patriotism; of credit, not honor" and "of dickering, not principle." Businessmen were crooked and untrustworthy, selfish and unenlightened. Since Wall Street could be reliably assumed to err consistently "on all social questions," Steffens automatically took the opposite side.[16]

This model positing a monolithic business community uncannily pursuing its own interests collided with Steffens's own experience and contradicted other views he expressed. In 1906, when that rule should have been fresh in his mind, he apparently voted for Hearst for governor of New York over the scourge of the life insurance industry, Charles Evans Hughes. He ignored Tom Johnson, a street railway magnate, and Charles R. Crane, the plumbing fixtures millionaire who was La Follette's financial angel and who invited Steffens into Russia in 1917. He apparently forgot Edward A. Filene, the eccentric merchant prince who saved Steffens's Carmel home in 1935. The *Autobiography* treats J. P. Morgan ("the boss of all the bosses") and Elbert Gary of U.S. Steel without rancor and praises Henry Ford as "the industrial leader in a land of industrial pioneering . . . a prophet without words, a reformer without politics, a legislator, a statesman—a radical."[17]

The rule Steffens claimed to have adopted was jettisoned in the 1920s, the decade when Allan Benson, the antiwar Socialist candidate for president in 1916, published a favorable biography of Ford; when Ida Tarbell, who remembered Steffens as the "most brilliant" of her colleagues on *McClure's Magazine* produced a sympathetic study of Judge Gary; and when Bruce Barton's best-selling *The Man Nobody Knows* depicted Jesus as a go-getter going about His Father's business. Sinclair Lewis later disclaimed that the eponymous hero of *Babbitt* was intended to be a figure of ridicule. "I understand that man," the novelist insisted; "by God I love him." And when Al Capone moved from Cicero, Illinois, to Miami, he tried to join the Rotary Club; perhaps he, too, really liked George Babbitt. To boost America was to mean business, and Steffens was also swept into the national mood, insisting that the proper "distribution of wealth was within sight in my amazing country."[18]

A HARD-BOILED EGGHEAD

Even though he was less hostile to big business as a "revolutionist" than he had been as a reformer, his stance in the twenties was hardly consistent. Steffens repudiated his earlier opposition to businessmen in politics and called government just another business, which wasn't so bad after all. Advocating more businessmen in control in Washington, he also apparently read Thorsten Veblen and called for the removal of businessmen from the boardroom. He hoped that managers devoted to production would replace investors hungry for profits; and he welcomed the administration of Herbert Hoover without understanding his troubled presidency as Veblen gone haywire—an engineer trying to save the price system. Steffens believed that Hoover would strengthen the polity by unifying its economic and political purposes. On the other hand, he predicted failure for Hoover—and that was good too, since the worse the crisis of capitalism was, the better the chances for revolution.

Steffens was so adept at the reconciliation of opposites that he formulated what Sovietologists call the convergence theory. Knowing how much Russian leaders marveled at "Fordismus," Steffens speculated that "the United States of America, which the Russians recognize as their chief rival, is, however unconsciously, moving with mighty momentum on a course which seems not unlikely to carry our managing, investing, ruling masters of industry, politics, and art—by our blind method of trial and error—in the opposite direction around the world to the very same meeting place." It was typical of him to assert that "Bolshevik Russia and the mass machine-making United States were more alike, essentially and politically, than any two countries I have seen." Fascinated by technique, he separated the ideal of efficiency from other questions of value, which he assumed were decisively shaped by impersonal economic forces anyway. Returning from Russia in 1919, he compressed American pragmatism and American optimism into his one memorable line. He had been polishing "I have seen the future and it works" even before entering the future from Sweden. Such theorizing simply dismissed facts; but in a way it did not matter, since the privately owned American industries were working too. The *Autobiography* quotes Ella Winter with approval: America "has what the socialists in Europe have always said they wanted, and more."[19]

Fascination with how the present works also drew Steffens toward the machine politicians, who opened up to him because he neither preached nor accused. He shared an interest in their craft, presenting himself (in David

Riesman's distinction) not as an indignant but as an inside-dopester. He showed Durham, for example, how Philadelphia's techniques for buying voters and legislators were less proficient than the system elsewhere. The Boss who "wanted to know how it was worked out in detail . . . became enthusiastic. . . . To Durham, a politician, the methods elsewhere were fascinating, and forgetting his use for them, I talked on like an enthusiast to a willing listener, as one artist to another."[20] And so Steffens continued, encouraged in the belief that he had what it took to catch a thief.

He was a hard-boiled egghead who stressed the disparity of effect between the intellectual and the man of action. Regarding his own academic training as top-heavy, Steffens had contemplated entitling his autobiography, *A Life of Unlearning*. He envied bold, practical men like Ford. Kerensky was an intellectual. Lenin was not, and therefore triumphed. D'Annunzio was an intellectual—and got as far as Fiume; Mussolini was not an intellectual—and marched on Rome. He who can, does; he who cannot, interviews—preferably a "romantic figure" like Il Dulce (Steffens knew everybody). Mussolini dumbfounded the journalist by telling him that those who did not realize that only action mattered had learned nothing from the war and its aftermath. The "divine Dictator" proved, apparently to Steffens's satisfaction, that the world could be changed by subverting theories, just as Einstein told Steffens in Berlin that the world could be better understood "by challenging an axiom." The *Autobiography* concludes with the credo that "as for the world in general, all that was or is or ever will be wrong with that is my—our thinking about it."[21] Perhaps an echo was intended of the Marxist injunction to change the world instead of describing it. If so, it is hard to accept such advice from Steffens, whose claim to preeminence among journalists lay in his flair for propounding axioms.

As a muckraker, he concluded that the nation's traditional ideals, like honesty, democracy, individual success and personal rectitude, were "antiquated. . . . These won't take us very far." But Steffens himself made little measurable advance in envisioning what might replace these norms. The *Autobiography*—itself an individual achievement in whose popularity Steffens took pride—chastises Roosevelt, Woodrow Wilson, and Mexico's Venustiano Carranza for having "no economics."[22] However, his own economics, apart from his belief in the inevitability of collectivism, was hardly crystalline. In his "life of unlearning" he became a baccalaureate of the Bolshevik revolution—but got no further. Steffens had a cause, but not a case that was stringently reasoned; a faith, but not a sensible and internally consistent justification for it; an image of a workable future, but not a vocabulary exact enough to prevent collapse upon inspection. He neither specified the meaning of those elastic terms like democracy, honesty, or morality, nor reflected upon the substitution of other values.

Steffens was scarcely a democrat, if the term refers to an advocate of maximal participation in the affairs of state. He showed no genuine sympathy for the common people, nor did he identify himself with their fate. His support of the bosses was due not to their popularity but to their power, and he was more interested in how cities might be run than in how the masses might be represented. He neither savored the flesh-pressing and crowd-pleasing instincts of the bosses, nor criticized those Progressives whose views narrowly reflected the class interests of the well-born. Such inoculation against the infectious spirit of democracy differentiated Steffens from most of his fellow citizens.

While he did not ordinarily call himself a democrat, he often described himself as a liberal, a term the *Autobiography* often deprecates. The effort to determine what Steffens meant by "liberal" is not rewarding, however. He was less interested in validating the claims of liberalism or in revitalizing its traditions than he was in validating his disenchantment and his frustration with its failures. Before a California audience in 1933, his semantic confusion (and his activist fervor) bubbled quickly to the surface: "I am introduced to you as a tired liberal. I am not a liberal, but I am tired . . . of liberalism. I mean that I am tired of this open-mindedness, this willingness to consider the facts of history and of the present and the next thousand years. I think as a liberal that we have come to the time when we must stop thinking and decide and do it." If liberals differed from Communists in their hesitation to board the locomotive of history, then it made no sense to call Lenin "the greatest of the Liberals," "a liberal by instinct."[23]

If a liberal is defined as a champion of freedom within the rule of law, either in seeking to maximize private economic rights or in defending civil rights and liberties, especially of the underprivileged, then Lincoln Steffens was not a liberal. Claiming to be "tired of this open-mindedness," he in fact exuded the receptivity and tolerance associated with the liberal temper. But he also had a most-favored nation policy, minimizing the importance of civil and political rights in the Soviet Union while condemning the violation of those rights in the United States. He was satisfied with the Leninist assurance that liberty in Russia would require a few generations but was impatient with the pace of economic justice in America, which would not be granted a millennium to achieve. After the Communist revolution was crushed in Hungary in 1919, Steffens blamed its failure on Bela Kun's refusal to unleash the red terror. He also justified the Soviet purges that began with the Kirov murder in 1934, though Steffens did not live long enough to gauge the full cost of the Stalinist *Walpurgisnacht*. He replied to criticism of Soviet tyranny by pointing to American workers, an entire class that he supposed was deprived of its freedom. Consistency would have required condemnation of terror in both the United States and the Soviet Union, but Steffens was as selective in his "liberalism" as he was in his reserves of patience. He thus exemplified what Sidney Hook called "totalitarian liberalism," which combined leftism on domestic issues with subservience to Russian policy and propaganda.

Further evidence of his repudiation of the ideal of liberty as a superannuated vestige of an earlier political culture can be found in his ambivalent treatment of Italian fascism. Steffens granted that the divine dictator "abolished free speech, free thought, free assembly, a free press." But even though fascism was highly oppressive, it was, like Bolshevism, alleviating the burdens of economic insecurity. Having resided in Italy during much of the twenties, Steffens recalled the "bracing sight" of "young black shirts walking through the streets, into an inn, or down the aisle of a railroad train, heads up, shoulders back, in command of the world."[24] Against such assured force, thought was impotent; and Steffens, who had earlier been sickened by the bloodied skulls of strikers in New York, raised no fundamental objections to a police state abroad.

A COLLISION WITH CHRISTIANITY

For all his insistence that honesty was as limited in value as democracy, "the moral advantage of self-knowledge" was one of the few ideals he held with any consistency and tenacity. If only for professional reasons, Steffens appreciated candor; but honesty defined as the absence of boodling held no appeal. Instead he cherished the freedom from illusion based on obedience to the Delphic injunction. He told an unconvinced Harvard president, Charles W. Eliot, that students should not become crooks inadvertently: "Intelligence is what I am aiming at, not honesty." The emotional center of the *Autobiography* is therefore the chapter in which the author muckraked himself. Having given the idea for an article on a labor union scandal to a *McClure*'s colleague, Ray Stannard Baker, Steffens found his own reporting overshadowed; and Josephine Steffens objected to her husband's excessive generosity. He replied that "it didn't matter who wrote the article"; besides, Baker would remember to whom credit was due. His wife suspected otherwise. "She invited him to dinner," Steffens recalled, "and asked him how he came to write that article. He told her the genesis of it, with no mention of me! She won, I smiled . . . and I felt—yellow. My wife, who had presence of mind, knew me better than I knew myself; and all she had to do was to scratch the surface and there it was: envy, jealousy, and all the rest." He resolved henceforth "to be intelligent, rather than good,"[25] fearing the supreme humiliation of being taken for a sucker (and, trusting foresight rather than conscience, become a dupe instead).

Steffens never explained why being right is incompatible with doing right. He never discerned self-knowledge in anyone but crooks and bosses, whose minds were uncluttered by cant. Only the old pols are presented in the *Autobiography* as unfettered by illusion, their roguish charm enhanced by their willingness to tell the truth (except under oath). Steffens felt compelled to exalt political and business behavior only when, like Mae West's diamond, goodness had nothing to do with it. The result was, once again, baffling.

Part of the difficulty is semantic since the repudiation of moralism does not in ordinary discourse extinguish moral categories. For example, when Steffens proposed a substitute for the system that necessitated corruption, he asked his readers to imagine "an environment in which men would be tempted to be good."[26] And when he underscored the value of "self-awareness," he was obliged to define it as a "moral advantage." Nor does the advocacy of clarity in itself answer the riddles of ethics. Clarity about what, if not ultimately about what human beings should desire and emulate? To fathom one's own character does not thereby silence the claims of conscience or resolve problems of conduct that are inescapably framed in the language of morality.

Steffen's attack on morality also collided with his acceptance of Christianity. In the wake of the dynamiting of the *Los Angeles Times* building in 1910, he became a star witness in one of the subsequent trials, during which the prosecuting attorney asked if Steffens were not "an avowed anarchist." It so happened that the journalist did consider himself an anarchist, a label which, with characteristic insouciance, he pinned on anyone disrespectful of the judicial system. But he told his interrogator that he was "worse than that . . . I believe in Christianity." The witness explained that he was "a muckraker, and I tell you that things are so bad in this world that justice won't fix them. It's too late for that. I believe that nothing but love will do the job. That's Christianity. That's the teaching that we must love our neighbors." In an atmosphere of very sour labor relations, Steffens played the picaresque saint, calling not for justice but for mercy, which he considered "scientific, as Christianity is." The conclusion of its most dedicated adherents that Christianity makes exorbitant demands upon humanity did not occur to Steffens, for whom the goods of this world were all interchangeable. Nor did he quite explain how the punishable sin could be completely separated from the absolved sinner. "The doctrine of forgiveness instead of punishment for the sinner," he asserted, "is sound, scientific, and—it is natural."[27]

It would be just as natural to wonder why Steffens did not urge upon Bolsheviks the doctrine of forgiveness but called for a reign of terror instead. The salient issue here is not only the discrepancies that can be located in anyone's life and thought; what is remarkable is Steffens's habitual failure to make the discriminations essential to intelligible discourse. He defied plausibility, if not the Aristotelian law of identity, in making Christianity and communism synonymous. "I believe that nothing but love will do the job," he announced from the witness stand in Los Angeles. After visiting Russia he believed that "only revolution could do the job"—but nowhere does the *Autobiography* suggest that the earlier view was abandoned. "The acts of the Apostles showed them practicing Communists!—as if . . . they could not practice Christianity under the system; they could not love one another under our intense competition." (Never mind that Steffens admired the scientific resourcefulness he claimed was common to both industrial capitalism and primitive Christianity.) Jesus "had evidently tried not only to preach Christianity, but proposed also a scheme to make it possible!" Best of all, like the future, "it worked."[28]

This was the pragmatist's ultimate accolade. But since Steffens argued that the municipal machines and the capitalist enterprises also worked, the advantages of Christianity/communism in this context become less impressive. He eventually chose the Bolsheviks over the bosses because they looked like winners—and in the world of Lincoln Steffens, nice guys never finished last. A year after Lenin's seizure of power, an article signed "Christian" reported that "the revolution in Russia is to establish the Kingdom of Heaven here on earth, now; in order that Christ may come soon: and coming, reign forever. Forever and ever, everywhere." The contributor to the *Nation* seemed only dimly aware of the practical difficulties in reconciling the brotherhood of man with the dictatorship of the proletariat; but insofar as he made a choice, he preferred to be cruel in order to be kind. A revolutionary situation, he wrote in 1933, imposes a dilemma "whether to be nice socialists or—socialists."[29] Since the Apostles were really Communists, Steffens reasoned that the Communists were really up-to-date Apostles; and armed with this exculpation, it was easy to be hard.

"Nothing that I used to think," he wrote in 1926, "could stand in the face of that Russian experience." Consistent support of the Soviet Union did not sharpen his thinking; instead, during the Great Depression, it only widened his influence. His certitudes, which terminated the doubts of young leftists like Granville Hicks "like a blast of machine gun fire,"[30] cloaked a restless, table-hopping mind. But neither the perverse ironies he concocted nor the canniness honed in the backrooms could assuage an indomitable will to believe. The paradoxes he spun so recklessly simply outpaced the responsibility to resolve them, the imperative to make sense. Here Steffens was reminiscent of Henry Demarest Lloyd, the muckraker who called himself "a socialist-anarchist-communist-individualist-collectivist-cooperative-aristocratic-democrat."[31] Such impossible containment of multitudes suggests that attacks on American capitalism are unlikely to be sustained by thinkers too wooly to understand it; and despite Steffens's mockery of intellectuals, revolutions elsewhere have often been led by men who spent time in libraries. Twentieth-century America has been replete with insurgents whose purposes became obscure, with tired liberals and totalitarian liberals, with socialists who were not radicals, with panthers who turned out to be pussycats. But Steffens's career is similar in the incorporation of this history in one man, and his thought circular in the futility of its effort to grasp what he was against and ultimately who he was.

Call him a muckraker—and he calls himself a revolutionist instead. Call him radical—and he calls himself a Christian. Probe his Christianity—and he praises crooks. Call him a defender of corruption—and he reserves his highest esteem for the La Follettes and the Tom Johnsons. Call him a reformer—and he wants the strong to rule instead of the good. Call him an apologist—and he defines self-awareness rather than force as the supreme virtue. Call him a philosophical journalist—and he derides intellectuals. Call him a shoddy thinker—and he scorns theory in favor of what works. Ask if the revolutionary future works—and he is reassuring: The Soviet Union "will save the world. That is my belief." Ask if Christianity works—and he responds, yes, that too, so long as we are unencumbered by "honesty" or "morality" or distaste for Fascist and Bolshevik thugs.[32] Ask him if capitalism works—and he answers, yes, so long as businessmen refrain from corrupting politics, or, alternatively, so long as they are allowed to centralize and rationalize the state apparatus. Then ask if democracy works—and he replies, yes, so long as his readers "understand . . . what a part dictatorship has to play in a democracy," how necessary the strongman is as the people's representative.[33] Ask if he is therefore a democrat—and he calls himself a liberal. Ask what he means—and he calls Lenin a liberal and Henry Ford a radical, and himself an anarchist, and the world no larger than our imagination. And then, like the Cheshire cat, he disappears, leaving behind only a wicked grin.

NOTES

1. Lincoln Steffens, *The Autobiography of Lincoln Steffens* (New York: Harcourt, Brace, 1931), 515, 541; Justin Kaplan, *Lincoln Steffens: A Biography* (New York: Simon and Schuster, 1974), 157, 243, 298.

2. Quoted in Ellen Fitzpatrick, ed., "Muckraking and Its Aftermath," in *Muckraking: Three Landmark Articles* (Boston: Bedford, 1994), 110; Granville Hicks, "Lincoln Steffens: He Covered the Future," *Commentary* 13 (February 1952): 147.

3. Quoted in Kaplan, *Lincoln Steffens*, 302.

4. Steffens, *Autobiography*, 416.

5. Quoted in Kaplan, *Lincoln Steffens*, 308.

6. Steffens, *Autobiography*, 244, 525.

7. Quoted in Kaplan, *Lincoln Steffens*, 332.

8. Elizabeth Hall, "The Freakish Passion: A Conversation with George Steiner," *Psychology Today* 6 (February 1973): 62.

9. Lincoln Steffens to Whittaker Chambers, June 18, 1933, in *The Letters of Lincoln Steffens*, 2 vols., ed. Ella Winter and Granville Hicks (New York: Harcourt, Brace, 1938), 2:961.

10. Quoted in Lothar Kahn, *Insight and Action: The Life and Work of Lion Feuchtwanger* (Rutherford, N.J.: Fairleigh Dickinson University Press, 1975), 218.

11. Richard Hofstadter, *The Age of Reform: From Bryan to F.D.R.* (New York: Alfred A. Knopf, 1955), 186–98.

12. Quoted in David P. Thelen, *Robert M. La Follette and the Insurgent Spirit* (Madison: University of Wisconsin Press, 1976), 44.

13. Steffens, *Autobiography*, 458; Mike Royko, *Boss: Richard J. Daley of Chicago* (New York: Signet, 1971), 201.

14. Steffens, *Autobiography*, 414, 614, 848.

15. Arthur M. Schlesinger Jr., *The Age of Jackson*, abr. ed. (New York: Mentor, 1949), 180; Lincoln Steffens, *The Shame of the Cities* (1904; reprint, New York: Hill and Wang, 1957), 3, 4–5; Steffens, *Autobiography*, 434.

16. Patrick F. Palermo, *Lincoln Steffens* (Boston: Twayne, 1978), 42–43; Robert Stinson, *Lincoln Steffens* (New York: Frederick Ungar, 1979), 54, 65; Steffens, *Autobiography*, 715.

17. Steffens, *Autobiography*, 590, 853.

18. Quoted in Kaplan, *Lincoln Steffens*, 100, and in Sheldon N. Grebstein, *Sinclair Lewis* (Boston: Twayne, 1962), 75; John Kobler, *Capone: The Life and World of Al Capone* (New York: G. P. Putnam's Sons, 1971), 221; Steffens, *Autobiography*, 855.

19. Steffens, *Autobiography*, 799, 851, 855, 872; Kaplan, *Lincoln Steffens*, 250.

20. Steffens, *Autobiography*, 414.

21. Ibid., 813, 815, 816, 873.

22. Ibid., 494, 514, 732, 743.

23. Quoted in Kaplan, *Lincoln Steffens*, 313, and in David Caute, *The Fellow-Travellers: Intellectual Friends of Communism* (New Haven: Yale University Press, 1988), 179; Steffens, *Autobiography*, 797; Lincoln Steffens, "The Greatest of Liberals" (1936), in *The World of Lincoln Steffens*, ed. Ella Winter and Herbert Shapiro (New York: Hill and Wang, 1962), 240.

24. Steffens, *Autobiography*, 818, 824.

25. Ibid., 521–525, 608, 611; Christopher Lasch, *The New Radicalism in America, 1889–1963: The Intellectual as a Social Type* (New York: Alfred A. Knopf, 1965), 267–270.

26. Steffens, *Autobiography*, 573.

27. Ibid., 525–526, 670–673, 688, 700–701; Geoffrey Cowan, *The People v. Clarence Darrow: The Bribery Trial of America's Greatest Lawyer* (New York: Random House, 1993), 383–388.

28. Steffens, *Autobiography*, 526, 804, 832.

29. Quoted in Kaplan, *Lincoln Steffens*, 219; Lincoln Steffens, "A Muckraker's Memoirs" (1933), in *The World of Lincoln Steffens*, ed. Winter and Shapiro, 260.

30. Lincoln Steffens to Marie Howe, January 8, 1926, in *Letters of Lincoln Steffens*, 2:724; Hicks, "Lincoln Steffens," 154.

31. Quoted in Harvey O'Connor, "Henry Demarest Lloyd: The Prophetic Tradition," in *American Radicals: Some Problems and Personalities*, ed. Harvey Goldberg (New York: Monthly Review Press, 1957), 79.

32. Quoted in Paul Hollander, *Political Pilgrims: Travels of Western Intellectuals to the Soviet Union, China, and Cuba* (New York: Oxford University Press, 1981), 64.

33. Steffens, *Autobiography*, 462, 543, 591.

6

Small-town Editor, Big-time Fight

James Kates

By the turn of the century in America, more people lived in cities than on farms. America's cities, brimming over with immigrants and corruption, were ripe for journalistic inquiry. The muckrakers took full advantage—from Charles Edward Russell's look at tenement life to Lincoln Steffens's chronicle of municipal corruption. While the efforts of the muckrakers in relation to municipal affairs have been well-documented by historians, journalistic efforts in rural areas have gotten less attention. The national mass-circulation magazines have gotten the attention of researchers, but just as Progressivism was a national and local phenomenon, so too was muckraking journalism. James Kates tells the story of a small-town Wisconsin newspaper editor who crusaded against a national lumber company on behalf of a "primitive rebel" who was resisting the company. In the process, Kates reveals how this editor became a rebel himself by allying his newspaper with a voiceless farmer and revealing how the muckraker's spirit—like all good journalism—was instinctually with the underdog. Reprinted with permission from the *Wisconsin Magazine of History* 79, 2 (winter 1995–1996): 83–108, in which it was entitled "A 'Square Deal' for a 'Primitive Rebel': Alfred E. Roese and the Battle of Cameron Dam, 1904–1910."

At 8:35 P.M. on Sunday, September 8, 1906, Alfred Eugene Roese boarded the eastbound Soo Line railroad at Osceola, along the St. Croix River in northwestern Wisconsin. As the 44-year-old newspaperman settled into his seat, the train pulled out of the Osceola station and skirted the south side of the village. From there it passed farm fields, dairy herds and rolling stands of oak, maple and other hardwood trees. As darkness fell and the train chugged eastward into Barron County, the hardwoods increasingly gave way to towering white pines. When he stepped off the evening limited at Cameron Junction, Alfred Roese stood at the edge of the great northern forest, an area he often referred to as "the wilderness."[1]

Traveling with his brother, Roese secured a wagon and horse team for the 5-mile journey north to Rice Lake. The next morning, the two men took an Omaha Line train 30 miles northeast to Winter, in Sawyer County. After a hearty noon meal, the Roese brothers walked 4 miles eastward on a dirt road, then another 6 miles through a dense hemlock forest "with nothing to guide one's footsteps . . . but the blazed trees on either side of the trail." After encountering a swamp, two porcupines and a "large yellow dog," the travelers reached their destination: the hardscrabble farm of John F. Deitz.[2]

For two years, Deitz had been vilified by lumber companies as an "outlaw" and "anarchist," but Alfred Roese found him to be neither. The farmer stood in shirtsleeves, with his hands in his pockets, as the visitors approached. "Then we introduced ourselves," Roese recalled, "and received such a welcome as can only be given by a man who is shut off from his fellow creatures and to whom the sight of a friendly face is almost unknown." Deitz escorted the Roese brothers to his home, a rude two-room cabin overlooking the Thornapple River. There they made acquaintance with the rest of the clan: Deitz's wife Hattie and their children Clarence, Leslie, Myra, Helen, Stanley and John Jr. Mrs. Deitz fed the visitors an "excellent supper," and the group carried their chairs outdoors, where they talked and laughed until past midnight.[3]

For all its levity, the talk had serious moments. Through the pages of his newspaper, the weekly *Osceola Sun*, Roese had reported on the travails of the Deitz family since 1904. That year, John Deitz had forbidden the Chippewa Lumber & Boom Company from sending logs through a dam on the Thornapple that touched upon his farm. The standoff had exploded into violence only weeks before Roese's visit. On July 25, 1906, Deitz and his family had been ambushed by a posse led by the Sawyer County sheriff and guided by a lumber-company foreman. John and his son Leslie had wounded one attacker with rifle fire, and Clarence had been shot in the head. The latter was still swathed in homemade bandages, a grim reminder of a wound that had exposed his brain and nearly killed him.[4]

Roese had believed from the start that the farmer was justified in his battle. But the editor also believed in seeing things first-hand, so he had undertaken the long journey to the Thornapple with an eye toward publishing a "full, true and complete account of this trouble." After two nights and a full day with the family, Roese's faith in Deitz was confirmed, and his commitment to the farmer's cause was sealed. "If there is a more peaceable, quiet, law-abiding and liberty-loving citizen of Wisconsin than John F.

Deitz, the editor of The Sun has yet to make his acquaintance," Roese told his readers in an eight-page special "Deitz Edition" published a few weeks later. Over the next few years, the editor would visit the Deitz homestead several times. Deitz's battle would culminate in a bloody shoot-out in 1910; public sentiment for him would grow, wane, and then grow again. Roese would support his friend to the last, though Deitz's stubborn manner appears to have strained their alliance. But in the autumn of 1906, the Osceola editor saw no gray areas in the epic struggle: "If the true character of John F. Deitz was generally known, if his worth was truly appreciated, his name would be emblazoned in Wisconsin's hall of fame as one of the greatest men this state has ever produced."[5]

HOME TOWN NEWS, OSCEOLA-STYLE

It is not my intent in this narrative to relate every incident in the Deitz affair. Rather, I am seeking to define the ethos that led an editor, Alfred Roese, to pursue the case with such incredible zeal. John Deitz epitomized the historical actors whom E. J. Hobsbawm has identified as "primitive rebels": persons to whom capitalism came "from outside, insidiously by the operation of economic forces which they do not understand and over which they have no control." Deitz had a swift and brutal introduction to the realities of corporate power, and he rebelled in ways that most people would never consider. But average citizens of Osceola, though their initiation into the twentieth century was much more gentle, also faced economic changes that may have been confusing, even frightening. In the *Osceola Sun*, Roese sought to show his readers that Deitz's dilemma was not really so different from their own. In doing so, he seems to have invoked a consistent set of values by which he expected Osceolans—and small-town Americans everywhere—to live.[6]

In *Home Town News: William Allen White and the Emporia Gazette*, Sally Foreman Griffith outlines the career of an editor who was almost Roese's exact contemporary. Griffith's White was an active "booster," an advocate of economic development and unabashed community spirit. As businessman, mediator, politician and definer of local interests (and often as the local scold), White "assumed that the interests of local businesses were identical with those of the community as a whole." The booster ethos, Griffith writes, served as a counterbalance to the brutal imperatives of laissez-faire capitalism: It "sought to channel individual competitive energies toward the interests of the community as a whole, arguing that the fortunes of each were tied to the prosperity of all." Growth and social cohesion, in this scheme, were entirely compatible.[7]

Roese's Osceola bore some resemblance to White's Emporia. It was primarily an agricultural village, a provider of goods and services to the farmer and an *entrepot* through which the farmer's products passed on their way to the great cities. But unlike Emporia, Osceola lay at the edge of an immense economic upheaval, one that threatened the small-town republican values that both White and Roese espoused. When Roese founded the *Osceola Sun* in 1897, the pine forests of northern Wisconsin were being mowed down to provide timber for the expanding settlements of the Great Plains. By 1910, when he sold the paper, the forests were virtually gone. Though Osceola was not itself a lumber town, it afforded a close view of the timber business and its potential threats to small-town republicanism: aggregation of capital, political corruption and the loss of small-town autonomy to outside interests. Roese, like White, was suspicious of Populist conspiracy theories. But he was quick to sound an alarm when he perceived that Deitz—and the ideal of small-town, face-to-face democracy—were imperiled by "the grasping greed of a great corporation."[8]

White and Roese occupied somewhat similar worlds, but it would be a serious mistake to lump them together as archetypes of the small-town editor. By the turn of the century, White was a famous man. He remained in Emporia all his life, but increasingly came to view his local activities in terms of national imperatives. Coupling his "booster" rhetoric with calls for Progressive reform, White sought to forge a community spirit that would place "public duties above immediate personal interests." In Griffith's view, White possessed a certain self-awareness about his role; he cast himself as a small-town sage even as he was becoming nationally prominent. Writing for national magazines, he offered his readers "an idealized image of the small town as the embodiment of essential virtues, from neighborliness and equality to unity, service, and morality." White presented these virtues "as characteristic of the animating spirit of the various reform causes of the time." The Emporia editor had much in common with Progressive reformers in the cities: He was affluent, he was educated, and he moved confidently in circles of power, whether in Topeka or in Washington. In addition, the Progressive crusade seemed to offer White not just a blueprint for national redemption, but a means of fulfilling his professional ambitions as well.[9]

Alfred Roese's options were far more limited, and they helped shape his narrower world-view. No national magazines clamored for his byline; no national politicians sought his counsel. Roese's "booster" rhetoric often was strikingly similar to White's, but its fundamental orientation was strikingly different. White viewed small-town virtues as a means of national salvation. His ethos, while not without its anxieties, was infused with Progressive optimism. Roese viewed the small town as a world apart, a place whose values could not be duplicated in the cities. While he embraced the "trust-busting" rhetoric of Theodore Roosevelt, Roese never accepted its underlying assumption: that concentrations of economic power had to be recognized as a fact of modern life. White's small town was a beacon on a hill. Roese's was a fortress under siege.

In championing John Deitz's cause, Roese invoked one idea time and again: that the poor farmer was entitled to a "square deal." In the narrowest sense, he meant a fair hearing in court, and just compensation for the use of his property. Convinced that fair treatment in Sawyer County was impossible, Roese sanctioned Deitz's repeated acts of civil disobedience. Deitz, it must be said, was not a rational man; he spurned several settlement offers and pressed his case far beyond the point of reason. His legal claims against the lumber interests were shaky, if not downright spurious. By covering the Deitz case, Roese was venting his anxieties that, someday, many Americans—and not just a bull-headed backwoods farmer—might be denied a "square deal." Several factors contributed to this "square deal" ethos:

- Suspicion of corporate power, particularly of "trusts" and other conglomerations of capital that undercut competitiveness and local control;
- Strong ties to fraternal organizations as outlets for "boosterism" and manly camaraderie;
- A sense of mutual obligation—in particular, a sense that a legal contract was a poor substitute for a handshake and a spirit of economic reciprocity;
- A strong belief in the superiority of small-town life, particularly the ideal of doing business face-to-face; and
- Intense parochialism and rivalry between small communities.

Roese believed that the lumber industry was ephemeral, extractive and exploitative. In short, it had no place in his conception of a "square deal," which was premised on fairness and long-term obligations. From there, it was a short path to championing John Deitz, the "Defender of Cameron Dam," as the antithesis of the "grasping" corporation, and as a symbol of virtue. In the pages of the *Osceola Sun*, the plight of the obstinate settler became an urgent jeremiad on the future of small-town life.

THE EDITOR COMES TO TOWN

The son of a Baptist minister, Alfred Roese was born on a farm near Osceola and spent almost all his life in northwestern Wisconsin. As a youth he worked on a railroad survey crew. Beginning in 1892, he edited the *Weekly Press* at Maiden Rock, the hometown of his wife. But the depression of the 1890s hit farmers hard, and with them local merchants. After five years on "the turbulent and annoying sea of Journalism," Roese concluded that the village could not support a newspaper. "We regret very much to leave you, for we have a warm spot down in our heart for you all," he told his readers in the farewell edition. With that, Roese packed up his type, his press and his young family, and moved north to Osceola.[10]

At least in his eyes, the village of 500 people was brimming with possibilities. Osceola occupied a pretty site on wooded bluffs above the St. Croix

River, a tributary of the Mississippi. In earlier days it had been a minor port and a center for shipbuilding. "Every steamboat goes down the river with all the wheat on board she will take, and a couple of wheat-laden barges made fast to her sides," Horace Greeley had written after a trip up the St. Croix in 1865. The railroad had displaced the river cargo business, but pleasure steamers still carried passengers to and from the Osceola landing, at the foot of Spring Street. By the late 1800s, most Polk County farmers had gotten out of wheat and into corn, oats and stock raising. The dairy business was growing, with a ready market at St. Paul, less than 50 miles away via the Soo Line. Proximity to the Twin Cities also spurred great hopes for tourism. Because of its mineral springs, Osceola was touted as the "Saratoga of the West."[11]

Osceola had little direct involvement in the lumber business. But to see this enterprise at work, one merely had to glance down from the bluffs, to the roiling waters of the St. Croix. On many days the river was choked with pine logs, floating toward sawmills at Stillwater, Minnesota, some twenty miles downstream. The St. Croix timber harvest had peaked in 1890, with 452 million board-feet of logs being shepherded through the floating "boom" at Stillwater. Roese occasionally reported the doings of the lumbermen, as in this brief notice in 1898: "The Boom company sluiced over a million feet of logs last Saturday." For Osceolans, the most tangible evidence of the timber business was the lumberjacks—affectionately known as "red shirts"—who trooped into town with money to spend each spring.[12]

Roese launched his newspaper in good "booster" fashion, with a banner headline reading "OSCEOLA, THE BEAUTIFUL." Below it he reprinted a Soo Line publicity piece boasting of Osceola's promise as a resort town, one that "tempts the lounger from the stuffy confines of the city." Local tidbits, usually no more than a sentence or two, dominated the front page. Roese made it clear that local news, no matter how obscure, was his top priority: "We want a good live correspondent from every hamlet in Polk county. Call at this office for stationery." (Within the week, a reader heeded the call for local news by bringing a two-pound potato to the *Sun* office. The new editor gave the spud front-page mention.) Roese printed four pages of his paper locally, stuffing it with another four pages of "patent insides" produced at St. Paul. The latter were heavy with illustrated fiction and ads for patent medicines. In his first editorial, Roese stated his objectives plainly. The *Sun*, he vowed, would be "non-partisan; but we reserve the right to criticize the acts of all public men." Coupled with that watchdog role, Roese promised that the newspaper would work for the "upbuilding of Osceola," and would advertise to the world its "varied natural beauties and attractions, as well as its commercial advantages."[13]

Despite the vow of non-partisanship, the *Sun* soon emerged as a Republican paper. But it kept its promise to criticize politicians regardless of party.

Almost from the start, Roese swore enmity to Robert La Follette, whom he considered a dangerous opportunist and grandstander.

Demand for the first edition exceeded two thousand copies. Roese soon recruited correspondents from much of Polk County; he printed their reports under alliterative headings, such as "Amery Actions," "Farmington Phrases" and the like. Within a month, the demand for advertising forced him to displace some local correspondence. By the end of 1897 he could boast that "The SUN has the largest circulation in Polk county of any newspaper in the world. This may sound odd, but nevertheless it is true."[14]

Roese joined the Odd Fellows and the Masonic Order, where he rubbed elbows with many of the small merchants who advertised in the *Sun*. However, his social contacts did not prevent him from criticizing businessmen, at least collectively, for what he considered their lack of community spirit. In the spring of 1897, Osceola's bridge across the St. Croix River to Minnesota had been badly damaged by ice. On December 22, 1897, just ten weeks after launching his newspaper, Roese mounted his first big public-improvement campaign, urging businessmen to raise $8,000 to repair the bridge. The project would "advertise the place and leave the impression . . . that Osceola was a live, wide-awake town," he wrote in a front-page article. For citizens who proposed a cheaper alternative of ferry service, Roese had nothing but scorn. Osceola's boosters had to "roll the stone of selfishness off of their heart" and provide the money for the bridge. As for the naysayers, they were "nothing but leeches on the back of a community that sap its strength and then throw its carcus [*sic*] to the buzzards."[15] The *Sun*'s badgering paid off, and the bridge was fixed. With no apparent irony, Roese called for a celebration of the community's less-than-spontaneous generosity.[16]

Always keen for a brawl, Roese soon showed his colors on the lumber business. Economic rivalry had been a fact of life in the St. Croix Valley since the Civil War era. Wisconsinites were intensely jealous of the Stillwater lumbermen, whom they dubbed the "Minnesota marauders." Much of the St. Croix timber came from the Wisconsin side of the river, but the capitalists, managers and laboring men who profited by it were mostly Minnesotans. Indeed, Osceola seemed almost entirely cut off from the timber industry's benefits. The huge white pines that sustained the industry were cut well to the north of the village; they were sawed into lumber well to the south. Osceola, it seemed, reaped few dollars and plenty of hardship from the business: Logs often clogged the St. Croix to the extent that navigation by pleasure steamers was impossible.[17]

On January 18, 1900, Roese and a delegation of valley businessmen rode the train to St. Paul to complain of the situation. Some of the editor's most faithful advertisers were included: a proprietor of a mercantile company, a dealer in agricultural machinery and a druggist. The men implored the Army

Corps of Engineers to impose restrictions on the St. Croix River Boom Corporation. Casting aside any pretense of objectivity, Roese paraphrased the complaint of one Polk County man: The timber barons "thought they had royal rights." They had transformed the virgin forests into a "dreary waste." Far from being benefactors, they were "the hardest of taskmasters and the veriest tyrants." Roese sneered at the arguments of the boom company's lawyer. "Those who heard him last Thursday say his speech was painful in the aggregate or some place else, and his charges were as wild as a 'pipe dream.' "[18]

A month later, the government ruled that pleasure boats would have first rights to the river on Decoration Day, Independence Day and during the month of August. Other than that, the timber interests held sway. Roese jeered this "open decision of preference to the boom company." He also condemned the daily *Stillwater Gazette*, which had complained that the decision was unduly harsh on the lumbermen. The Stillwater editors had "mutilated several columns with the soreness they feel," Roese wrote, adding: "If there were less Stillwater and fewer dam boom companies there would be a more equitable distribution of enterprise and a greater and more prosperous growth in the upper valley." The interests of the valley as a whole were not helped by the "centralization of capital at Stillwater," Roese fumed.[19]

In contrast to this "centralization of capital," the landscape of southwestern Polk County presented an almost Jeffersonian aspect. Osceola Township, which surrounded the village, was a land of small farms. Most were less than a quarter section; the biggest, at 200 acres, belonged to the merchant J. N. Johnson. Roese would not condone sniping between village and country. He insisted that they shared mutual interests, and the advertising in the *Sun* bore out this claim. Osceola served the farmer, and the farmer in turn gave life to the village. Livery stables, harness-makers, and purveyors of general merchandise supported the *Sun* week after week. Roese accepted national advertising—much of it from patent-medicine peddlers—but he relegated it to the paper's back pages and refused to sell contract space at a discount.[20]

For Roese, much like William Allen White, the key to growth was a spirit of economic reciprocity. The *Sun* boosted Osceola; in return it expected the support of local merchants and urged Osceolans to spend their money at home. Roese regarded the mail-order houses with fear and suspicion, and he railed against catalogue shopping almost weekly after 1900. An Osceolan who sent a dollar beyond the county's boundaries should feel that he or she had "sinned." The *Sun* noted that farmers had no control over commodity prices; their fates were determined by "the grain operators of large cities." Now the "concentration of business in cities" was robbing rural people of the last vestige of local control by "requiring" them to send their money away. That would mean "the ruining of beautiful and home like towns.

When you have depleted the home town you have done much toward depreciating the value of the farm lands." Roese "talked up" Osceola, and he expected his advertisers to "talk up" the *Sun*: "Now is it just fair for The Sun to be preaching your good qualities, asking and urging people to patronize you, when you never think of saying a good word for The Sun?"[21]

To some extent, Osceola retained elements of what Thomas Bender has called the "premodern moral economy." Business activities were grounded in social relationships, and the work of individuals was still strongly linked to the work of the community. Bender has written of the "bifurcation" of American society, by which he means the rise of a market system with "justification independent of community." He dates this phenomenon to the latter half of the nineteenth century, though it came to different communities at different times.[22] Roese's rhetoric, beyond its obvious self-interest, reveals a profound unease over this "bifurcation" and its consequences for the community. The editor never spoke of bald economic motives, but of mutual obligations and the common good. Even when dealing with mundane matters, such as the *Sun*'s solicitation of job printing, Roese could impart a tone of moral duty: "A paper such as The Sun, costs a 'lot' of money every week to produce, and it can only be kept up to its present standard, by securing such business *as by right belongs to it*."[23]

William Allen White often spoke of business in terms of "reciprocity and loyalty" while simultaneously championing its "rationality and efficiency." In the process, the Emporia editor revealed a "fundamental contradiction in the booster ethos." White embraced Progressive reform as a way of assuaging his anxieties about this contradiction. For him, the Progressive values of efficiency and aggressive government oversight held promise that a level playing field might be maintained, even as Emporia abandoned its isolation and tied itself into the national market economy.[24]

Roese did not possess White's talent for reconciling the booster contradiction. Instead, he gave short shrift to arguments that businesses should be "rational," and he insisted that business ethics were inseparable from larger questions of morality. Sounding every bit like the minister's son he was, Roese argued that a businessman who gave to the community would be rewarded many times over. As a small-town schoolboy, Roese probably had not been exposed to the theories of classical economics, but as an adult he would have distrusted them. Individualistic self-interest, in his view, did not give rise to an "invisible hand" that elevated the community's common interest. Instead, the unbridled quest for profits was a centrifugal force that inevitably would tear the community apart. In this sense, Roese's ideal of business conduct was less contradictory than White's—and many times more fragile. That may explain why Roese was far more critical than White of businesses that he believed had gone astray.[25]

Despite Roese's anxieties, his own business flourished. On September 28, 1905, he celebrated the *Sun*'s eighth anniversary by printing a special edition on book-quality paper. Engravings of the newspaper's new equipment were printed throughout the edition in bright blue ink. Circulation stood at 1,700. Roese had long since abandoned the "patent insides," printing all eight pages of the paper in his own shop. He announced that he had replaced his old set of type, which had served him since his days at Maiden Rock. In an editorial, he eulogized the well-worn bits of lead in a manner that imbued them with mystical spirit: "Week by week and day by day the dress that has been discarded chronicled the happenings of the world, and especially the part that is the world to us, our county and state. It told the incidents and events, the hopes and ambitions and pleasures and sorrows that made up the history of the weekly life of our friends, our neighbors and ourselves."[26]

"Bro. Roese, of The Osceola Sun, is evidently prospering," a fellow editor (and apparently a fellow Mason) wrote in one of many bouquets the paper printed two weeks later. Marveled another: "We have often wondered how Roese made things go so blamed fast over his way."[27]

DISCOVERING THE DEITZ CASE

Roese's prosperity had only tangential connections to the lumbermen who were denuding the great forests of the north. Still, the *Sun* occasionally printed tidbits about the timber business, which by the early twentieth century was flagging. Late in 1905, Roese reprinted an item from the *Stillwater Gazette* that sounded the death knell for the St. Croix logging industry. The boom at Stillwater had handled just 102 million board-feet of logs in 1905, and the figure was expected to fall to 90 million in 1906. After that, "the output of the boom will be gradually reduced . . . until all the logs on the St. Croix and its tributaries have been cut."[28]

In the pages of the *Sun*, the passing of the lumber business might have remained a footnote if not for the intransigence of a farmer named John F. Deitz. Dozens of miles from Osceola, in the dense forests of Sawyer County, Deitz had begun to make trouble for the lumber companies in the spring of 1904. The scene of battle was a small, unimposing dam on the Thornapple River.

The Cameron dam had been built in 1875, under a state charter issued to an Eau Claire lumberman. It was a crude structure of hewn timber and earthen reinforcements, 15 feet high and just 25 feet wide. But by regulating the flow of water, it allowed lumbermen to float millions of dollars' worth of timber down the Thornapple to the Chippewa River, and from there to the "Big Mill" of the Weyerhaeuser lumber conglomerate at Chippewa Falls.[29]

Deitz's dispute sprang from the fine print of a real-estate deal. In 1900, the Deitz family bought 160 acres of Sawyer County land from Jennie Cameron, a widow. A corner of the Cameron dam lay on the property. Mrs.

Cameron's deed contained an easement that permitted the Chippewa Lumber & Boom Company to use the dam. But for reasons unknown, no such provision was included in the title when the Deitzes acquired the farm. After years of working itinerantly at the site, the Deitz family occupied the land in February 1904. John Deitz submitted a claim for $1,700 to the Chippewa Logging Company for his work as a watchman on a dam on the Brunet River, where the family had previously lived. The claim was denied, and Deitz roughed up two loggers in an ensuing fistfight. Seething with anger, the farmer vowed to get even. "They've got to go through my dam," he noted. "I've wrote the company, and I'm going to get a little money out of it. When they're counting their millions, the few crumbs that fall to the floor ought to be mine." Besides his back wages, Deitz claimed he was owed $8,000 in royalties for logs that had passed through the dam since 1900. Loggers who arrived at the property in April 1904 were amazed to find a sign warning against trespassing. Deitz stood over the dam, backing up his words with a Winchester rifle. The lumberjacks fled to the woods.[30]

The lumber company obtained state and federal injunctions against Deitz, but the farmer insisted he had never been properly served with legal papers. (On one occasion, fearing that a package of warrants was an "infernal machine," Deitz hoisted it with a pitchfork and threw it into the river.) Authorities at Hayward, the county seat, made several bungled attempts to capture the lawless woodsman. William Irvine, manager of the Chippewa Lumber & Boom Company, proposed that the Masonic Order arbitrate the dispute. Deitz and Irvine were both Masons, as were many of the lumber company's managers. Deitz, suspicious that corporate ties were more powerful than fraternal ones, refused the overture. In April 1906, water from dams above the Deitz farm was released as if on cue, and the Cameron dam was destroyed. The lumbermen apparently had intended to wash all the timber downstream, but they only partially succeeded. Thousands of logs were stranded above the dam, in a marshy area on and around the Deitz property.[31]

The *Osceola Sun* took early notice of the case, as did most other newspapers in northern Wisconsin. In the plainest sense, the Deitz drama was an exciting story, and the farmer's blustering rhetoric made for good copy. Roese culled items from his exchange papers and reprinted them, often on the front page. He also reprinted editorials from papers sympathetic to Deitz, such as the *Rice Lake Leader*. One such piece, in 1905, condemned a "low lived sneaking trick" by two men who had called at the Deitz home claiming to be lost and hungry, and then had tried to serve the farmer with legal papers. Deitz had bodily thrown them from the cabin. Roese quoted a *Minneapolis Tribune* piece in which the settler told why he refused to take his grievances before the legal system: "I am a poor man and have no money to fight a millionaire corporation in the courts."[32]

But it was not until July 1906, when Clarence Deitz was wounded in a "shower of leaden hail" from the Sawyer County posse, that Roese resolved to investigate the situation first-hand. On August 30, the *Sun* announced that it had received a 22-page, handwritten manuscript from Deitz outlining his side of the controversy. "It will be of great interest to everyone who believes in a 'square deal,' " Roese told his readers. "This case has attracted wide attention, and The Sun congratulates itself and its thousands of readers on the 'scoop' it has accomplished." A week later, the editor made his first trip to the cabin on the Thornapple.[33]

For several weeks, Roese trumpeted his forthcoming "Deitz Edition." Until then, most Osceolans probably had viewed the case as a spectacular entertainment. But suddenly they were implored to regard it as a personal challenge, and an opportunity to express community solidarity with a down-trodden family in the far-away woods. Roese announced that extra copies of the edition would be sold for 25 cents, with proceeds going to a Deitz benefit fund: "Here is an opportunity for every friend of this persecuted man to help a good cause. In addition to the newspapers, photos of the Deitz family and views of the famous farm will be on sale at 50 cents each." In late October, Roese's gasoline-powered press worked overtime. Besides the regular *Sun* of October 25, it cranked out 1,700 copies of the "Deitz Edition" for subscribers, and an additional 4,000 copies of the edition for individual sale.[34]

"JOHN F. DEITZ BEFORE ALL MEN," read the edition's main head-line, suggesting that the farmer was standing before the citizenry and invit-ing judgment. Deitz's own disjointed statement occupied a dozen columns; among other things, he charged that a young woman who was sent to the home to tutor the Deitz children had rifled through the family's belongings looking for incriminating evidence. Roese urged readers to "exchange places with Mr. Deitz," and to imagine that, after years of toil, they had somehow incurred "the enmity of a powerful corporation, and that corporation, backed by its millions of dollars and its armed gangs of desperadoes and thugs should attempt to despoil you of your home. . . . [W]ouldn't you do just exactly as John F. Deitz is doing today?"[35]

In his top story, Roese betrayed severe anxiety over the case and its mean-ing to American democracy. Without "regard to class or political affiliation," all citizens were entitled to a "square deal," he wrote. But the machinery of democracy had been corrupted. Great wealth, instead of conveying ben-efits to the many, had enabled a privileged few to seize control of the gov-ernment. Grafters dominated politics, and "money-ruled judges" had sullied the justice system. Money had become "the controlling power," and "the possessor of unlimited quantities of gold" seemed to be above the law. In Roese's eyes, great wealth necessarily sprang from great wrongdoing. For any Osceolan who viewed the Deitz case as a far-away amusement, Roese had an ominous warning: "No one is safe from these vultures."[36]

Advance publicity for the "Deitz Edition" had rattled nerves in Sawyer

County. Roese had been warned by F. L. McNamara, the county's district attorney, that "as a man who owns property and relies on the state to protect that property," he should not "defend criminals and crime." McNamara labeled Deitz's resistance as "an attack on our organized form of government which is nothing but anarchy." Roese assured his readers that the *Sun* was not opposed to settling disputes by "the ordinary course of law." But in this case, Roese was convinced that a fair trial was impossible, and that the defiant Deitz was "pursuing the one course open to him."[37]

Thus began an extraordinary alliance that was to last more than three years. Roese visited the Deitz home again in late November. The family was under siege; they dared not venture into town for fear of ambush or arrest. With the long northern winter approaching, they had nothing to eat but venison and a cellar full of root crops. "Hold the fort, for we (your friends) are coming to the front to help you out, all that we can," Roese wrote to the family on Christmas Day. He enlisted the help of several Deitz supporters, including Charles Broughton, editor of the *Fond du Lac Bulletin*. Another comrade, a man named Jacobson, invoked fraternal ties in his pledge to join the battle. He wrote to Roese: "I see you think that I am a Bro. Mason, but am sorry I am not, but that does not matter. I am for what I think is right . . . I am an Odd Fellow, also an Elk, and I think their teachings are very much the same as the Masons. The first qualification for either, *is to be a man*. When it comes to starving women and little children, in order to satisfy *greed, I want to fight, if I get killed in the first fire*."[38]

Early in 1907, Roese put the *Sun*'s columns to work for a cause far distant from Main Street: the relief of the Deitz family. The lumber company had tried "to cut off Mr. Deitz from his base of supplies, and, with hunger gnawing at the vitals of himself, wife and little ones, force him to give up," Roese told his readers on January 17. Osceolans already had donated "400 pounds of clothing, etc.," which were delivered to the Thornapple on Christmas Eve. Editor Broughton of Fond du Lac raised half a ton of various "provisions," which he took to the cabin in January along with four barrels of flour from Osceola. Meanwhile, John Deitz declared glumly that the lumber company was certain to kill the entire family that summer: "I am satisfied that I will be the last one to be murdered, as there would be no excuse for murdering the rest if I were dead."[39]

The rhetoric intensified in February, when Roese launched a massive re-supply campaign. Deitz was "a prisoner in his own home," never knowing when the lumber company thugs might shoot him "like a beast." The farmer had invoked the wrath of the lumber barons by refusing to "humbly bow" to their demands. By supporting Deitz, the *Sun* suggested, Osceolans could take a stand for justice and individualism; they could reaffirm not just Deitz's liberty, but their own. Roese presented a bold challenge to his readers, in-viting them to think of the Deitz case not in terms of particular circum-stances, but as a referendum on inalienable rights: "Do you recognize the right of a citizen of Wisconsin to live and support himself and family in the manner he sees fit, so long as he does nothing to conflict with the laws of the state?"[40]

In this manner the Deitz case was imbued with a key element of "booster-ism": The good of one was tied to the good of all. Roese asked readers to bring donations of food or money to the newspaper's office. "The liberty-loving, oppression-hating citizens of Wisconsin have never been asked to contribute to a more worthy cause than this."[41]

The campaign succeeded. Early in March, Roese and several other men took the supplies to Winter by train, then loaded them on a horse-drawn sleigh for the journey through the forest. The goods would last through the fall. In a front-page letter in the *Sun*, the Deitzes thanked "the hundreds who have so quickly come to our assistance." Roese, meanwhile, paid the family's property taxes for 1906 to prevent the Weyerhaeuser interests from obtaining a tax deed on the dam site. To foot the bill, Hattie Deitz stitched mittens from deer hides, which were shipped to Roese for sale at Osceola at one dollar a pair. In addition to the editor's everyday duties, the burden on his time must have been tremendous, but Roese seems never to have complained. "It certainly gives me pleasure to know that you have so much faith in me," he wrote to Deitz in January.[42]

SEEKING AN ENEMY

Alfred Roese's anger over the treatment of John Deitz coincided with Progressive indignation over the cutting of the northern forests. To that extent, the "enemy" in the Deitz case was clearly defined. The Chippewa Lumber & Boom Company and the Mississippi River Logging Company, Deitz's prime adversaries, were subsidiaries of the nation's biggest lumber empire: the vast syndicate controlled by Frederick Weyerhaeuser. Though not entirely secretive, Weyerhaeuser and his colleagues had a "habit of si-lence." Thus they escaped—at least for a while—the scrutiny accorded John D. Rockefeller and other high-flying capitalists of the early twentieth cen-tury. But by 1905, the systematic destruction of the woods was becoming apparent. Having logged off the Midwest, Weyerhaeuser was turning his sights to the Pacific Northwest. Instead of being replanted, most of northern Wisconsin was simply abandoned, and allowed to revert to the counties for nonpayment of taxes. Speaking to the American Forest Congress in 1905, Theodore Roosevelt epitomized the growing resentment over lumbermen who "skin the country and go somewhere else . . . whose idea of developing the country is to cut every stick of timber off of it, and leave a barren desert."[43]

Alfred Roese was deeply troubled by the rise of the "trusts," and clearly ambivalent over the meaning of wealth. Though he might not have admitted it, Roese was a nineteenth-century man, one who felt at home in the "pre-

modern moral economy" of Osceola. The specter of corporate power fright-
ened him. Thus he could reprint, in the guise of the *Sun*'s lead story, a
1905 press release from *Everybody's* magazine advertising a forthcoming article called "Frenzied Finance": "It will only be a few years, [the author
believes], when ten men will be absolute legal owners of the entire United
States and the rest of the people will be legally their slaves." When aroused,
as he had been in writing the "Deitz Edition," Roese declared flatly that
bigness meant corruption and chicanery. At another juncture, he stated that
"The corporation is a business necessity and if it lives up to the laws is no
more a menace than an individual." Corporations were a threat only when
they became "powerful enough to control the machinery of government,"
he wrote. Roese's own politics fueled his indecision. He tended to follow
the dictates of his hero, Theodore Roosevelt, and to abhor what he considered the unreasoned populism of Robert La Follette and William Jennings
Bryan. In 1904, Roese quoted approvingly a speech given by Roosevelt a
year before in Milwaukee. There was no place in society for wealthy men
who used their riches to "oppress and wrong" their neighbors, Roosevelt
had said. But neither was there a place for the "demagogic agitator" who
attacked capitalists or corporations without regard to "whether they do well
or ill." Such "ignorant rancor," Roosevelt had warned, could "overthrow
the very foundations upon which rest our national well being."[44]

Roese gained some ammunition late in 1906, with the publication in
Cosmopolitan of an article asserting that Weyerhaeuser's fortune "overshad-
ows that of John D. Rockefeller." The piece claimed the lumber baron
controlled "everything in the Mississippi River lumber district," which certainly was a gross exaggeration. Roese reprinted the article in the *Sun*. Weyerhaeuser broke his accustomed silence just long enough to sputter that the
story was the product of the "diseased Hearst mind."[45]

Historian Robert H. Wiebe has written that "attributing omnipotence to
abstractions—the Trust and Wall Street, the Political Machine and the System of Influence—had become a national habit by the end of the nineteenth
century. This was the American way of expressing the contrast between a
familiar environment and the strange world beyond." For Roese, this contrast was unambiguous and deeply disturbing. In the person of Frederick
Weyerhaeuser, he seems to have found a villain whose wicked ways would
excuse almost any transgression by the hotheaded John Deitz. Such for-
bearance would prove increasingly necessary, for the "Defender of Cameron
Dam" was veering onto a dangerously irrational course.[46]

DEFIANCE AND DISASTER

There is no evidence that the *Sun* suffered economically from its advocacy
of Deitz. The paper's advertising volume appears to have grown after 1906.
In May 1907, a dozen angry subscribers canceled the paper—not because

of the Deitz coverage, but because Roese had belittled the talents of the winners of a high school declamatory contest. "If anybody thinks that by threatening to stop his paper or withdraw his patronage he can dictate what or what shall not appear in its columns, he will do well to disengage himself from that fallacy at once," Roese thundered in reply. Despite such petty skirmishes, which appear to have greatly frustrated him, Roese expanded the *Sun* to a six-column format in June of 1907. A handsome new masthead featured the state seal and motto, "Forward," at its center. The editor thanked readers and advertisers for their "able support." To Deitz, who feared that he would sell out, Roese expressed constant reassurance. "I am still possessor of The Sun and I guess I will be for some time to come," he wrote in February of 1908. "It's paid for and that's more than most of the country prints can say." Even if he sold, he vowed, he would try to "go nearer to the seat of war"—by which, presumably, he meant buying a newspaper in Sawyer County.[47]

In the meantime, the terms of the dispute had shifted markedly. On June 10, 1907, W. E. Moses, an independent logger acting as an agent for Frederick Weyerhaeuser, called at the Deitz cabin and offered a settlement. Weyerhaeuser would pay Deitz his back wages for his work on the Brunet River dam. In return, Deitz would allow the lumbermen to remove 4 million board-feet of logs from above the Cameron dam and haul them overland to the Flambeau River. The farmer would get to keep 300,000 feet of logs lying on his own property. Moses explained that Weyerhaeuser wanted no violence. Deitz agreed to the settlement. On September 16, Moses returned to the Thornapple and paid the family $1,717 in cash—without a doubt, the largest sum of money they had ever seen.[48]

Roese learned of the accord from a newspaper article, and wrote to Deitz:

I could not sleep after reading the story, and then all night long I could see you and your family clustered around the fireplace talking over the all important matter. . . .

If God ever had anyone on his footstool that are more deserving than the family who have been holding the fort at Cameron dam, I've never heard of them. *"Praise God From Whom All Blessings Flow"* is my humble prayer to each and every member of your family. . . .

Mrs. R. and myself send to you our heartfelt blessings and hope . . . that we will be able to soon grasp the hand of the one man who has been able to hold his own with the lumber thieves of Wisconsin. . . .

From a true friend even unto death

Alfred.[49]

Other newspapers heralded the announcement as a Deitz victory. JOHN DEITZ WINS HIS GREAT FIGHT, said one headline. But for three months, the *Sun* was strangely silent on the matter. Roese visited the farm twice more in November, taking along his son, Harry. On December 26,

1907, the *Sun* published a photo of a deer-hunting group taken at the Deitz homestead. Besides Roese and his son, the hunters included W. E. Moses, the Weyerhaeuser agent, who was supervising removal of the logs from above the dam that winter.[50]

The editor apparently was waiting for a cue from Deitz; it wasn't long before he got it. In a letter published in the *Sun* on January 2, 1908, Deitz reported that Moses' hirelings "have been sneaking around our field looking for a sure shot at us." The farmer claimed he still was owed $8,000. Frederick Weyerhaeuser, he blustered, "has millions for conspiracy to murder, but hasn't money to pay his honest debts." Emboldened by his settlement, Deitz clearly was gunning for more.[51]

Thus Roese was placed in a tough position. For years, the editor had campaigned for a "square deal" for Deitz. But now that a settlement had come, who was to define whether it was fair? Deitz seemed to feast on his own notoriety. Beginning in 1908, he cast himself in the role of revolutionary martyr. Toward the end of the battle, Deitz abandoned his Republican leanings and embraced socialism. That seemed to make no difference to Roese, who stated that socialists, like everyone else, were entitled to a fair hearing.[52] In the Cameron dam dispute, Roese gave Deitz the benefit of the doubt, allowing the farmer to define what "fairness" meant. When it became clear that Deitz probably never would be satisfied, Roese still allowed him regular access to the columns of the *Sun*. The Weyerhaeuser interests were troubled by Deitz's continued noisemaking; through Roese, they tried to effect a financial settlement that would remove Deitz from the land altogether. Deitz taunted his friend, suggesting that Roese was an "easy mark" for the lumber companies and that they would co-opt him. Behind his bravado, the farmer probably was feeling increasingly isolated. Roese remained steadfast in his support: *"I gave you my word once and that is all that is necessary."*[53]

Roese editorialized on the case infrequently after that, but Deitz continued to rail in print against the "lumber trust." In 1909, the *Sun* published a Deitz poem blasting Frederick Weyerhaeuser:

> And now this man of foreign birth
> Owns this part of the earth
> That is called the land of liberty,
> Where the people are so E.Z.;
>
> He owns the law-making bodies too,
> He owns everything but me and you,
> He owns the courts as you own your dog,
> What he doesn't own he'd slaughter like a hog.[54]

Alfred Roese, meanwhile, had problems of his own. In letters to Deitz, he complained of a heavy workload, dissatisfaction with employees, and bouts of sickness. In the autumn of 1909, he spent ten days on the road soliciting subscriptions throughout Polk County. The pressures of the newspaper business—what he liked to call the "editor's burden"—apparently were wearing him down. Roese was frustrated by the dormancy of the local Business Men's Association, and on February 14, 1910, he made one last plea for "boosterism": "Boom your town. If you don't, who will? Make all the newcomers and prospective residents think it is going to be the metropolis of this part of the country, and soon it will be." Osceola, at the time, had a population of about 600.[55]

On May 5, 1910, Roese announced that he had sold the *Osceola Sun* to two business partners, Robert Truax and Fred Barrett. He attributed the sale to poor health. Disposal of the newspaper had caused him "a bitter pang," he said, adding: "The knowledge that if I was to prolong my life to anywhere near man's allotted three score years and ten I must sever my connection with the paper, did not make the task any easier." With that, Roese packed up and left Osceola, the town whose fortunes had been linked to his own for thirteen years. The family took an extended trip through the western United States, where Roese investigated business prospects and, apparently, regained his health.[56]

He returned to Wisconsin just in time to catch the climax of the Deitz drama. In September 1910, Roese bought the *Star-Observer*, in the Wisconsin village of Hudson, just east of St. Paul. Early that same month, John Deitz went to the village of Winter to vote. He became involved in an argument with the president of the local school board. A logger named Bert Horel intervened, and Deitz pulled a pistol and shot Horel in the neck, badly wounding him. Deitz retreated to his cabin. The *Sawyer County Record* called him a "crazy anarchist outlaw terror," and many people in the county apparently agreed. Public opinion, which previously had been favorable to Deitz, now turned sharply against him. Then, on October 1, the Sawyer County sheriff and two posse members shot Myra and Clarence Deitz. Myra, a young woman of about 20, was hit in the back. After two days of intense suffering under arrest at Winter, she was loaded on the baggage car of a train and shipped to an Ashland hospital. The public was indignant over such callous treatment, and its sentiment turned pro-Deitz once more.[57]

The sheriff's ambush seemed to reenergize Alfred Roese, who had always been fond of the Deitz children. He railed against the "savagery" of the attack: "Handcuffing the delicate girl, faint with the loss of blood, helpless and in an agony of pain is cruelty unparalleled in this present century. . . . [C]an any sane person, outside of Sawyer county, deny the widest sympathy with John F. Deitz and every individual member of his family from the baby up?"[58]

Deitz refused a last-minute peace offer, including a personal pledge from Governor James O. Davidson that he would receive a fair trial and free legal counsel. Likening himself to John Brown, he vowed to fight to the end. On Saturday morning, October 8, about three dozen deputies, a score of newspapermen and a horde of townspeople trooped through the frost-covered woods to the Thornapple for the final showdown. Just before 10 o'clock, the deputies opened fire. At least a thousand shots were fired in a gunbattle lasting more than five hours. John Deitz took refuge in the loft of his barn, where he held the posse at bay with his deer rifle. Deitz was wounded in the hand. A deputy, Oscar Harp, was killed. At the begging of his family, John Deitz gave himself up. John, Hattie and Leslie Deitz were taken into custody, eventually to be charged with murder. The story of the battle made the front page of the *New York Times*.[59]

Free on bail, Deitz and his family took to the vaudeville circuit, but a tragic denouement was waiting in the wings. Early in 1911, the Deitzes spoke at the Shubert Theater in Minneapolis. An orchestra played "patriotic airs" as John, Myra and Leslie took the stage. John Deitz, facing a battle for his freedom, was full of his usual bluster. "They used plenty of funds to get the whole Deitz family and they couldn't even get the dog," he bellowed, to the crowd's great approval and shouts such as "You're all right, John!" But Deitz's bravado did him no good in court. On May 13, 1911, Hattie and Leslie Deitz were acquitted, and John Deitz was convicted of murder and sentenced to life in prison. At Hudson, Alfred Roese gave the story front-page play, but the unidentified copy seems not to have come from his own pen. It referred to Deitz's "uncontrollable madness" and "sinister grin," terms that Roese never would have used in reference to his friend. Deitz served ten years in prison before being pardoned amid a wave of public sympathy in 1921; he died in 1924. He was 63. The *Milwaukee Journal* eulogized him in heroic terms: "Beside Cameron dam, on the Thornapple river, Sawyer county, he staked it all."[60]

Roese left Hudson in 1912. He had an itinerant and apparently only marginally successful career, editing small newspapers in Minnesota and Wisconsin until 1919. He was working as a representative for the *Milwaukee Journal* and the *Duluth Herald* when he died in 1920. He was 58 years old.[61]

THE STORY AND THE FABLE

Americans reacted to the rise of corporate power in strikingly different ways during the Progressive era. In *The Search for Order*, Robert Wiebe documents the ascent of an "aggressive, optimistic, new middle class" in the large cities, people who possessed deep faith that they could rationalize American society by means of "efficiency" and sound management. Alfred Roese was 38 years old when the century turned; to an extent he was a prisoner of his rural upbringing and his modest education. Unlike the new professional class, which sought to remake the nation, Roese clung tenaciously to the premodern values that had served him well in Osceola. His ethos was backward-looking, but it also was admirable for its integrity and its commitment to simple justice. Wiebe, looking beyond his own concern with the rise of the professional middle class, has suggested that Progressivism might best be viewed in terms of broader responses to modernization. Such a framework is applicable to Alfred Roese, for the Osceola editor—despite all his talk of local development—was in many respects an antimodernist.[62]

It is noteworthy that Roese did not view the Deitz case in terms of forest conservation, which in the early 1900s was the province mostly of college-educated professionals. Roese, like most other people in northern Wisconsin, assumed that the cut-over lands would be turned into farms. Indeed, he believed that the stench of wrongdoing in Sawyer County had retarded agricultural development. His chief quarrel with the lumber companies was not that they cut down trees, but that they corrupted politics and treated people badly.[63]

If he saw it, Roese must have scoffed at the epilogue to the Deitz case written by the *New York Times*. A week after the shoot-out of 1910, the *Times* devoted the front page of its Sunday magazine section to the battle at Cameron dam. The story seemed to view the case as a backwoods anomaly, an object lesson in the perils of socialism and the "blood lust among primitive men." The dispute, the *Times* said, was "symbolized by the solitary figure of Deitz, brooding over an idea in the loneliness of his forest home."[64]

In the pages of The *Osceola Sun*, the Cameron dam affair was not an anomaly but a vital test case on the future of the United States. Roese was an unusually skillful small-town journalist. By combining "booster" rhetoric with a vivid sense of drama, he sought to invest the story with a sense of urgency that all Osceolans could feel. The community's response to his appeals for aid suggests that, to a great extent, he succeeded. As portrayed by Roese, John Deitz was not a "solitary figure" at all, but a vital symbol for small-town citizens, a man whose struggle epitomized their own. The structure of power in the northern woods—not to mention Deitz's own penchant for self-destruction—tested the "square deal" ethos severely, and perhaps even crushed it. But Roese's crusade was a worthy one, and a prime example of how an editor could cast an out-of-town story as a local fable with an enduring moral.

NOTES

1. *Osceola Sun*, October 25, 1906; C. M. Foote and E. C. Hood, *Plat Book of Polk County, Wisconsin* (Minneapolis, 1887); *Facts About Selected Hardwood Farming Lands in Polk Co., Wisconsin* (Eau Claire, 1902), pamphlet collection, State Historical Society of Wisconsin, Madison. The author would like to acknowledge the encouragement and assistance of Professor James L. Baughman of the University of Wisconsin-Madison and Paul H. Hass of the State Historical Society of Wisconsin.

2. *Osceola Sun*, October 25, 1906; *Wisconsin Atlas & Gazetteer* (Freeport, Maine: DeLorme Mapping Co., 1992), 72, 84–85. Newspaper stories variously spell the name "Deitz" and "Dietz." The farmer signed his name "Deitz," so I have used that spelling throughout.

3. *Osceola Sun*, October 25, 1906.

4. Ibid.; Hass, "The Suppression of John F. Deitz: An Episode of the Progressive Era in Wisconsin," *Wisconsin Magazine of History* 57 (1974): 255–309.

5. The *Osceola Sun*, October 25, 1906.

6. E. J. Hobsbawm, *Primitive Rebels: Studies in Archaic Forms of Social Movement in the 19th and 20th Centuries*, 3rd ed. (Manchester, England: Manchester University Press, 1974), 3.

7. Sally Foreman Griffith, *Home Town News: William Allen White and the Emporia Gazette* (1989; Baltimore: Johns Hopkins University Press, 1991), 3–5.

8. *Osceola Sun*, February 14, 1907.

9. Griffith, *Home Town News*, 113–114, 142–143.

10. Biographical sketch in Alfred E. Roese papers, State Historical Society of Wisconsin, Area Research Center, Eau Claire (hereinafter referred to as Roese papers); *Weekly Press* (Maiden Rock, Wis.), September 16, 1897.

11. James Taylor Dunn, *The St. Croix: Midwest Border River* (New York: Holt, Rinehart and Winston, 1965), 58, 204; *Osceola Sun*, March 8, 1956; *Facts About Selected Hardwood Farming Lands*, 5.

12. Dunn, *St. Croix*, 113; *Osceola Sun*, April 27, 1898, March 15, 1956. A board-foot is a measure of wood 1 foot square by 1 inch thick.

13. *Osceola Sun*, October 6, 13, 1897; September 24, 1908.

14. *Osceola Sun*, October 13, November 3, December 1, 1897. The *Sun* boasted a circulation of about 1,300 during its early years, a figure that rose to more than 2,000 by the time Roese sold the paper, in 1910. These figures were unaudited, of course.

15. *Osceola Sun*, December 22, 1897.

16. *Osceola Sun*, March 30, 1898.

17. Dunn, *St. Croix*, 108.

18. *Osceola Sun*, January 25, 1900.

19. *Osceola Sun*, February 15, 22, 1900.

20. *Plat Book of Polk County, Wisconsin*; *Osceola Sun*, November 10, 1897. Parts of northern and eastern Polk County showed heavy ownership by timber interests. These lands were largely in hardwoods. Unlike pine, hardwood usually could not be floated to market; it was cut during the winter and hauled to the railroad on enormous sleds. Roese appeared to regard the heavily wooded townships of Polk County as hard-luck cousins to the more prosperous farming areas.

21. *Osceola Sun*, November 30, 1905; July 12, December 20, 1906.

22. Thomas Bender, *Community and Social Change in America* (1978; Baltimore: Johns Hopkins University Press, 1982), 110–113.

23. *Osceola Sun*, November 30, 1905.

24. Griffith, *Home Town News*, 40.

25. As an example of Roese's business ethos, consider his endorsement of the druggist C. W. Staples for a seat in the Wisconsin Assembly in 1906. Staples was a socialist, but Roese saw fit to transcend party loyalty and endorse his friend who was "temperate in all things." Staples put "character above everything," "will sacrifice

private interests to public good," and "does not have one brand of honesty for business purposes and another for private life," Roese wrote. *Osceola Sun*, October 18, 1906.

26. *Osceola Sun*, September 28, 1905.

27. *Osceola Sun*, October 12, 1905.

28. *Osceola Sun*, October 19, 1905. The last log went through the St. Croix boom on June 12, 1914. Dunn, *St. Croix*, 113.

29. Hass, "The Suppression of John F. Deitz," 268–269.

30. Ibid., 268, 270.

31. Ibid., 270–277.

32. *Osceola Sun*, April 13, 1905.

33. *Osceola Sun*, August 2, 30, 1906.

34. *Osceola Sun*, September 20, October 25, 1906.

35. *Osceola Sun*, October 25, 1906.

36. Ibid.

37. Ibid.

38. *Osceola Sun*, December 6, 1906; Alfred E. Roese to Deitz family, December 25, 1906, Roese papers (emphasis in original). Roese, aware that the Deitz family was desperate for kind words, often quoted other people's letters in his correspondence. He also sent press clippings, which the Deitz family assembled in a scrapbook. Broughton, as editor of the *Sheboygan Press*, would become one of Wisconsin's most prominent journalists.

39. *Osceola Sun*, January 17, 31, 1907.

40. *Osceola Sun*, February 14, 1907.

41. *Osceola Sun*, February 21, 1907.

42. *Osceola Sun*, March 14, 1907; Roese to Deitz family, January 27, 1907, Roese papers.

43. Ralph W. Hidy, Frank Ernest Hill, and Allan Nevins, *Timber and Men: The Weyerhaeuser Story* (New York: Macmillan, 1963), 290, 297.

44. *Osceola Sun*, January 26, 1905; February 6, 1908; June 30, 1904. At least once a month, Roese had something nasty to say about John D. Rockefeller. One front-page article noted that the oil titan was not as rich as commonly supposed; in fact, he was making just $59,523 a day. "By Exercising Frugality He Manages to Keep the Wolf From the Door," Roese declared in a headline. *Osceola Sun*, February 28, 1907.

45. Weyerhaeuser: Richer than John D. Rockefeller," *Cosmopolitan Magazine* 42 (holiday edition, 1906–1907): 252–259; *Osceola Sun*, February 7, 1907; Hidy, Hill, and Nevins, *Timber and Men*, 302.

46. Robert H. Wiebe, *The Search for Order, 1877–1920* (New York: Hill and Wang, 1967), 164.

47. *Osceola Sun*, May 2, June 6, 1907; Roese to Deitz, February 18, 27, 1908, Roese papers.

48. Hass, "The Suppression of John F. Deitz," 290.

49. Roese to Deitz, September 19, 1907, Roese papers (emphasis in original).

50. "The Suppression of John F. Deitz," 290; Roese to Deitz, October 10, November 21, 1907, Roese papers; *Osceola Sun*, December 26, 1907. According to historian Paul H. Hass, Moses regarded Deitz as "a misguided but honest and hospitable man, almost insanely suspicious and extremely violent in speech." In 1909,

Moses circulated a petition in Sawyer County asking that criminal charges against Deitz be dropped.

51. *Osceola Sun*, January 2, 1908.

52. For example, in 1910 Roese stated that the new socialist government of Milwaukee should be given a chance, and he doubted fears that businesses would flee the city. Hass, "The Suppression of John F. Deitz," 271–272, 292; *Osceola Sun*, April 14, 1910.

53. Hass, "The Suppression of John F. Deitz," 290–292; Roese to Deitz, January 17, February 6, March 6, 1908, Roese papers (emphasis in original).

54. *Osceola Sun*, July 29, 1909. Deitz was a prolific back-woods poet. Some of his early verse, lampooning political conditions in Sawyer County, is quite clever. It is probably indicative of Deitz's state of mind that, in later years, his wit gave way to rambling doggerel.

55. Roese to Deitz, December 10, 14, 1908; January 29, October 23, 1909, Roese papers; *Osceola Sun*, February 24, 1910. The Roese-Deitz correspondence that has been preserved stops at the end of 1909. The two men apparently did not see each other after 1908.

56. *Osceola Sun*, May 5, 1910; *Hudson Star-Observer*, September 15, 1910. The *Sun* continued to print letters from Deitz after the change of ownership. It printed news stories on the case, too, though the new editors didn't show the zeal for the battle that Roese had. Editorially, they shared the rather widespread suspicion that Deitz was a crackpot.

57. Hass, "The Suppression of John F. Deitz," 292–294; *Hudson Star-Observer*, October 6, 1910. Clarence Deitz was shot in the hand. Myra recovered from her back wound. She went on to marry, then divorce, a Chicago film director who made a movie about the Deitz affair.

58. *Hudson Star-Observer*, October 6, 1910.

59. Hass, "The Suppression of John F. Deitz," 296–298; *Hudson Star-Observer*, October 13, 1910; *New York Times*, October 9, 1910.

60. Undated, unidentified clipping (Minneapolis, February, 1911) in scrapbook of John F. Deitz papers, State Historical Society of Wisconsin, Madison; Hass, "The Suppression of John F. Deitz," 300–302, 307; *Hudson Star-Observer*, May 18, 1911; *Milwaukee Journal*, May 9, 1924.

61. Biographical sketch of Alfred E. Roese, in Roese papers; *Osceola Sun*, May 27, 1920.

62. Wiebe, *Search for Order*, 166; David M. Kennedy, "Overview: The Progressive Era," *The Historian* 37 (1975), 453–468.

63. *Osceola Sun*, October 25, 1906.

64. *New York Times*, October 16, 1910.

7

Did the Muckrakers Muck Up Progress?

Thomas Leonard

The mass circulation journalism of the magazines of the turn of the century was not unlike the television "magazines" of today, such as "60 Minutes" or "20/20" or "Dateline." It reached huge audiences with a variety of content that ranged from soppy fiction and features to hard-hitting political exposé. Even some of the fiction, appearing in serial fashion, was highly political—and constituted a frontal assault on the political establishment. Of course, this is what made much of the exposé so attractive; it had shock value for readers who were often not very politically sophisticated. But the exposés, as Thomas Leonard finds, both attracted and repelled the audience. While the muckrakers' goal seems to have been to arouse the public with a healthy dose of facts and force them to badger their elected representatives with demands for change, an odd and unexpected result was created. The public instead began to pull back from political life, fearing perhaps that the political system was so corrupted that civic engagement had no purpose. And so, the muck-rakers may have inadvertently created the first generation of citizens who tuned in to the media but then dropped out because of the tunes they heard. Leonard's chapter first appeared as a chapter in his book, *The Power of the Press: The Birth of American Political Reporting*, which was published in 1986. It is reprinted with the permission of Oxford University Press.

The political reporting of the Progressive Era has often been viewed as a grand civics lesson. Muckraking, the investigative journalism in the success-ful magazines of the day, has usually been understood as a way of waking up citizens to their political responsibilities. There is much evidence to support this view. From the beginning of the century to World War I, the magazines with progressive themes sounded a call to political action in both the facts and the fiction they published. Readers were asked to raise their voices against illegitimate power. Over and over again, the case was made to extend the citizen's power through the direct primary, initiative, and recall so that the simple act of marking a ballot could choose a candidate, depose an official, or make law directly. Part of the credit for women's suffrage belongs to this literature of reform. More than this, progressive journalism tapped the national genius for voluntary organization. In leagues, clubs, churches, and social settlements, reformers built a fellowship around political goals and the periodicals of the movement often helped to bring citizens together in these ways. Lincoln Steffens alone convened the citizens of several New England communities to lead them through a civics lesson.

The impact of all this on political parties was greater than any other reform movement of the twentieth century. Theodore Roosevelt's Bull Moose campaign of 1912 was the most successful third party challenge of modern times. In the decade before 1912, both Republicans and Democrats sought the banner of progressivism, and the leading figures were devoted to the magazines of reform. A number of progressive senators had familiar bylines in the muckraking magazines. Senator Robert M. La Follette of Wisconsin started his own weekly. It survived into the 2000s as the *Progressive*. Even before the Wilson administration, reform journalists frequently took government jobs. Ray Stannard Baker, George Creel, and Brand Whitlock, for example, were as immersed in the details of state politics as officeholders. There were celebrated cases of muckraking in which public officials simply told what they had learned at work. Christopher Powell Connolly, for example, had been a district attorney in Montana before exposing the state for the readers of *Collier's*.[1]

There is a paradox to the civics lesson provided by progressive journalism: overall political participation declined in America as this reporting gained strength. For all the new constituencies we may credit to Progressives, for all their skill in mobilizing protest, it remains true that this age of reform was an age of voter apathy.[2]

In the Progressive Era the percentage of the electorate that voted was sharply down from the extraordinary high turnouts in the decades when citizens could expect little in the way of inspired investigation of political ills on a national stage. In 1912, the population was a fifth greater than during William Jennings Bryan's futile campaigns for the presidency, but Wilson gained the White House with fewer votes than Bryan had attracted. In that year of passion, the total vote for President Taft, ex-President Roosevelt, and Wilson was lower than Taft and Bryan combined drew in 1908. At the national level there was a steady fall-off in voting by those eligible in the progressive years. Most of the large industrial states lost 15 to 20 percent of their voters in presidential campaigns between the election of McKinley and Wilson. At the local level this was not always so, but many urban and state reformers won during periods of decreased voting participation. At a time of easier transportation as well as communication, this drop-off in interest at election time is a puzzle.

It is not possible to explain the slide in voting by demographic changes, the fracture of parties, or new voting rules. The immigrants of the 1870s and 1880s marched to the polls, and it is hard to find anything in the newcomers of the turn of the century that should have held them back. Besides, in sections of rural America where new immigrants were rare, the same decline occurred as in the major cities. The decline in national vote totals is not simply a result of the practical disfranchisement of so many blacks and poor whites in the South at the end of the nineteenth century. The graph of electoral participation makes a deep valley in the Progressive Era for the North and East as surely as in the South. Twenty-six of the thirty-four non-southern states participating in both the 1896 and the 1916 elections showed a decline in participation. Women, of course, did not skew the figures in national elections until 1920.

Progressives did crack party loyalties, but that by itself need not have discouraged participation. In 1896, Bryan repudiated the traditional economic policy of fellow Democrats, dismissed the party establishment, and drove "gold Democrats" away. His appeal for the free coinage of silver also split the GOP. Yet for all this damage to party loyalties, the Democrats and Republicans managed to attract more voters than in the election of 1892. Insurgency by itself is no explanation for voter apathy. Nor is the existence of party machines the heart of the matter. Today, states with abundant patronage and efficient party organizations do *not* have greater participation in elections than the "reform" states.[3] When Progressives attacked political machines they were not bringing down a way of conducting elections that was inherently better at turning out voters. Progressive support for the secret ballot and tighter registration laws undoubtedly discouraged some voters, but these reforms do not account for what happened. The downturn in voting preceded the secret ballot in many states. Where rural voters did not have to register, their participation dropped along with the urban voters faced with controls.

The decline in voting was not an isolated sign of decreased participation. That venerable institution, the monster campaign rally, also dwindled. As the presidential candidates divided on progressive issues, their organizations were not able to match the "Sound Money" parades of 1896 (in Chicago, the procession took five hours to pass the reviewing stand). The new century brought no spectacles of commitment to compare with those extraordinary gatherings at the front porches of Republican candidates. In 1888, Benjamin Harrison drew nearly 200,000 well wishers to his home in Indiana, a figure approaching 80 percent of the Republican voters in the state. The crowds outside William McKinley's home in Canton, Ohio, during the campaign of 1896 equaled more than 10 percent of the Republican vote nationwide in November.[4] Judged from the candidates' front porches, as well as at the polls, something fundamental was happening within this political culture to reduce interest in elections.

Recent scholarship has demonstrated that the origins of nonvoting lie in strategies of the national party organizations in the 1880s and 1890s. For a number of reasons (not all of them pragmatic) the old rituals fell out of favor in high party committees. Distaste for "ignorant" voters and the spectacles that moved them to the polls led both parties to try to raise the intellectual level of campaigns. Some of the most thoughtful journalists of the Gilded Age, such as Edwin L. Godkin of the *Nation*, favored this course and hoped it would leave the unqualified voter behind. Journals that deplored mass democracy to a small group of readers influenced American politics because they reached a party elite ready to listen. Metropolitan dailies with more talk of their "independence" and less space available for national party materials also signaled the end of the full mobilization of the voter that had been possible before 1900. The daily paper now had too many new interests and sources of support to be effective missionaries for their party.[5]

The new priorities for party and newspaper do not by themselves explain why voting lost its appeal. Party professionals often do not get what they want and must backtrack. There must have been a powerful cultural sanction for their efforts to dispense with the ritual that had carried so many Americans to the polls. The independent dailies were evidently not crucial to the change, for turnout also fell in small towns where dependable party newspapers remained to urge on voters.

The fashion of muckraking in popular literature of the Progressive Era does much to explain why the habit of voting declined. It must be admitted that the best-known generalizations about muckraking shed little light on this change. Reporting bad news about American institutions and branding some politicians scoundrels was not a new activity of the press. It would appear that if press attacks on the competence of government could drive voters from the polls, that would have happened early in the course of American democracy. To show that muckraking eroded trust in government is not the same thing as showing why the habit of voting weakened. There is some evidence that today the cynical and the disaffected vote at about the same rate as citizens with confidence in their government. Broad statements about the "negative" tone of the muckrakers are little help in explaining the drop in political participation.[6]

To understand the impact of the muckraking texts, one must read them with the common sense of nineteenth-century politics clearly in mind. For it was the discrediting of some basic assumptions about how democracy worked that made muckraking both shocking (as the authors intended) and (as they did not wish) a message to pull back from political life.

Before the Progressive Era, Americans voted for two fundamental reasons: The issues touched their deepest concerns as members of an ethnic or religious group, and the parties drilled citizens to act on their feelings. The best local studies we have suggest that class interest and economic factors do little to explain the late nineteenth-century electorate. Religious orientation and ethnic loyalties were the basis of politics. They set the tone and defined the issues for orderly party conflict. Mobilizing these powerful loyalties was the business of politicians.

The imagery of war does not distort the democratic process of the nineteenth century. The two parties *looked* like armies. In election campaigns they marched in review before their leaders, wearing uniforms, chanting slogans, carrying flags, stepping to brass bands. The attitude toward the small number of citizens not in the ranks—the swing voters—was that of a regular army toward mercenaries: It was necessary to buy their services, and questions of honor were beside the point. Patronage (the "spoils") was the chief objective of each party. The partisan dailies of the nineteenth century were heavy with speeches—there was an abundance of information about the issues of the day—but editors saw to it that citizens could make simple choices. Blind loyalty was more often a virtue than a vice in these publications, and at election time the drumming for loyalty grew louder as many new party newspapers were created. National magazines did not reach a large public with a more complex view.[7]

Progressivism, and especially its journalism, undermined the ritual of political participation. The reformers lacked the enthusiasm of party regulars for indoctrination, social pressure, and, if need be, the payoff. Progressives asked the public to overturn old assumptions and to view issues in new ways. Muckraking magazines attacked the notion that a citizen's vote should be an act of loyalty set by tradition and sprung by election spectacle. Political participation was redefined as a thoughtful search for that true principle obscured by the "surface play" of the parties. Implicit here was a heresy to both Republicans and Democrats of an earlier generation—that detachment was the right course if there was no clear choice or the issues seemed too complex. In 1903, the *Independent* called on reformers to recognize that "the more conscientious and the more intelligent the voter is the more likely will he be at certain times to decide that duty and common sense admonish him to play golf or go fishing on election day."[8]

The old politics had anticipated the difficulties of the new. In 1892, Democrats and Republicans emphasized educational measures over the traditional ritual. The result was the lowest rate of voter turnout in twenty years. It appears that both parties pursued citizens with open minds so well that they left some of their loyalists confused and distracted. The drill of the

faithful was sloppy. Progressive journalism was a major disruptive shift toward political education, confusing the voter's cues and teaching him to
hesitate.[9]

Party loyalty itself was a virtue of the old politics that progressive journalism helped turn into a vice. This was the lament of that Tammany stal-
wart, George Washington Plunkitt, in his "very plain talks" on American
government. When a leader "hustles around and gets all the jobs possible
for his constituents," Plunkitt thought that a "solemn contract" was made
and voters must return him to office "just as they're bound to uphold the
Constitution of the United States." Plunkitt spoke out in the midst of progressive attacks on this self-evident moral truth. There had always been the
"crime" of ingratitude in Tammany, he admitted, but reformers were worse,
for they added ridicule to moral turpitude. Plunkitt cited *The Shame of the
Cities* as a sign of this confusion about the proper basis of politics and he
probably had in mind cartoons of the type that *McClure's Magazine* featured: party voters with rings in their noses, pulled by the reins of party
leaders. In the eye of leaders like Plunkitt, reporting by Progressives turned
the moral order upside down.[10]

Progressives exposed the forced system of participation. In some of the
most prominent muckraking texts, the manipulation of voters made electoral
politics a chamber of horrors. *Cosmopolitan* ran a four-part series by Charles
E. Russell, "At the Throat of the Republic," to demonstrate "that nine of
every ten elections are decided solely by the methods of the vote broker and
the ballot box stuffer." When Ben Lindsey and Harvey J. O'Higgins made
patronage and electioneering part of *The Beast* (1910), they used a term no
stronger than was common in the new reporting about city elections in that
decade.[11]

It is less well-known that muckrakers delivered the same shocking news
about the voting of rural America. This theme was so striking to reporters
and editors that it was used many times. Early in his series on the states,
Lincoln Steffens noted that voters in Rhode Island's villages had sold out.
Ray Stannard Baker found that the swing votes of Springfield, Ohio were
for sale in every election. David Graham Phillips began *The Plum Tree* with
Hoosiers at the polls lined up like addicts, exchanging their vote for the
favor of the local party official. Brand Whitlock created an antipastoral scene
in rural Illinois with *The Thirteenth District* (1902). Every autumn, Whitlock
wrote, campaigns drew the small-town lawyers and businessmen to a terrible
harvest: "Amid all this beauty and mystery, men were fighting one another,
bribing, deceiving and coercing one another, in order that the offices of the
republic might be taken from one set of men and turned over to another
set of men." Adams County, Ohio, where both parties ran buggies down
country lanes delivering payoffs to farmers for their vote, was exposed several
times. Whitlock concluded that "if the muckrakers were to report to their
magazines what they know on this subject, I am sure they would reveal

conditions that are worse than those urban States they have so minutely examined."[12]

For all this criticism, the face-to-face community of the small town attracted and bedeviled progressive journalists. Reform required coalitions of urban voters, citizens united in politics by recognition of their common interests, not from trust developed in living together. Muckraking was ambivalent about whether democracy could survive in America's cities of enlightened strangers.

Ray Stannard Baker argued both sides of the question. He put his name on major investigations of industrial America and posed issues that required close study and mobilization of voters if solutions were to be found. Baker's faith in an informed public spanned the Progressive Era. At the same time, he published the "Adventures in Contentment" series under the name David Grayson. These were idylls in the countryside of a freethinker. The Grayson stories began in that bright new hope of progressive journalism, the *American* magazine. Sometimes the stories appeared in the same issues as Baker's investigative pieces. He did all he could to keep authorship of the Grayson stories a secret. There was no reason for the reader to think the same man was responsible for the fiction as well as the facts. One of the earliest stories contrasted politics in the city and in the country. Grayson confessed that, in the city, he and others dodged political responsibilities and were hopelessly confused. Grayson said this was perfectly natural. In the country there was "elbow knowledge" of public issues gathered in the plain talk of one neighbor to another. In the city, Grayson found only newspapers and books on politics offering "sham comfort" and "mock assurance." "It was good to escape that place of hurrying strangers," Grayson said, to gain neighbors who could help make sense of politics. The Grayson stories acknowledged that country folk needed to educate themselves, but there was more than a hint that citizens who did not keep a cornfield or one-room school within sight could not be trusted to govern. Written by a muckraker, edited by reformers, and loved by readers drawn to progressivism—the Grayson stories imply that the literature of exposure was beside the point. In the cities there would be apathy and confusion for in the absence of community, reporting did not matter.[13]

America's cities were "a wilderness of careless strangers," William Allen White said. With his home in Emporia, Kansas, and his eye on reform across the country, White addressed an urban nation that (by his own analysis) could not respond adequately because the "instincts of humanity" decayed as citizens grew up outside a country town. White helped edit the *American* magazine and fought for insurgents in the Republican Party, finally carrying the banner for Roosevelt in the Bull Moose campaign of 1912. But all of this work to draw readers to national reform was undermined by White's writing that was designed to make urban citizens feel misplaced and damaged by the rhythms of their daily life. Like Baker, White sometimes made political participation forbidden fruit. The citizen from the big city could not taste it.[14]

The eclipse of rural communities worried a great variety of social critics and cast a shadow over the ideal of political participation in reform literature. The "small-town fetish" (as one scholar has called it) helped to channel progressivism to the urban neighborhood. This reform movement placed so much emphasis on community organizations, particularly social settlements, because nostalgia for the country towns was widely shared and cut across many other differences. Several progressives dreamed that newspapers could aid them in re-creating an intimate community in the city by supplementing personal contact, relaying conversation, and helping citizens to act as they were if members of a town meeting. The reality was that much reporting in reform journals added to the traditional fears about democracy in cities. Voting studies show that this cognitive dissonance hurt the Democratic Party. Progressivism got into the same trouble. Anti-urban appeals had been effective in nineteenth-century politics and remained potent in the new century. But they were drawbacks in a reform movement attempting to mobilize America's growing cities. Muckraking opened up the perplexing variety of urban scandals to the whole nation and gave a vivid, documented picture of how far the metropolis departed from fond memories (and folklore) of democracy in face-to-face communities.[15]

Progressives wished to populate both rural and urban America with different citizens than the ones who happened to form the electorate at the turn of the century. Reform journalism was directed at Americans whose ethnic or religious ties left them free to be disinterested voters. There was to be a "new citizenship" in which all ethnic or religious loyalties touching on politics were suspect. It was wrong, muckrakers said, to use politics to protect parochial interests, either by enforcing the moral rules of one group on another or by using politics for tribal advantage. Much ink has been shed arguing about whether this conception of politics was the narrow vision of a middle-class, Anglo-Saxon, Protestant group. It is certainly true that some progressive measures, like prohibition, were in part the revenge of some ethnic groups on others. It is not necessary to face the difficult questions about the exact tensions within this broad reform movement. Whether there was a cosmopolitan ideal or a coercive "Americanization" plan at the heart of progressivism (and both had a role), the attitude toward ethnic or religious loyalties was usually the same: they must give way to make a good citizen.[16]

The muckrakers wrote to refute the notion that some ethnic groups were at fault for the troubles of American government and also to show that parochial appeals would do no good. Thus Lincoln Steffens set out to explode the theory of scapegoats in the cities. He examined old immigrants (St. Louis), new immigrants (Pittsburgh), and Yankees (Philadelphia) to show that political systems were not determined by ethnicity. All these cities were corrupt. Steffens taught that no one group in society had inbred talent for governing. Confidence in any ethnic community was misplaced. Similarly, Upton Sinclair's *The Jungle* (1906) paid close attention to Lithuanian and Polish families in Chicago to show that they had no special standing as victims in Packingtown. A socialism embracing and transcending all parochial loyalties was the lesson of Sinclair's investigation.

Muckraking was troubled by the loyalties that kept urban Americans apart and ambivalent about the city itself. But this was where this journalism brought the reader. Muckraking usually meant reporting on the work place and tenements, on urban vices and concentrations of power best revealed in cities. Washington itself became the focus for most of these concerns in the reform magazines.

In this respect, the journalism of the Progressive Era followed the reform-minded presidents. The office became a "bully pulpit," using Theodore Roosevelt's phrase. Presidential press conferences and regular opportunities to interview the chief executive replaced congressional debates as the most important news from Washington. The muckrakers were only a part of this shift of attention, but their national magazines had the greatest reach.[17]

A STARTLING LOOK AT THE GOVERNORS

In the first years of the twentieth century David Graham Phillips took political reporting where few journalists had dared to go. His steps were the ones reporters dreamed of; his conclusions were bolder than successful journalists had been willing to make. Phillips was a celebrity and a scoffer. The gray routine of a reporter's life was not for him, nor was pulling punches. Phillips snarled at the political process. He brought to the surface an antagonism toward government that was at the center of muckraking.

Phillips led a double life: the man of letters standing free of the demands of the newsroom and the reporter in harness who would chase any story. Phillips is easy to spot in the photographs of the press corps of this era, the peacock amidst the dark, wrinkled suits. His first editor in Cincinnati was so appalled by his fashionable tailoring that he would not speak to the young man for several days. In New York, conversations started over his white flannels and the large chrysanthemum he chose each morning for his lapel. Editors could not find an assignment too trivial, humiliating, or dirty to discourage him. He scored on the stories other reporters found hopeless. Colleagues credited Phillips with finding a missing child and then wringing the last tear from the discovery. He got a full account of a British naval disaster into the *New York World* before the Admiralty knew the details.

Phillips's advancement followed the daydreams of a generation of colleagues in the newsroom. Reporters were paid the wages of clerks and often lived as if they were paid less. Phillips commanded the unprecedented sums that Pulitzer and Hearst bid for star talent in New York. Many reporters worked themselves sick as they supplemented writing for a newspaper with stories for other publishers. Phillips could take or leave newspaper work as he chose, and for a time he happily covered a beat during the day and wrote fiction through the night. He published seventeen novels, seven short stories, and one play before his death at age 43. Phillips was assassinated in Gramercy Park in 1911 by a deranged reader of his novels. Somehow this self-sufficient, nocturnal dandy thrust himself into the middle of the great public questions of the Progressive Era. It was Phillips's series on government for a Hearst magazine in 1906 that provoked President Theodore Roosevelt to brand it "muckraking" and to warn the American people where such reporting was taking them.[18]

Any reader who even skims the nine installments of "The Treason of the Senate" soon notices two things: the pictures that tell Phillips's story and the reporter's insistence, over and over again, that the words of senators mean nothing. These may be the most important things about this reporting, for they upset the conventional way of telling political stories.

William Randolph Hearst had purchased *Cosmopolitan* in 1905, and the Senate exposé was his first opportunity in a magazine to show his characteristic extravagance. Phillips was allowed to name his price. Talented researchers were hired. The series was relentlessly advertised. There was full-color artwork on the first covers, and important cartoonists produced frontispieces. The most striking feature was the photographs Hearst obtained. The first installment of March 1906 began with New York's junior senator, Chauncey Depew, tilting his head back and laughing in the reader's face. This shot was followed by photos of the senator's three imposing residences and his drawing room in Washington. Depew was shown at play in his automobile and at work at the Republican convention. Three more senators were caught on the street with snap shots in the first six installments, and the story was frequently interrupted by architectural specimens. The fine modern edition of "The Treason of the Senate" reproduces only the cartoons from this run of illustration, and this is unfortunate. The photos said something about politics as startling as Phillips's words.

Cosmopolitan was the first magazine to find a place for photographs in the tested format of the exposé. Juxtaposing public servants with their lavish possessions had been a staple of illustrated journalism since the rise of *Harper's Weekly* a half century earlier. Without making an argument, without attempting to prove graft, the sumptuous setting of men in power was a visual indictment. Hearst used the new half-tone process to fit photographs into this scheme, and editors made sure readers got the point. The photo of Senator Depew in his auto had been published a year earlier by *Leslie's Weekly* captioned "A Statesman-Automobilist-Senator Depew, of New York, en route to the Capitol at Washington in his Horseless Carriage." The wide view of the avenue did make it seem the senator was going to work. *Cosmopolitan* cropped the photo to take the senator off the road and chose a caption to make it seem that he was idly sitting in his plaything—"one of the Senator's Favorite Recreations." Hearst's editors added the off-guard shot to this syntax of derision. Officeholders no longer controlled their public face. They could be "snapped," feet in the air or frozen to the sidewalk; they usually appeared to be fleeing the camera or caught at playing a children's game of statue.[19]

The governed were not used to seeing the governors in this way outside a cartoon. *Cosmopolitan* had not published an unposed photo of an American politician before "The Treason of the Senate." The magazine had gone beyond the studio portrait before Hearst took control, showing reformers bent over a desk or gripping a telephone. Also, like the Hearst newspapers, candid shots of the rich at play were common, but *Cosmopolitan* had never printed a photograph designed to fit a political exposé. *McClure's* had been just as conservative with pictures. The boodlers and bosses of Lincoln Steffens's series appeared as they chose to appear before the camera. "Snap shots" in political stories were not unprecedented in 1906, but they had not stung. Wounding photographs linked to an attack with words formed a new arsenal for the press. A few months after the Phillips series, for example, a photograph of the political establishment in California appeared in most of the progressive publications in that state as well as in national muckraking magazines. The camera had caught a Republican celebrating his nomination for the governorship in the company of the biggest moneymen in the state. The candidate's fingers gripped the shoulder of Boss Abraham Ruef of San Francisco. The photograph acquired a name, "The Shame of California." Veteran reformers, especially those working for Hearst, made much bolder use of photographs towards the end of the first decade of the century. Muckraking had hit upon a new way to picture men in power, anticipating candid shots and even the "ambush" techniques of television.[20]

"The Treason of the Senate" overturned conventional reporting because it changed what the reader was to hear as well as see. Phillips had contempt for the debates of Congress, and he wanted the public to stop listening. He rarely quoted a senator and gave only the haziest account of what their positions were on the issues. Repeatedly, he dismissed public debate as "sham battles" designed only to fool naive citizens. "Orators of the treason" pretended to disagree in order to disguise the conspiracies arranged in the committee rooms. To listen to these men was to be caught up in this deception, Phillips explained, for "all the speeches of these secret traitors to country and people . . . abounded in virtue, piety, and patriotism." An honest minority felt bound by senatorial courtesy and muffled criticism so the hyprocisy of the majority was never exposed. Phillips spoke of "the dust of the senatorial debates" and described an atmosphere so close and fetid that a healthy citizen must keep away. He marveled that the senators who sat through the debates did not break into laughter.[21]

"The Treason of the Senate" began by pointing out the "stupidity" of the electorate and frequently offered a sneer at the gullible public. Taunts of the average citizen crept into muckraking after the first discoveries about government. The general public was scorned in *The Jungle* by Upton Sinclair, an exposé that was frightening Americans at the time Phillips's series appeared. After 1906, Americans were not allowed to forget how little they knew or to escape blame for their ignorance. The deceptions worked! This was the chorus of the investigative magazines, with Phillips and Sinclair the loudest voices. Sinclair took his story through several election campaigns, showing how bread and circuses produced any outcome the capitalists wanted. Voters were handled as efficiently as cattle in Packingtown. Phillips drew attention to the occult nature of politics, "the mysteries of the Senate—all its crafty, treacherous ways of smothering, of emasculating, of perverting legislation." A reader might reasonably conclude that the upper house consisted of nothing but speeches that were bunk. Behind the "black art of politics" stood "the Interests"—a term Phillips coined to describe the American plutocracy. He predicted that the lower and middle classes would be crushed by this exercise of power in Washington. The humble citizen had only himself to blame. Phillips baited his readers, asking if the Senate's contempt was not justified.[22]

Phillips had built his reputation in fiction by mocking the political process, so his reports on the Senate could not have surprised his large number of faithful readers. The Americans in these novels, like Jurgis in Sinclair's *The Jungle*, lived through an anticivics lesson. Machines decided elections. Bosses controlled their own party and, usually, the other one as well. Higher up "the interests" bought the outcome plutocrats favored. Politics was a matter of "puppet peoples and puppet politicians," according to *The Cost* (1904). This was a tour of the "sewers of politics." "The Plum Tree," or, the "Confessions of a Politician," made the cover of *Success Magazine* a month before the nation elected a president in 1904. The novel was a great success on the book lists the following year. In sending Phillips to the Senate in 1906, Hearst was asking little more than to make fact follow popular novels of the day.[23]

Phillips's point in fiction was the same he made as a reporter. America's trouble was not merely that the plutocracy ruled, but that honest exchange of views was impossible. In *The Great God Success* (1901) an editor who dared to give space to all sides and to crusade for right finally sold out. The general reader was cast as a helpless victim of the commercial ties of the press. One Hampden Scarborough was the hero of these bleak novels in which everyone else with virtue is impotent. He was the progressive cast as savior and modeled after Phillips's college friend, Albert J. Beveridge. Beveridge, a senator from Indiana, was eloquent, but also pragmatic, as he worked for reform within the GOP. It is noteworthy that Scarborough's career was free of all those activities that would seem central to governing a democracy. There was no debating of positions or adjustments as more facts became known. Compromise and reconciliation were never goals, and minds were changed only as the leader cast a spell over a confused and frustrated public.

It was politics, itself, that was attacked in a good deal of the literature of reform. In *Success Magazine*, Charles E. Russell condemned "the fatal virus of 'practical politics,' the very name of which is always a sign of something rotten." Alfred Henry Lewis told readers of *Human Life* that "politics is the art of arousing the ignorance of mankind." There was contempt, not only for the compromises a practical politician must make, but also for the calculating mind that seeks partial good in the political process. Muckrakers like Phillips and Sinclair turned from the dissection of democracy, as it was, to an orgiastic vision of what it might become. At a convention, Scarborough's first words set off "huge waves of adulation, with his name shouted in voices hoarse and voices shrill like hissing foam on the triumphant crests of billows." Pauline Dumont, the betrayed wife of a corruptionist, listened to this voice and was seized: "Pauline felt as if she were lifted from her bodily self, were tossing in a delirium of ecstasy on a sea of sheer delight."[24]

Sinclair's Jurgis found political virtue the same way. He had learned that citizenship was a license to stuff ballots and that political work was all trickery and payoffs. He sank so low that he had only the warmth of a GOP rally to save him from the streets—"he must listen—he must be interested!" But a senator's address made him snore, and Jurgis was kicked out into the cold. Finally, a Socialist rally was salvation. The image of the slumbering labor giant brought the workers to their feet

and Jurgis was with them, he was shouting to tear his throat; shouting because he could not help it, because the stress of this feeling was more than he could bear . . . There was an unfolding of vistas before him, a breaking of the ground beneath him, an upheaving, a stirring, a trembling; he felt himself suddenly a mere man no longer—there were powers within him undreamed of, there were demon forces contending, age-long wonders struggling to be born; and he sat oppressed with pain and joy, while a tingling stole down into his finger-tips, and his breath came hard and fast.

Sinclair needed several hundred more words to describe a political conversion that was at once an ecstasy of body and soul.[25]

Progressives rarely made good cynics, and neither Phillips nor Sinclair could walk away from the political institutions that each condemned. Sinclair gave advice to the president—sometimes more than once a day—on how to regulate the meat packing industry through legislation. It was not until many months later that Sinclair acted as if he believed what he had shown readers of *The Jungle*: piecemeal reform through the parties was a delusion. (Packingtown had federal meat inspectors, and this troubled the bosses not at all.) The *Cosmopolitan* articles fit into Hearst's campaign for the direct election of senators, and Phillips, too, put stock in this reform. He expected great things from a few insurgents in the Senate and believed an attack on the plutocracy might yet come from this body. The GOP, he once wrote, "has become chiefly a mask for burglarious operations and nauseating exploitations of helplessness and ignorance. But the moment of awakening is at hand."[26]

What were readers supposed to make of this reporting? How could a political process worthy of such contempt be fixed so quickly? How could a government of traitors doing the bidding of the wealthy disappear? Theodore Roosevelt touched the play of defeatism and hope within reform sentiment in an address on April 14, 1906, "The Man with the Muck-Rake."

Roosevelt's remarks, made during the dedication of the House Office Building on Capitol Hill, were calculated. He had tried out the argument weeks earlier before journalists likely to be in good spirits at a Gridiron Club dinner. The public address identified not a single story or reporter and was filled with encouragements to honest criticism, embracing even the attacks of "merciless severity." More, the president closed with a deep bow to the left and gave vague endorsement of a progressive tax on large fortunes. Some social critics did feel that the nice things they heard before Roosevelt punched them were not enough. As the reporters took offense at the suggestion that they delighted in filth, TR [Theodore Roosevelt] rushed to assure them *their* work was not being questioned. The president also conducted a long correspondence with Sinclair and lured Phillips to the White House for soothing treatment.[27]

TR's private papers show that he had Phillips and Sinclair uppermost in mind and that the term "muckraker" was designed to blacken their names and discredit their point of view. Writing in confidence to William Howard Taft, the president credited these muckrakers with "building up a revolutionary feeling." This was probably not TR's deepest concern in the spring of 1906. He reminded Taft that Republicans had stopped such threats before. In private as well as in public, the president seems to have worried more about political indifference than about revolution. Roosevelt told the crowd on Capitol Hill that an indiscriminate attack on the "powerful means the searing of the public conscience." He worried about "the hard scoffing spirit" and "the vacant mind" of citizens nurtured on exposés. In private, the president fumed about what literature was now doing to politics. He had stopped halfway through Phillips's *The Plum Tree* in disgust but returned to it shortly after the muckrake speech on the urging of the editor of the *Saturday Evening Post*. In a letter to the journalist that was longer than any published review of the novel, TR spoke in confidence about how little the political process matched the story. "Now, I feel that almost each individual fact brought forward by Phillips is true by itself," the president conceded, "and yet these facts are so grouped as to produce a totally false impression."[28]

The criticism at base was that Phillips did not know politics, the mixture of motives that seemed so obvious to Roosevelt after a quarter century of public life. What most exasperated the president was that *sincere* men stood against his policies! Men "with no earthly interest at stake" could frustrate his will! TR seems to have grown angrier as he thought about it, and eleven days later he added a note to this letter about "The Treason of the Senate." Phillip's reporting was now more dangerous, the president said, for the articles "excite a hysterical and ignorant feeling against everything existing, good or bad."[29]

This was not quite fair. The editors of muckraking magazines were obsessed by charges that they were too negative, and they responded with demonstrations that this was not so. As in Phillips's and Sinclair's work, exposés were almost always connected with legislation that would set things right. Open one of these magazines at random and read for a half-hour: there is assurance (probably more than once) that an aroused public opinion will fulfill the promise of democracy. But this said, the president was a discerning critic of the literature of muckraking. The process of government was usually denigrated so effectively that participation in it—even as a voter—was made to seem futile. The imaginative literature and reporting repelled the citizen from political life.

Of all the progressive journalists, Brand Whitlock knew best what he was talking about when he developed this theme. In the 1890s, he left the Chicago press corps to become an assistant to the reform governor of the state. In the early years of the century, Whitlock's name was continually before the nation as the mayor and great innovator of Toledo, Ohio, and the author of stories about how America was governed. The voters of Toledo returned Whitlock to office three times and such was his popularity that he was continually asked to baptize, marry, and eulogize his constituents.[30]

Editors, especially at *McClure's*, sensed that Whitlock had something new to say about public life. Mere cynicism and elegantly expressed disgust were not by themselves new in political literature. There had been plenty of that in the bohemian world of Chicago journalism, and many across the nation knew of Mark Twain's fulminations as well as that wicked novel written by Henry Adams and published anonymously, *Democracy* (1880). The worst that could be said about the American experiment in government had already been said. Again, the distinctive feature of the muckrakers was not that they were first to say things, but that they were the first to say these things from *within* the political culture they described. What impressed writers of Twain's generation was that Whitlock wrote as someone who breathed the air of politics on the ward level and could create believable characters at home in this world.[31]

Whitlock was vastly more knowledgeable than Phillips about how public questions are settled, but the mayor's eye was just as cold. During the Progressive Era, Whitlock issued an autobiography testifying to his "disgust" with the old parties and customs. In much of his fiction, the political process was an invitation to nausea or boredom. Washington, for this muckraker, was not peopled with the lively rascals Twain and Adams had seen. Politics was posturing and indolence. Congressman Jerome Garwood in *The Thirteenth District* lived only to dodge any coalition that could send him back to his wife and law practice in Grand Prairie. Power and position translated into stuporous loafing: "To saunter over to the House at noon, to saunter back, to lean at that corner of the little bar in the Arlington, one foot cocked over the other, his broad hat on the back of his head, and the Havana cigar between his teeth tilted at an angle parallel with the line of his hat brim, thus preserving to the eye the symmetry of the whole striking picture he knew he made—this was existence for him." Whitlock was surely one of the first moralists to suggest that corruption in America did not keep bad rulers busy.[32]

The muckrakers scoffed at politics as they labored to make politics better. They said that traditional outlets for political feeling led the wrong way. Party and ethnic loyalty were snares that the good citizen must avoid. The agenda for the nation now consisted of complex, sobering problems. Was it likely that some in the electorate were driven away from politics by this message? Were some Americans less impressed by the example of activism the muckrakers set than by the perplexing and discouraging course of politics they wrote about so well? We do not have modern survey data to profile the citizens who stopped voting (and attending rallies) at the beginning of this century, but magazine circulation figures offer important clues to the impact of muckraking.

Between 1902 and 1912 about a dozen popular journals tried many times with exposé material. The effect in the marketplace was unpredictable. The circulation of *Everybody's* went from 150,000 to 700,000 in the course of the "Frenzied Finance" series. *Ridgway's* (under the same editorial hand that guided *Everybody's*) never caught on and quickly went bankrupt. *McClure's* simply found in muckraking a way to hold onto the large readership it had won in the 1890s. For all of Hearst's money, *Cosmopolitan* attracted few new readers with muckraking. The staff from *McClure's* that took charge of the *American* magazine achieved no breakthrough in circulation. Both *Cosmopolitan* and *American* magazine boosted their readership only after editors gave up, reluctantly, on investigative reporting. *Collier's* doubled its readership, to over half a million as it featured reform themes. The *Saturday Evening Post*, serializer of six novels by Phillips, climbed to one million circulation by 1910. The popular appeal of social criticism in the magazines was volatile but the editors' commitment to these stories was remarkably steady. This has become a familiar state of affairs in the mass media. The magazine business in the Progressive Era looked very much like television networks in later decades, convinced by a political mood in the nation and a few hits, that the public had unlimited appetite for programs blended to a formula. The popular recipe is the one sure to be, in time, force-fed.[33]

MUCKRAKERS AND CELEBRITIES

Perhaps the most important feature of muckraking was that it became such a ubiquitous and insistent trade practice. The number of magazines truly dedicated to reform has often been set too high, but the error stems from a correct perception by researchers: the investigation of social problems and impatience with the political status quo seems to be everywhere one looks in the periodical literature. It is reasonable to assume a readership in 20 million American homes. In a total population of about 90 million people, the great majority of American families with anything topical to read were exposed to muckraking material. No wonder Senator Beveridge in 1910 called the exposés a "people's literature" amounting to "almost a mental and moral revolution." Not all of this, of course, carried an extreme critique of government. But writers such as Phillips, Russell, Sinclair, and Steffens had a great deal of exposure, both as contributors and as celebrities in the news. As with any heresy, we may assume that their outlook grew congenial to citizens as it was merely described, or, indeed, as it was refuted. If muckraking did nothing more than break the silence over the wisdom of political participation in America, it did a great deal.[34]

What today would be called the "demographics" and "reader profile" of muckraking was discussed in 1905 by those sure judges of public taste, Finley Peter Dunne's Irishmen in the Archey Road saloon:

" 'It looks to me,' said Mr. Hennessy, 'as though this counthry was goin' to th' divvle.'

'Put down that magazine,' said Mr. Dooley. 'Now d'ye fell betther? I thought so. But I can sympathize with ye. I've been readin' thim mesilf.' "

Mr. Dooley said that he rarely read magazines before or when he did open one, "I'd frequently glance through it an' find it in me lap whin I woke up. Th' magazines in thim day was very ca'ming to the' mind.' " No more, Hennessy and Dooley agreed, as they reviewed the exposés of muckrakers. "Is there an institution that isn't corrupt to its very foundations? Don't you believe it."[35]

The extraordinary reach of muckraking meant that much of its audience had nothing like the first-hand knowledge and love of politics of a Mr. Dooley. The magazine distribution system was so efficient and the price so low that historians have spoken of a "revolution" in publishing. There was little cost in money or time to read these stories. Even citizens who did not ask for this material found it without looking far. Indeed, there was a system of rewards to see that they found it. In 1906 when *Success Magazine* organized a "People's Lobby" to fight a corrupt Congress, the editors offered deep discounts to subscribers who would take magazines such as *Good Housekeeping, Country Gentlemen*, and *Yachting*. These "clubbing" subscription plans also allowed a reader to combine magazines with a taste for reform, but the offers were advertised to sweep in readers with the widest variety of interests.[36]

The Americans who were exposed to muckraking were usually not experienced consumers of political revelations, and there is no sign that the Progressive Era brought an increase in the number of politically sophisticated readers. The circulation of the older, serious political journalism (such as the *Arena* and the *Nation*) remained small. A magazine even modestly successful at muckraking might have ten times the readers of these political journals. In the Progressive Era there was no sign that the public wanted more investigation of social problems than the popular magazines furnished. There is some reason to think that readers wanted less. Book publishers did not have the captive readers represented by a magazine subscription list, and they found no vast public existed for muckraking books. *The Jungle* was a bestseller and Phillips's fiction made respectable sales, but these were exceptions. *The Shame of the Cities* sold 3,000 copies. "The Treason of the Senate" did not attract a book publisher in the Progressive Era. The mass taste for exposure was fully met by the magazines, reaching a public much larger than those actively curious and generally informed about political life.[37]

Modern students of communications have measured the effect of critical political reporting on a mass public with the aid of representative samples and control groups. This research has paid close attention to the signs of political malaise that we also seek to explain in the Progressive Era. Methodological disputes still flash between these researchers, but a growing body of evidence points to a connection between negative reporting of political life and the public's trust in government and sense of political efficacy. The crucial point for students of progressivism is the way less sophisticated consumers of political information seem most affected by critical reporting. Conclusions drawn from the response to news documentaries on television need little translation to apply to the public reached by muckraking in popular magazines at the beginning of the century:

News organizations have been compelled to bombard the American television audience with interpretive, sensational, aggressive, and anti-institutional news items. This content reaches and holds a unique audience, larger and more volatile than that attracted by any other medium. Many of the members of this unique audience are inadvertent to it. These inadvertent viewers tend to lack political sophistication: they cannot cope well with the type of news and information that the networks provide. But because the networks are too credible to be dismissed in their messages, these viewers respond to the content by growing more cynical, more frustrated, more despairing; they become increasingly less enamored of their social and political institutions.[38]

Today, this malaise probably has only a small direct effect on voting for the simple reason that American leadership has adjusted. In modern presidential elections, especially, candidates run against politicians as a class, politics as a profession, and Washington as a community. At the beginning of the century, neither party knew how to co-opt this diffuse discontent so skillfully. The anticivics lesson of the popular press was, in its reach and clarity, new. In the Progressive Era the disillusionment with politics affected participation because neither the Plunkitts nor the Roosevelts could connect with a broad new cynicism about how the game was to be played.

Sermons on good citizenship are apt to spring from such discoveries. Serious students of politics—of the Progressive Era or today—will not rush to judgment. Is democracy better off if ill-informed citizens feel more comfortable? Are wiser choices made by confident voters who are untouched by controversy? If the electorate shrinks to those who can surmount their frustrations, does the political system suffer? At the end of the Progressive Era, Walter Lippmann cited the lower turnouts for elections as a sign of what he had learned to accept in journalism and politics: there was now a "phantom public." The community to be counted on for informed choice and participation was small, and even these citizens had to delegate important decisions to an elite. A recent summary of theories of democracy finds a consensus "that high levels of participation and interest are required from a minority of citizens only and, moreover, the apathy and disinterest of the majority play a valuable role in maintaining the stability of the system as a whole." The value of broad public interest in politics must not be taken for granted."[39]

A history of the press alone cannot fully explain basic changes in political behavior. Patterns of work, family life, and religious belief have much to do with notions of political efficacy and the appeal of elections. The way political stories are told in the press has special importance in the study of what makes citizens willing or unwilling to participate in government. Journalism can change more quickly than the fundamental relationships in life. In a society in which fundamentals are changing, journalism is common ground, defining and offering agendas for what is important (if anything) about the political process. Muckraking was important not because it was the source of alienation, but rather because it was a rapid transmitter of this anxiety among communities with different reasons to feel lost in the new urban nation. The language for politics in the investigative magazines was one of the few innovations of the Progressive Era pervasive enough to account for the broad withdrawal from elections.

What of the opinion leaders, the men and women with a stock of knowledge about political institutions? Did muckraking in the magazines weaken their faith in traditional politics? Conservatives in the Progressive Era thought this was happening. The "Treason of the Senate" was answered in the *New England Magazine* with the lament that, in this slick form, "the educated, discriminating element of the populace are prone to accept as gospel truth statements of alleged fact that would be laughed at if published in the ordinary newspaper channels of news."[40] Again, the breadth of the muckraking appeal gave it special power. These glossy magazines were not shunned by serious people, and the celebrity journalists were not quickly dismissed. Walter Lippmann, a college prodigy, was courted by his professors at Harvard, but just before he graduated in 1910, he turned to Lincoln Steffens to define his career. "What I have dreamed of doing is to work under you," Lippmann told Steffens. Unlike earlier reform, the progressive movement was not hobbled by the reaction of an elite against the breakthroughs in mass publicity.[41] As in all successful periods of reform, there had to be a suspension of disbelief, a granting of some truths, however vaguely stated or wrong in detail. This is what the muckraking magazines brought about. Political reform turned on this consensus, but so, too, did a new disenchantment with politics.

In life as well as in their art, the muckrakers wished to adjourn the traditional politics of party debate and conflict. Sinclair and Russell fled to the Socialist movement, then moved to more idiosyncratic political stands. A host of muckrakers relished their experiences engineering a unified public opinion in Washington during World War I. Lincoln Steffens set a classic model of dreamy, radical-sounding detachment. Disillusionment with the mainstream of American political life obviously owed much to the course of the war, but it was implicit in what the muckrakers had found as political reporters. This was a lesson they had taught well in an age of reform.

NOTES

1. There are two quantitative studies of this reporting: Judson A. Grenier Jr., "The Origins and Nature of Progressive Muckraking," Ph.D. diss., UCLA, 1965, and Peter N. Barry, "The Decline of Muckraking: A View from the Magazines," Ph.D. diss., Wayne State University, 1973. In Barry's sample between a quarter and a third of the muckrakers held jobs in government in the course of their careers, see p. 57.

2. I have relied on the voting analysis in Walter Dean Burnham, "The Changing Shape of the American Political Universe," *The American Political Science Review* 59 (March 1965): 7–28; Burnham, *Critical Elections and the Mainsprings of American Politics* (New York: Norton, 1970), ch. 4, see especially 84; and Paul Kleppner, *Who Voted? The Dynamics of Electoral Turnout, 1870–1980* (New York: Praeger, 1982). Richard L. McCormick, *From Realignment to Reform, Political Change in New York State, 1893–1910* (Ithaca, N.Y.: Cornell University Press, 1981), confirms this trend and shows that, in New York, lower turn-out was not an artifact of changed voting procedures (see 187–89, 241–42, 252–53, 262, 269). See also Michael Paul Rogin and John L. Shover, *Political Change in California: Critical Elections and Social Movements, 1890–1966* (Westport, Conn.: Greenwood Press, 1970), 26–28; and John Francis Reynolds, "Testing Democracy: Electoral Participation and Progressive

Reform in New Jersey, 1888–1919," Ph.D. diss., Rutgers University, 1980. Puzzlement about the decline of voting began during the Progressive Era. See, for example, William G. Brown, "The Changing Character of National Elections," *Independent* January 19, 1905): 121–26, Charles E. Russell, "The Break Up of the Parties," *Success* January 1909): 9; and "New Anxieties about Voting," *Century Magazine* (December 1912): 311–12. Recognition of this problem by historians is remarkably recent, see Daniel T. Rodgers, "In Search of Progressives," *Reviews in American History 10* (December 1982): 113–32, especially 115–17, and Thomas C. Leonard, "The 'Bully Pulpit': Who Listened?" *Reviews in American History* II (March 21, 1983): 104–7.

3. Raymond E. Wolfinger and Stephen J. Rosenstone, *Who Votes?* (New Haven: Yale University Press, 1980), 100.

4. Burnham, *Critical Elections,* 73. Richard Jensen, *The Winning of the Midwest, Social and Political Conflict, 1888–1896* (Chicago: University of Chicago Press, 1971), 13. Warren E. Miller, "Disinterest, Disaffection, and Participation in Presidential Politics," *Political Behavior* 11 (1980): 12, 14, suggests that voter turnout by itself may not be an adequate measure of political interest. In the past two decades, for example, citizens have reported a stronger habit of writing letters to representatives in government: At the same time turnout for elections has declined. No one has data from the Progressive Era to permit fine distinctions, but I know of no evidence of broader participation in politics by males in this period.

5. The most sophisticated and comprehensive study of this matter is Michael E. McGerr, *The Decline of Popular Politics: The American North, 1865–1928* (New York: Oxford University Press, 1986).

6. Jacob Citrin, "The Alienated Voter," *Taxing & Spending* I (October–November 1978): 10–11. For a more ambiguous reading of the evidence, see Richard Brody, "The Puzzle of Political Participation in America," in *The New American Political System*, ed. Anthony King (Washington, D.C.: American Enterprise Institute, 1978), 287–324, especially 308–10.

7. Jensen's extensive discussion of campaign styles in *The Winning of the Midwest* should be supplemented with Jean H. Baker, *Affairs of Party: The Political Culture of Northern Democrats in the Mid-Nineteenth Century* (Ithaca, N.Y. Cornell University Press, 1983), 288–97 on martial forms in political life.

8. "Cheerful Vanity," *Hampton's Magazine*, January 1910: 152–53. "Political Duty," *Independent* May 14, 1903, 1159. See also "The Revolt of the Plain Citizen," *World To-Day*, April 1905, 345–46.

9. On the varied causes of anti-partyism in the 1890s see, in addition to McGerr cited above, Jensen, *The Winning of the Midwest*, 164, 174–75, 306–7. Paul Kleppner, *The Cross of Culture: A Social Analysis of Midwestern Politics, 1850–1900* (New York: Free Press, 1970), is another convincing demonstration of the primary of religious and ethnic factors in elections and the importance of ritual in political participation. That a more complex presentation of issues hurts turn-out is axiomatic in social science literature, see for example Miller, "Disinterest, Disaffection, and Participation," 30–31. Both historians and students of contemporary political behavior have good reason to be modest in speculation. Rodgers, "In Search of Progressivism," observed that "no one really knows" why a complex withdrawal from politics occurred early in this century, 116. Wolfinger and Rosenstone, *Who Votes* (1980, 2)

cautioned that "research on this topic has not progressed much beyond a few very broad (and sometimes false) propositions."

10. William L. Riordon, *Plunkitt of Tammany Hall* (1905; New York: Dutton, 1963), 36, 81–83. *McClure's Magazine*, March 1905, 525 has this cartoon by Dan Beard. Steffens filed a concise plea against party loyalty in "Enemies of the Republic," *McClure's*, August 1904, 395–408.

11. Charles E. Russell, "At the Throat of the Republic" *Cosmopolitan*, December 1907, January 1908, February 1908, April 1908, 146–57, 259–71, 361–69, 475–80 (150 quoted).

12. Lincoln Steffens, "Rhode Island: A State for Sale," *McClure's*, February 1905, 342. Ray Stannard Baker, "What Is Lynching?" *McClure's*, February 1905, 422. David Graham Phillips, *The Plum Tree* (Indianapolis: Bobbs-Merrill, 1905), 12–13. Brand Whitlock, *The Thirteenth District, The Story of A Candidate* (Indianapolis: Bowen-Merrill, 1902), 116–17, see also 236–37; Whitlock, "The City and Civilization," *Scribner's Magazine*, November 1912, 628. The wide attention to rural Ohio in the reform press is fully documented in Genevieve B. Gist, "Progressive Reform in a Rural Community: The Adams County Vote-Fraud Case," *Mississippi Valley Historical Review* 97 (June 1961), 60–78.

13. David Grayson, "Adventures in Contentment, The Politician," *American Magazine*, October 1907, 646–50. For a discussion of the antiurban theme in the later Grayson stories see John F. Semonche, *Ray Stannard Baker: A Quest for Democracy in Modern America, 1870–1918* (Chapel Hill: University of North Carolina Press, 1969), 168–71. Similar sentiments in muckraking magazines: "Confessions of a Country Mouse in the City" and "The Call of the Tame," *Independent*, February 11, 1904, 310–11 and 339–40. George Creel, "Mending Broken Men," *Success,* June 1911, 18–19, 38–40, esp. 39. In light of the analogy I shall make between muckraking and the mass media of contemporary America, it is significant that Herbert J. Gans found "small-town provincialism" a basic value shaping coverage, in *Deciding What's News: A Study of CBS Evening News, NBC Nightly News, Newsweek, and Time* (New York: Pantheon, 1979), 48–50.

14. White, *Gazette*, February 1, 1912 and June 20, 1912, cited in Jean B. Quandt, *From the Small Town to the Great Community: The Social Thought of Progressive Intellectuals* (New Brunswick, N.J.: Rutgers University Press, 1970). "Emporia and New York," *American* magazine, January 1907, 258–64. Helen O. Mahin, ed., *The Editor and His People: Editorials by William Allen White* (New York: Macmillan, 1924), 252–53, 309–11).

15. Quandt, *From the Small Town to the Great Community*, ch. 10, is an illuminating discussion, see especially 66, 70. See Kleppner, *The Cross of Culture*, 304, on Bryan's campaign of 1896.

16. David P. Thelen, *The New Citizenship: Origins of Progressivism in Wisconsin, 1885–1900* (Columbia: University of Missouri Press, 1972), 288. There is a vast literature on ethnic tensions within progressivism. Some of the most valuable discussions are John Higham, *Strangers in the Land: Patterns of American Nativism, 1860–1925* (New York: Pantheon, 1963), 116–22, 174–79; John D. Buenker, *Urban Liberalism and Progressive Reform* (New York: Scribner, 1973), 163–97. David H. Hollinger, "Ethnic Diversity, Cosmopolitanism and the Emergence of the American Liberal Intelligentsia," *American Quarterly* 47 (May 1975): 133–51.

17. The definitive study of the changed focus of reporting in the capital is George

Juergens, *News from the White House: The Presidential-Press Relationship in the Progressive Era* (Chicago: University of Chicago Press, 1981). The press corps moved camp from Capitol Hill to the White House, a building not routinely covered before the end of the 1890s.

18. The photo of Phillips is in Isaac F. Marcosson, *David Graham Phillips and His Times* (New York: Dodd, Mead, 1932). Bailey Millard, "David Graham Phillips, His Work and His Clothes," *Human Life*, June 1909, 9–23.

19. *Leslie's Weekly*, March 20, 1905, 304. All of the photographs, save one, are reproduced in the reprint edition published in New York in 1953.

20. The only precedent I have found for the snap shots of senators appeared in a story favorable to the upper house: Walter Wellman, "Operating the United States Senate," *Success*, October 1904, 559–61. What the *New York Times* called "promiscuous photographing" (snap shots of the Democratic presidential candidate) arose in the 1904 campaign, July 16, 1904, 2. "The Shame of California-Photographed," appeared in *American* magazine, December 1907, 144 as part of Lincoln Steffens, "The Mote and the Beam." George E. Mowry, *The California Progressives* (Chicago: Quadrangle Books, 1951), 60, 174.

Charles E. Russell's series, "What Are You Going To Do About It?" *Cosmopolitan* July–October and December 1910 is a striking example of how composite photos brought a new element to the work of a veteran muckraker. In his earlier, celebrated work on the Beef Trust and the tenements owned by Trinity Church, documentary photographs had come without theatrical effects. James Creelman, "The Romance and Tragedy of Wood Engraving," *Pearson's Magazine*, March 1907, 293, called the half-tone process a "revolution" in illustration and emphasized the economy. A master engraver fetched $150 to $200 for a picture that could now be made ready for the press for $6 to $30. The savings in time was just as dramatic. See also Neil Harris, "Iconography and Intellectual History: The Half-Tone Effect," in John Higham and Paul K. Conkin, eds., *New Directions in American Intellectual History* (Baltimore: Johns Hopkins University Press, 1979).

21. Phillips, *The Treason of the Senate*, ed. George E. Mowry and Judson A. Grenier (Chicago: Quadrangle Books, 1964), 59, 85, 92, 99, 114–15, 121, 126, 146; "orators of the treason" appeared in a conclusion at the end of the third installment in *Cosmopolitan*, the phrase is not reproduced in this edition. Phillips also dismissed speeches in the Senate writing in *Appleton's Magazine* (April 1906). David J. Rothman, *Politics and Power: The United States Senate, 1869–1901* (Cambridge, Mass.: Harvard University Press, 1966), is the best single demonstration of how little of his subject Phillips understood. The "Treason of the Senate" was longer, but not more extreme than other exposés of Congress in these magazines. Alfred Henry Lewis said that his political reporting was modeled after the rattlesnake's approach to intruders, and Lewis was frequently as good as his word. See, for example, "Confessions of a Newspaper Man," *Human Life* November 11, 1905, 4; "Some Presidential Candidates," Ibid., April 1908, 9–10, 32–33; "What Is 'Joe' Cannon?" *Cosmopolitan*, April 1910, 569–75. Samuel Merwin, "Taking the Hoe to Congress," *Success*, September 1906, 604–5, 647–48. Hearst's long, drawn-out release of the "Archbold Letters" was an assault on the integrity of the Senate, see *Hearst's Magazine, The World To-Day*, May 1912, 2201–16, and Ibid., June 1912, 2362–2776.

22. Phillips, *The Treason of the Senate*, 60, 69, 92, 99, 104, 194, 214. Upton Sinclair, *The Jungle* (1906; New York: Bantam Books, 1976). Virtually all of the

fiction I use first appeared in muckraking publications. I cite the books as a convenience. There was much taunting of the reader in Russell, "At the Throat of the Republic," 150, 260, 475. Alfred Henry Lewis spoke of "a numskull public" in "The Revolution at Washington," *Cosmopolitan*, July 1910, 245.

23. John Graham (David Graham Phillips), *The Great God Success, A Novel* (New York: Frederick A. Stokes), 173; Phillips, *The Cost*, 241; Phillips, *The Plum Tree*, 220, 252. For dispiriting testimony about how politics worked see, for example, Eltweed Pomeroy, "An Outsider's Experiences with Inside Politics" and the editorial "Popular Government; 1904," *Independent*, May 5, 1904, 1006–10 and 1039–40; William Hemstreet, "The New Primary Law," *Arena*, December 1902, 585–95.

24. Alfred Henry Lewis, "Mr. Lewis' Editorial Comment" *Human Life*, November 1906, 17. Charles E. Russell, "The Break-Up of the Parties," *Success*, January 1909, 6. Phillips, *The Cost*, 252. Similarly, the posthumously published *George Helm* (New York: A. Appleton & Co., 1912) treated politics as a black art whose deceptions corrupted the best citizens. This novel ran as a serial in Hearst's *The World To-Day*, during the presidential campaign of 1912.

25. Sinclair, *The Jungle*, 339–41, 366–67.

26. "Albert J. Beveridge: A Character Sketch," *Success*, August 1905, reprinted in Louis Filler, ed., *Contemporaries: Portraits in the Progressive Era by David Graham Phillips* (Westport, Conn.: Greenwood Press, 1981), 125 (quoted).

27. I have quoted from the Roosevelt text in the Mowry and Grenier edition of *The Treason of the Senate*, 218, 223. For a full account of the Roosevelt-Sinclair exchange and each man's role in the reform legislation see Robert M. Crunden, *Ministers of Reform* (New York: Basic Books, 1982), 163–99.

28. Mowry and Grenier, *The Treason of the Senate*, 220. Elting E. Morison et al., eds., *The Letters of Theodore Roosevelt*, 8 vols. (Cambridge, Mass.: Harvard University Press, 1951–54), 5: TR to Alfred Henry Lewis, 17 Feb. 1906, 156–57; TR to William H. Taft, 15 March 1906, 184; TR to George H. Lorimer, 12 May 1906, 264–65. George W. Alger had made similar points earlier in the *Atlantic* about the depressing and isolating effects of exposure for the ordinary reader, see his *Moral Overstrain* (Boston and New York: Houghton Mifflin, 1906), 124–27.

29. Morison, ed., *The Letters of Theodore Roosevelt*, 5: TR to George H. Lorimer, 12 May 1906, 269.

30. Robert M. Crunden, *A Hero in Spite of Himself: Brand Whitlock in Art, Politics, and War* (New York: Knopf, 1969), 107.

31. Ibid., 74.

32. In Whitlock's disgust with the political process see Crunden, *A Hero in Spite of Himself*. Whitlock, *Forty Years of It* (Westport, Conn.: Greenwood Press, 1968), 94–95. This autobiography was published in book form in 1914; it had reached the public through magazines a year earlier. Whitlock, *The Thirteenth District*, 433.

33. Barry, "The Decline of Muckraking" has the most comprehensive and carefully qualified circulation figures, see 26–27 and Appendix 11.

34. David H. Chalmers estimated that 12 million monthly readers, encompassing 20 million families were reached by periodicals with muckraking themes, "The Muckrakers and the Growth of Corporate Power: A Study in Constructive Journalism," *American Journal of Economics and Society* 18 (April 1959): 297. Beveridge quoted by David P. Thelen, *Robert M. La Follette and the Insurgent Spirit* (Madison: University of Wisconsin Press, 1976), 76.

35. Finley Peter Dunne, "National Housecleaning," *Collier's*, December 16, 1905, 12.

36. "The Publishers' Outlook," *Success Magazine*, October 1909, 613, reviews clubbing schemes. The editors said that there had been a five-fold increase in the circulation of subscription agency catalogues since 1900. Ibid., October 1903, 621.

37. Richard Hofstadter, *The Age of Reform: From Bryan to FDR* (New York: Vintage Books, 1955) 186–98. According to the letter to Lincoln Steffens from Doubleday, Page & Co., 25 Jan. 1909, *The Shame of the Cities* sold twenty-nine copies from July 1908 to November 24, 1908. A letter from this publisher on August 1, 1909, reported that thirty-nine copies had been sold in the preceding six months (both in Lincoln Steffens Papers, Columbia University). For the total sales figures of this book and others see Barry, "The Decline of Muckraking," 215–17.

38. Michael J. Robinson, " 'Public Affairs Television and the Growth of Political Malaise: The Case of 'The Selling of the Pentagon,' " *American Political Science Review* 70 (June 1976): 426. Thomas A. Kazee, "Television Exposure and Attitude Change: The Impact of Political Interest," *Public Opinion Quarterly* (winter 1981): 507–18, is a confirming study of the Watergate era with a valuable review of the literature on the ways reporting may decrease the public's sense of its political efficacy. Austin Ranney, *Channels of Power: The Impact of Television on American Politics* (New York: Basic Books, 1983) is a particularly lucid consideration of the implications of this research. Ranney follows Herbert Gans in drawing attention to similarities between progressivism before WWI and television newspeople in the 1980s (53–54). Gans, *Deciding What's News*, 203–6. Arthur H. Miller, Edie N. Goldenberg, and Lutz Erbring, "Type-Set Politics: Impact of Newspapers on Public Confidence," *American Political Science Review* 73 (March 1979): 67–84 shows that the effects of political criticism was greatest on those whose education had not prepared them to account for complexity. The authors take issue with earlier methods of studying this problem. During the Progressive Era, some editors of the older magazines made a dark prognosis of the new exposés; see, for example, "The Cheap Magazines in Politics," *Harper's Weekly*, January 25, 1913, 5.

39. Walter Lippmann, *Public Opinion* (New York: Harcourt, Brace & Co., 1922) and idem, *The Phantom Public* (New York: Harcourt Brace, 1927). Carole Pateman, *Participation and Democratic Theory* (1970; New York: Cambridge, Eng.: Cambridge University Press, 1980), 7. This book is a careful examination of the inadequacies of contemporary democratic theory.

40. David S. Barry, "The Loyalty of the Senate, *New England Magazine*, October 1906, 141. *McClure's* itself published letters of its elite, appreciative readers, see June 1904, 221–24.

41. Ronald Steel, *Walter Lippmann and the American Century* (New York: Little, Brown, 1981), 34. Even Hearst's editors had an appetite for theoretical work by Progressives, see for example Walter E. Weyl, "The New Democracy," *Hearst's Magazine, The World To-Day*, June 1912, 2489–94. Leonard L. Richards, "Gentlemen of Property and Standing," *Anti-Abolition Mobs in Jacksonian America* (New York: Oxford University Press, 1971), see especially 71–73, 162–70.

Epilogue: Muckraking and the Ethic of Caring

Howard Good

Progressive Era muckrakers practiced the literature of exposure because they hoped it would bring about the moral regeneration of a corrupt, overly materialistic American society and because they believed it allowed them to carry on Christ's work in the world. Contemporary journalists, on the other hand, tend to practice exposure for exposure's sake—because it creates excitement, uproar, attention. "What the mob thirsts for is not good government in itself," H. L. Mencken once observed, "but the merry chase of a definite exponent of bad government."[1] While it has lost none of its merriment, the chase has speeded up and spread out since the advent of communication satellites and computerized newsrooms. The news media now seem to operate full time on the assumption that there is nothing quite as enticing to an audience as the greasy smell of scandal.

It is the investigative style that matters most in journalism today, not the subject or outcome of an investigation. Thus a TV newsmagazine asks the momentous question, Who gets hit on more in singles bars, blondes or brunettes? The defining visual characteristics of a tough investigative report are all there—the high-angled shot from a hidden camera, the grainy black-and-white footage, the computer-altered faces in order to preserve the anonymity of sources. The only thing missing is an authentic issue.

There are, of course, investigative stories of real weight and purpose also being produced. In Chicago, a Northwestern University journalism professor and several of his students dig up evidence that helps free a man who has spent 16 years on death row for a double murder he didn't commit.[2] In New York City, Mike McAlary of the *Daily News* sneaks into a hospital to interview a Haitian immigrant who was sodomized with a broom handle by police and then publicizes the outrage in a series of front-page columns.[3] In Allentown, Pennsylvania, a staff writer for the *Morning Call* exposes the dangerous lack of sprinklers in high-rise buildings, leading to new laws and an award from the Pennsylvania Women's Press Association.[4]

So is the old muckraking spirit still alive in the press after all? Not exactly. The context in which contemporary journalists do their work is far different from that in which the original muckrakers did theirs. As previous authors in this book have made clear, the original muckrakers shared a common outlook, a common set of values. Their journalism was a heartfelt expression of a sweeping ideological vision of Progressive reform. By contrast, the examples of investigative reporting cited above sprang more from happenstance than from moral fervor or political conviction. Both McAlary and the *Morning Call* reporter, Elliot Grossman, probably would never have begun their respective investigations if they hadn't received tips. And even after Grossman ran down his story, he had rather modest goals for it. "I wasn't trying to get any laws passed," he admitted. "I was just trying to get sprinklers installed."[5]

Investigative reporting as currently practiced shouldn't be confused with muckraking. Muckraking belonged to a particular era and culture, and the conditions that gave rise to it—a ruthless and unregulated capitalist system, rapid urbanization, a massive influx of non-English-speaking immigrants, governmental paralysis—no longer exist in the same form. What's more, the original muckrakers had a ready outlet for their writings in popular national magazines, an outlet that has considerably narrowed over the years. Although news organizations still undertake investigations and crusades, none is as thoroughly identified in the public mind with this type of journalism as, say, *McClure's* once was. Their efforts are sporadic and haphazard and unrelated to each other or any overarching social objective.

But even if it were possible to replicate the muckraking journalism of old, it isn't certain that would be entirely desirable. Most of the original muckrakers were white male Protestants who came from rural or small-town America, and they brought with them into the larger world an array of small-town fears and prejudices. They were frequently antisaloon, anticity, antiimmigrant. Such censoriousness would be out of place—or at least not very productive—in the big, buzzing, polyglot society America has become.

Is there no positive lesson, then, that we can draw from the Progressive Era muckrakers? Actually, there is. We just have to grope around under the bed to find it. The vast majority of journalists today are better educated, better paid, and better dressed than their turn-of-the-century predecessors, but despite that, they aren't necessarily better journalists. How one rates their abilities depends in part on how one defines the primary function of journalism. Is it to inform, entertain, or advocate? Is it to give people what they want or what they need? Is it to serve democracy or the economy?

These questions have grown increasingly difficult to answer as the lines between information and entertainment—and between the various mass media themselves—have blurred. The *New York Times*, the *Washington Post*, and the Knight-Ridder newspaper group, for example, have all announced separate plans to transform their Web sites into portals or gateways for online advertisers to reach Internet users. "It's a recognition that they need to move beyond the news," a publishing industry analyst for Merrill Lynch said. "People don't only want local news—they want more entertainment listings and other services."[6]

Meanwhile, the *Wall Street Journal* has hired Creative Artists Agency, one of Hollywood's top talent agencies, to represent it in pitching and fielding proposals for TV shows and movies. "Our front-page stories are often narrative accounts with strong characters and strong plot lines, and so sometimes they bear some resemblance to movie plots," Stephen J. Adler, an assistant managing editor, explained. He hastened to assure the trade magazine *Editor & Publisher* that the deal would not get in the way of "good journalism."[7] But as news and entertainment merge, both in terms of corporate ownership and social function, the criteria for what constitutes journalism, let alone good journalism, have turned problematic. Once considered "the first draft of history," journalism is now considered the first draft of a screenplay.

It is here, amid the mounting confusion over journalistic roles and responsibilities, that the original muckrakers can perhaps offer guidance. Their work was deeply moral. As historian John Crunden has pointed out, the muckrakers were "preachers within an evangelical Christian moral environment."[8] They espoused the brotherhood of man and believed that the application of the Golden Rule to politics and business created the only real possibility for reform. This may have been naive of them, but whatever their limitations as social thinkers, they generally sought the common good.

Journalists in the 1990s don't seek the common good as much as stories or information. Consequently, their relationship to the public is colder and more remote. At a time when journalists are widely distrusted—only 25 percent of those recently surveyed said journalists would ever tone down a story to avoid hurting people[9]—the muckrakers can suggest a better way of doing journalism. They fought, in the words of their premier publisher, S. S. McClure, "for those unable to defend themselves."[10] Contemporary journalists can learn from their example the importance of grounding journalism in an ethic of caring.

A lack of caring has led to what Harvard ethicist Sissela Bok calls "a morally toxic environment." In her 1998 book, *Mayhem: Violence as Public Entertainment*, Bok writes that ethics is about establishing the conditions under which human beings thrive. She notes that caring, or empathy, is the very basis of a morally healthy environment, for without "some rudimentary perception of the needs and feelings of others, there can be no beginnings of felt responsibility toward them." It is her position that media violence, which occupies an increasingly large proportion of journalism and entertainment, erodes empathy. Citing social science research, she argues that excessive exposure to media violence results in desensitization and an appetite for yet more violence, particularly among at-risk members of the audience, such as children. Media companies indifferent to everything but their own security and profits breed, she contends, human beings indifferent to everything but their own sordid amusement.[11]

One doesn't have to agree with the whole of Bok's analysis to accept the validity of her claim that the media possess enormous influence over public life, but exercise it with little or no moral discernment. And issuing newsroom codes of ethics isn't the solution. "Such codes," Jeremy Iggers reminds us in *Good News, Bad News: Journalism Ethics and the Public Interest*, "are part of the ideology of professionalism and have sustained the idea that journalism is properly the domain of a specialized class."[12] What is needed instead is a reorientation of journalism from the side of wealth and power to the side of the public. Rabbi Abbahu, a teacher circa A.D. 300 counseled that a person should always strive to be of the persecuted rather than of the persecutors.[13]

In at least a few newsrooms around the country, efforts are already underway to reorient the press. Some refer to this movement as "civic journalism," others as "public journalism," but by any name, its goal is to strike through the mask of traditional journalistic objectivity and give the press a more human face, one the public will recognize as trustworthy, concerned, and helpful. "Defining a newspaper as a tool, rather than as an information medium," Iggers remarks in his book, "implies a deeper kind of relationship. The information function is fulfilled when the reader learns something. The tool function is fulfilled when the reader does something"—for example, attends a school board meeting or calls a legislator.[14]

When President Theodore Roosevelt attacked reform journalists as filth-obsessed "muckrakers" in his famous 1906 speech, he was worried about "the hard scoffing spirit" and "the vacant mind" of citizens brought up on exposés. Thomas E. Leonard, in a chapter republished in this volume, asserts that Roosevelt's fears were largely justified and that the muckrakers turned the public off to politics by making political participation seem inherently corrupting and futile.[15] If Leonard's interpretation is correct, then the very thing civic journalism is committed to overcoming—public cynicism—began in earnest with the rise of muckraking.

Yet civic journalism can also be related in a much more positive way to the muckraking tradition. In the Progressive Era battles to control the excesses of capitalism, the muckrakers analyzed the problems, aroused public opinion, worked for legislative change, and then saw dozens of laws enacted.[16] At newspapers that have experimented with civic journalism, such as the *Charlotte Observer* and the *Wichita Beacon*, a similar approach has been followed. Journalists identify a problem, facilitate the search for possible solutions, and watch to see that the best solution is applied.[17]

Predictably, the civic journalism movement has attracted numerous critics, including the *New York Times*, the *Washington Post*, the *Wall Street Journal*, the *Boston Globe*, and the *Philadelphia Inquirer*. Some object to it on practical grounds. For example, Max Frankel wrote in the *New York Times Magazine* that newsroom budgets are frequently tight and devoting big bucks to civic journalism projects might bankrupt basic newsgathering. Others complain that civic journalism encourages journalists to get involved in what they cover, thereby betraying the first principle of the modern American press, objectivity. "Our central mission is to report the news, to set priorities, to analyze but not to shape or direct events or outcomes," Jane R. Eisner, editorial page editor of the *Philadelphia Inquirer*, told her readers. "Subsume or diminish the central mission, and we become like any other player in society, like any other politician, interest group, do-gooder, thief. I am not willing to relinquish this unique role."[18]

But perhaps the most brutal assessment of civic journalism has come from Jack Fuller, Pulitzer Prize–winning former editor of the *Chicago Tribune* and president and chief operating officer of the Tribune Publishing Co. At a recent meeting of the Organization of News Ombudsmen, Fuller declared that the real problem with civic journalism isn't that it violates objectivity or that it devours scarce resources, but that it is "unbearably dull. The execution of some of the things I've seen," he said, "you'd have to be someone's parent to make your way through it."[19]

Change is always hard, but it may be particularly hard within the media. Robert W. McChesney pointed out in his study, *Corporate Media and the Threat to Democracy*, that "several powerful myths" combine to "make it nearly impossible to broach the subject of media reform in U.S. political culture." The myths include: "that professionalism in journalism will protect the public interest from private media control; that the Internet and new digital technologies with their billions of potential channels eliminate any reason to be concerned about corporate domination of media"; and that the market is the best possible organization for a media system because it forces media firms to "give the people what they want."[20] So long as media corporations enjoy significant economic and political power—and six now control virtually everything shown on television[21]—these myths will form an ideological Maginot line designed to repel civic journalists and others with similarly "foreign" ideas.

Although its critics like to portray civic journalism as a reckless departure from standard operating procedure, it can also be portrayed as a return to a core ethic of empathy, resilience, and respect for others. "The superior journalist," Jay Newman observed in *The Journalist in Plato's Cave*, "recognizes that his greatest influence is exerted through the advancement of ideas and attitudes to which he is personally committed and not simply through service as the agent of those who already possess manifest power"—editors, publishers, keepers of social institutions.[22] American journalism history provides brilliant isolated examples of journalists who wanted to make a difference rather than just a career. We can count the original muckrakers—Ida Tarbell, Lincoln Steffens, Charles Edward Russell, Upton Sinclair—among these. But their relevance for today doesn't primarily lie in the effectiveness of their crusades against this or that wrong; it lies in the ethical values that fueled their writings and that represent a humane alternative to the prevailing callous style of journalism.

According to the Book of Genesis, God finally grew so tired of man's sins He unleashed a flood that washed the world clean. The flood that destroyed downtown Grand Forks, North Dakota, in spring 1997 may not have been a sign of divine anger, but it was morally transforming. Like Noah's ark, the *Grand Forks Herald* rode the floodwaters, and when the Red River of the North at last receded, the 36,800–circulation daily newspaper found itself with a new understanding of its responsibilities and in a new relationship to its community. The *Herald* won a Pulitzer Prize for public service for its coverage of the flood and subsequent fires. Despite its offices burning down, the paper published every day. Its newsroom staff was forced to relocate four times, at one point moving into an elementary school. They also had to deal with the upheaval the flood caused in their personal lives.[23]

By virtue of the codes and customs of their profession, journalists usually occupy a privileged position, covering even disaster stories with detachment, a kind of immunity from pity and awe. *Herald* staffers, however, were caught in the flood and got wet themselves. The experience changed their perspective forever. "Our point of view was not as bystanders," the paper's editor, Mike Jacobs, said, "but as people who were involved in the news. So, now we look for ways to see a story from the point of view of the person who is inside the story, rather than just the point of view of the person telling the story." This is civic journalism on a comprehensible scale, conducted without a lot of celebratory fanfare or self-righteous attacks on the concept of objectivity, just with a profound empathy for the day-to-day struggles of one's neighbors. "I'm not asking people to be part of the story," Jacobs explained, "I'm asking them to see the story and the point of view of the people who are in it—that it's happening to—and try to imagine ways to be helpful."[24]

Jacobs and his staff have carried on the values of justice and brotherhood embodied in muckraking and, as a result, stand out from the general run of journalists. Most newspapers continue to do the same old tawdry things in the same old tawdry way, even though public impatience with the press is growing. Fifty-three percent of those surveyed in 1999 by the First Amendment Center at Vanderbilt University think the press has too much freedom. Only 65 percent said papers should be able to publish a story without government approval—down from 80 percent in 1997. Sizable majorities also believe the news media shouldn't be allowed to endorse or criticize political candidates, use hidden cameras for newsgathering, or publish government secrets. "The survey doesn't address why," Ken Paulson, the center's executive director, noted, "but common sense tells you that the airwaves and newspaper columns have been filled with Monica Lewinsky, Marv Albert and the aftermath of the O. J. Simpson case. They've all contributed to a sense that the American press has lost its perspective."[25]

Something needs to be added to the journalistic mix, and a drop or two of the milk of human kindness might just be it. There will be cynics who say this can't be done, as there will be apologists who will say it shouldn't be, that the American press system is the best ever devised and tampering with it only invites trouble. But look around. Look at the journalists posturing in front of the cameras while poisoned rivers sicken and die; look at the media corporations absorbed in maneuvering for commercial advantage while cities and schools and industries crumble; look at the big headlines spotlighting the gruesome and freakish while real life goes unreported.

The muckrakers and their world vanished long ago, but the moral example of their work remains, capable of inspiring today's journalists to greatness and, better yet, to goodness. How wonderful would it be if the term "good journalist" was defined expansively—if it meant more than being accurate with the facts or quick on deadline, if it meant being caring as well? Pretty wonderful.

NOTES

1. H. L. Mencken, "Newspaper Morals," in *Gang of Pecksniffs*, ed. Theo Lippman Jr. (New Rochelle, N.Y.: Arlington House, 1975), 47.

2. "New evidence helps free death-row inmate," *Middletown (N.Y.) Times Herald Record*, Feb. 6, 1999, 2.

3. Regina Brett, "Putting the Column First," *Editor & Publisher*, May 29, 1999, 62.

4. Joe Strupp, "Series Fires Up Local Pols," *Editor & Publisher*, May 22, 1999, 16.

5. Ibid.

6. "Major Newspapers Expand Web Sites," *Middletown (N.Y.) Times Herald Record*, June 24, 1999, 49.

7. David Noack, "Wall Street Goes Hollywood," *Editor & Publisher*, June 26, 1999, 12.

8. John Crunden, *Ministers of Reform: The Progressives' Achievement in American Civilization, 1889–1920* (New York: Basic Books, 1982). See especially, "It Is Sin to Be Sick: The Muckrakers and the Pure Food and Drug Act," 163–199.

9. This was one of the findings of a survey by the American Society of Newspaper Editors shared with the author by Jim Goldbold, managing editor of the *Eugene* (Oregon) *Register-Guard*, in an e-mail, November 1998.

10. Quoted by Bruce J. Evensen in chapter 1, "The Muckrakers as Evangelicals."

11. Sissela Bok, *Mayhem: Violence as Public Entertainment* (Reading, Mass.: Addison-Wesley, 1998), 65, 70, 89.

12. Jeremy Iggers, *Good News, Bad News: Journalism Ethics and the Public Interest* (Boulder, Colo.: Westview Press, 1998), 137.

13. Quoted by Simon Wiesenthal, *The Sunflower* (New York: Schocken Books, 1976), 179.

14. Iggers, *Good News*, 154.

15. See this volume, chapter 7, "Did the Muckrakers Muck Up Progress?"

16. This argument is made in various studies of muckraking. See, for example, Crunden, *Ministers of Reform.*

17. Mike Hoyt, "Are You Now, Or Will You Ever Be, A Civic Journalist?" *Columbia Journalism Review*, September–October 1995.

18. Quoted in ibid.

19. Mark Fitzgerald, "The Boredom of Civic Journalism," *Editor & Publisher*, May 15, 1999, 6.

20. Robert W. McChesney, *Corporate Media and the Threat to Democracy* (New York: Seven Stories Press, 1997), 7–8.

21. " 'Free Speech' Must-See-TV," *Middletown (N.Y.) Times-Herald-Record*, June 8, 1999, 32.

22. Jay Newman, *The Journalist in Plato's Cave* (Rutherford, N.J.: Fairleigh Dickinson University Press, 1989), 63.

23. Chad Graham, "Flood Stories Hit Close to Home for Grand Forks Editor," *Iowa Journalist* (spring 1999): 2.

24. Quoted in ibid.

25. Marta W. Aldrich, "Americans Give Freedom of Press A Beating in Survey," *Poughkeepsie (N.Y.) Journal*, July 4, 1999, 3A.

Selected Bibliography

Alger, George W. *Moral Overstrain*. Boston and New York: Houghton Mifflin, 1906.

Applegate, Edd. *Journalistic Advocates and Muckrakers: Three Centuries of Crusading Writers*. Jefferson, N.C.: McFarland, 1997.

Bagdikian, Ben. *Media Monopoly*. 4th ed. Boston: Beacon Press, 1992.

Baker, Jean H. *Affairs of Party: The Political Culture of Northern Democrats in the Mid-Nineteenth Century*. Ithaca, N.Y.: Cornell University Press, 1983.

Baker, Ray Stannard. "The Case Against Trinity," *American*, May 1909.

———. *The Spiritual Unrest*. New York: Frederick A. Stokes, 1910.

———. *American Chronicle: The Autobiography of Ray Stannard Baker*. New York: C. Scribner's Sons, 1945.

———. *Woodrow Wilson and World Settlement*. Garden City, N.Y.: Doubleday, Page & Co., 1972.

Baldasty, Gerald. *The Commercialization of the Press in the 19th Century*. Madison: University of Wisconsin Press, 1993.

Bannister, Robert C., Jr. *Ray Stannard Baker: The Mind and Thought of a Progressive*. New Haven, Conn.: Yale University Press, 1966.

Barry, Peter. "The Decline of Muckraking: A View from the Magazines." Ph.D. diss., Wayne State University, 1973.

Bender, Thomas. *Community and Social Change in America*. 1978; reprint, Baltimore: Johns Hopkins University Press, 1982.

Black, Jay, ed. *Mixed News: The Public/Civic/Communitarian Journalism Debate*. Mahwah, N.J.: Erlbaum, 1997.

Bok, Sissela. *Mayhem: Violence as Public Entertainment*. Reading, Mass.: Addison-Wesley, 1998.

Brady, Kathleen. *Ida M. Tarbell*. New York: Macmillan, 1984.

Braeman, John. "Seven Progressives," Business History Review 35 (196).

Bremner, Robert. *From the Depths: The Discovery of Poverty in the United States.* New York: New York University Press, 1956.

Bridgeman, Charles T. *A History of the Parish of Trinity Church in the City of New York.* New York: Trinity Church, 1962.

Brody, Richard. "The Puzzle of Political Participation in America." In *The New American Political System,* ed. Anthony King. Washington, D.C.: American Enterprise Institute, 1978.

Buenker, John D. *Urban Liberalism and Progressive Reform.* New York: Scribner, 1973.

Burnham, Walter Dean. "The Changing Shape of the American Political Universe," *The American Political Science Review* (March 1965).

———. *Critical Elections and the Mainsprings of American Politics.* New York: Norton, 1970.

Cawelti, John G. *Apostles of the Self-Made Man.* Chicago: University of Chicago Press, 1965.

Chalmers, David M. "The Muckrakers and the Growth of Corporate Power: A Study in Constructive Journalism," *American Journal of Economics and Society* 28 (April 1959).

———. *The Social and Political Ideas of the Muckrakers.* New York: Citadel, 1964.

———, ed. *The Muckrake Years.* New York: P. Van Nostrand, 1974.

Charity, Arthur. *Doing Public Journalism.* New York: Guilford, 1996.

Crunden, Robert M. *A Hero in Spite of Himself: Brand Whitlock in Art, Politics, and War.* New York: Knopf, 1969.

———. *The Superfluous Men: Conservative Critics of American Culture, 1900–1945.* Austin: University of Texas Press, 1977.

———. *Ministers of Reform: The Progressive Achievement in American Civilization, 1889–1920.* New York: Basic Books, 1982.

Dillon, Michael. "A Smart Live Journal: E. H. Butler's *Buffalo News* and the Rise and Decline of an Open Public Forum, 1873–1914." Ph.D. diss., Pennsylvania State University, 1995.

———. "From Patriarch to Patrician: Edward H. Butler's *Buffalo News* and the Crisis of Labor, 1877–1892," *American Journalism* (Winter 1999).

Dix, Morgan, ed. *A History of the Parish of Trinity Church in the City of New York.* New York: Putnam, 1898.

Dooley, Patricia. *Taking Their Political Place: Journalists and the Making of an Occupation.* Westport, Conn.: Greenwood Press, 1997.

Dorman, Jessica Ann. " 'Deliver Me from this Muckrake': The Literary Impulse Behind Progressive Era Muckraking." Ph.D. diss., Harvard University, 1996.

Dunn, James Taylor. *The St. Croix: Midwest Border River.* New York: Holt, Rinehart and Winston, 1965.

Emery, Michael, and Edwin Emery. *The Press and America: An Interpretive History of the Mass Media.* Englewood Cliffs, N.J.: Prentice Hall, 1988.

Faulkner, H. U. *The Quest for Social Justice, 1898–1914.* New York: Macmillan, 1931.

Filler, Louis, *The Unknown Edwin Markham.* Yellow Springs, Ohio: Antioch Press, 1966.

———. *Crusaders for American Liberalism.* 1939; reprinted as *The Muckrakers.* University Park: University of Pennsylvania Press, 1976.

―――. "The Muckrakers in Flower and Failure." In *Essays in American Historiography*, ed. Harvey Shapiro. Boston: Heath and Co., 1968.

―――. ed. *Contemporaries: Portraits in the Progressive Era by David Graham Phillips*. Westport, Conn.: Greenwood Press, 1981.

Fitzpatrick, Ellen, ed. *Muckraking: Three Landmark Articles*. New York: Bedford Books, 1994.

Ford, James. *Slums and Housing*. Westport, Conn.: Negro Universities Press, 1936.

Fox, Paul. *The Poles in America*. New York: Arno Press, 1970.

Francke, Warren T. "Investigative Exposure in the Nineteenth Century: The Journalistic Heritage of the Muckrakers." Ph.D. diss., University of Minnesota, 1974.

Gans, Herbert J. *Deciding What's News: A Study of CBS Evening News, NBC Nightly News, Newsweek, and Time*. New York: Pantheon, 1979.

―――. "The Progressive Spirit Today," *The Quill* 72 (November 1984).

Gist, Genevieve B. "Progressive Reform in a Rural Community: The Adams County Vote-Fraud Case," *Mississippi Valley Historical Review* 97 (June 1961).

Goldman, Eric. *Rendezvous with Destiny/A History of Modern American Reform*. New York: Vintage, 1959.

Goodbody, John C. *One Peppercorn: A Popular History of the Parish at Trinity Church*. New York: Parish of Trinity Church, 1982.

Graham, Chad. "Flood stories hit close to home for Grand Forks editor." *Iowa Journalist* (spring 1999).

Graham, John (David Graham Phillips). *The Great God Success, A Novel*. New York: Frederick A. Stokes, 1902.

Grayson, David. (Ray Stannard Baker). "Adventures in Contentment, The Politician," *American Magazine* (October 1907).

Greenfield, Meg. "Why We're Still Muckraking." *Newsweek*, March 25, 1985.

Grenier, Judson A., Jr. "Muckrakers and Muckraking: An Historical Definition," *Journalism Quarterly* 37 (autumn 1960).

―――. "The Origins and Nature of Progressive Muckraking." Ph.D. diss., UCLA, 1965.

Griffith, Sally. *Home Town News*. New York: Oxford University Press, 1989.

Habermas, Jurgen. *The Structural Transformation of the Public Sphere*. Cambridge, Mass.: MIT Press, 1989.

Harris, Leon. *Upton Sinclair. American Rebel*. New York: Crowell, 1971.

Hass, Paul H. "The Suppression of John F. Deitz: An Episode of the Progressive Era in Wisconsin." *Wisconsin Magazine of History* 57 (1974).

Hays, Samuel P. *The Response to Industrialism, 1885–1914*. Chicago: University of Chicago Press, 1957.

―――. *Conservation and the Gospel of Efficiency: The Progressive Conservation Movement, 1890–1920*. Cambridge, Mass.: Harvard University Press, 1968.

Hidy, Ralph W., Frank Ernest Hill, and Allan Nevins. *Timber and Men: The Weyerhaeuser Story*. New York: Macmillan, 1963.

Higham, John. *Strangers in the Land: Patterns of American Nativism, 1860–1925*. New York: Pantheon, 1963.

Higham, John, and Paul K. Conkin, eds. *New Directions in American Intellectual History*. Baltimore: Johns Hopkins University Press, 1979.

Hobsbawn, E. J. *Primitive Rebels: Studies in Archaic Forms of Social Movement in the 19th and 20th Centuries.* 3rd ed. Manchester, England: Manchester University Press, 1974.

Hofstadter, Richard. *The Age of Reform: From Bryan to FDR.* New York: Vintage Books, 1955.

Hollinger David H. "Ethnic Diversity, Cosmopolitanism and the Emergence of the American Liberal Intelligentsia," *American Quarterly* 47 (May 1975).

Horton, John Theodore. *History of Northwestern New York.* New York: Lewis Historical Publishing Company Inc., 1947.

Horton, Russell M. *Lincoln Steffens.* New York: Twayne, 1974.

Howe, Irving. *World of Our Fathers.* New York: Harcourt, Brace, Jovanovich, 1976.

Hoyt, Mike. "Are You Now, or Will you Ever Be, A Civic Journalist?" *Columbia Journalism Review* (September–October 1995).

Iggers, Jeremy. *Good News, Bad News: Journalism Ethics and the Public Interest.* Boulder, Colo.: Westview Press, 1998.

Jensen, Richard. *The Winning of the Midwest, Social and Political Conflict, 1888–1896.* Chicago: University of Chicago Press, 1971.

Johnson, Walter, ed. *Selected Letters of William Allen White: 1899–1943.* New York: H. Holt & Co., 1947.

Jones, Maldwyn Allen. *American Immigration.* Chicago: University of Chicago Press, 1993.

Juergens, George. *News from the White House: The Presidential-Press Relationship in the Progressive Era.* Chicago: University of Chicago Press, 1981.

Kaplan, Justin. *Lincoln Steffens: A Biography.* New York: Simon and Schuster, 1974.

Kazee, Thomas A. "Television Exposure and Attitude Change: The Impact of Political Interest," *Public Opinion Quarterly* (winter 1981).

Kennedy, David. "Overview: The Progressive Era," *The Historian* 37 (1975).

Kennedy, Samuel V. "The Last Muckraker: Samuel Hopkins Adams." Ph.D. diss., Syracuse University, 1993.

———. *Samuel V. Hopkins Adams and the Business of Writing.* Syracuse, N.Y.: Syracuse University Press, 1999.

Kleppner, Paul. *The Cross of Culture: A Social Analysis of Midwestern Politics, 1850–1900.* New York: Free Press, 1970.

———. *Who Voted? The Dynamics of Electoral Turnout, 1870–1980.* New York: Praeger, 1982.

Kolko, Gabriel. *The Triumph of Conservatism: A Reinterpretation of American History, 1910–1916.* Glencoe, Ill.: The Free Press, 1963.

Lawson, Thomas. *Frenzied Finance: The Story of Amalgamated.* New York: Ridgeway-Thayer, 1904.

Leonard, Thomas C. "The 'Bully Pulpit': Who Listened?" *Reviews in American History* 11, March 21, 1983.

———. *Power of the Press: The Birth of American Political Reporting.* New York: Oxford University Press, 1986.

Lewis, Alfred Henry. "Confessions of a Newspaper Man," *Human Life* (Nov. 11, 1905).

Lippmann, Walter. *Public Opinion.* New York: Harcourt, Brace, 1922.

———. *The Phantom Public.* New York: Harcourt Brace, 1927.

Lloyd, Henry Demarest. *Wealth Against Commonwealth.* New York: Harper, 1894.

Lubove, Roy. *The Progressives and the Slums: Tenement House Reform in New York City, 1890–1917*. Westport, Conn.: Greenwood Press, 1962.

Mahin, Helen O., ed. *The Editor and His People: Editorials by William Allen White*. New York: Macmillan, 1924.

Marcosson, Isaac F. *David Graham Phillips and His Times*. New York: Dodd, Mead, 1932.

Markham, Edwin. *The Man with the Hoe*. New York: Doxey's, 1899.

———. *Lincoln and Other Poems*. New York: McClure, Phillips, & Co., 1901.

———. *The Shoes of Happiness and Other Poems*. 1913; reprint, Garden City, N.Y.: Doubleday, Doran & Co., 1932.

———. *Gates of Paradise and Other Poems*. Garden City, N.Y.: Doubleday, Doran & Co., 1920.

Marzolf, Marion. *Civilizing Voices: American Press Criticism 1880–1950*. New York: Longman, 1991.

May, Henry F. *The End of American Innocence: A Study of the First Years of Our Time*. New York: Oxford University Press, 1959.

McChesney, Robert W. *Corporate Media and the Threat to Democracy*. New York: Seven Stories Press, 1997.

McClure, S. S. *My Autobiography*. New York: F. Ungar, 1963.

McCormick, Richard L. *From Realignment to Reform: Political Change in New York State, 1893–1910*. Ithaca, N.Y.: Cornell University Press, 1981.

———. "My Discovery That Business Corrupts: A Reappraisal of the Origins of Progressivism," *American Historical Review* 86 (April 1981).

McGerr, Michael E. *The Decline of Popular Politics: The American North, 1865–1928*. New York: Oxford University Press, 1986.

McKee, John DeWitt. *William Allen White: Maverick on Main Street*. Westport, Conn.: Greenwood Press, 1988.

Mencken, H. L. "Newspaper Morals." In *Gang of Pecksniffs*, ed. Theo Lippman Jr. New Rochelle, N.Y.: Arlington House, 1975.

Millard, Bailey. "David Graham Phillips, His Work and His Clothes. *Human Life* (June 1909).

Miller, Arthur H., Edie N. Goldenber, and Lutz Erbring. "Type-Set Politics: Impact of Newspapers on Public Confidence," *American Political Science Review* 73 (March 1979).

Miller, Warren E. "Disinterest, Disaffection, and Participation in Presidential Politics," *Political Behavior* 11 (1980).

Miraldi, Robert "The Journalism of David Graham Phillips." Ph.D. diss., New York University, 1985.

———. "The Journalism of David Graham Phillips," *Journalism Quarterly* 63 (spring 1986).

———. *Muckraking and Objectivity: Journalism's Colliding Traditions*. Westport, Conn.: Greenwood Press, 1991.

———. "Charles Edward Russell: 'Chief of the Muckrakers.' " *Journalism Monographs* (April 1995).

Morehouse, Clifford P. *Trinity: Mother of Churches; an Informal History of Trinity Parish in the City of New York*. New York: Seabury Press, 1973.

Morison, Elting E., et al., eds. *The Letters of Theodore Roosevelt*. 8 vols. Cambridge, Mass. Harvard University Press, 1951–54.

Mott, Frank Luther. *American Journalism: A History.* New York: Macmillan, 1962.

Mowry, George E. *The California Progressives.* Chicago: Quadrangle Books, 1951.

———. *The Era of Theodore Roosevelt, 1900–1912.* New York: Harper and Row, 1958.

Newman, Jay. *The Journalist in Plato's Cave.* Rutherford, N.J.: Fairleigh Dickinson University Press, 1989.

O'Neill, William. *The Progressive Years.* Chicago: University of Chicago Press, 1957.

Painter, Nell Irvin. *Standing at Armageddon: The United States, 1877–1919.* New York: Norton & Co., 1987.

Park, Robert. "The Natural History of the Newspaper," *The American Journal of Sociology* (November 1923).

Pateman, Carole. *Participation and Democratic Theory.* 1970; reprint, New York and Cambridge, Eng.: Cambridge University Press, 1980.

Patterson, Margaret Jones, and Robert H. Russell. *Behind the Lines: Case Studies in Investigative Reporting.* New York: Columbia University Press, 1986.

Phillips, David Graham. *The Plum Tree.* Indianapolis: Bobbs-Merrill, 1905.

———. *George Helm.* New York: A. Appleton & Co., 1912.

———. *The Treason of the Senate.* Eds. George Mowry and Judson A. Grenier. Chicago: Quadrangle, 1964.

Plunz, Richard. *A History of Housing in New York City.* New York: Columbia University Press, 1990.

Protess, David L., et al. *The Journalism of Outrage: Investigative Reporting and Agenda Building in America.* New York: Guilford Press, 1991.

Quandt, Jean B. *From the Small Town to the Great Community: The Social Thought of Progressive Intellectuals.* New Brunswick, N.J.: Rutgers University Press, 1970.

Rammelkamp, Julian S. *Pulitzer's Post and Dispatch, 1878–1883.* Princeton, N.J.: Princeton University Press, 1967.

Ranney, Austin. *Channels of Power: The Impact of Television on American Politics.* New York: Basic Books, 1983.

Reaves, Sheila. "How Radical Were the Muckrakers? Socialist Press Views, 1902–1906," *Journalism Quarterly* 61 (winter 1984).

Regier, C. C. *The Era of the Muckrakers.* Chapel Hill: University of North Carolina Press, 1932.

Reynolds, John Francis. "Testing Democracy: Electoral Participation and Progressive Reform in New Jersey, 1888–1919." Ph.D. diss., Rutgers University, 1980.

Richards, Leonard L. "Gentlemen of Property and Standing," *Anti-Abolition Mobs in Jacksonian America.* New York: Oxford University Press, 1971.

Riis, Jacob. *How the Other Half Lives: Studies Among the Tenements of New York.* New York: Charles Scribner's Sons, 1902.

Riordon, William L. *Plunkitt of Tammany Hall.* 1905; reprint, New York: Dutton, 1963.

Rischin, Moses. *The Promised City: New York's Jews, 1870–1914.* Cambridge, Mass.: Harvard University Press, 1962.

Roberts, Eugene. "The Finest Reporting Is Always Investigative." *IRE Journal* (winter 1988).

Robinson, Michael J. " 'Public Affairs Television and the Growth of Political Malaise: The Case of 'The Selling of the Pentagon,' " *American Political Science Review* 70 (June 1976).

Rodgers, Daniel T. "In Search of Progressives," *Reviews in American History* 10 (December 1982).

Rogin, Michael Paul, and John L. Shover. *Political Change in California: Critical Elections and Social Movements, 1890–1966.* Westport, Conn.: Greenwood Press, 1970.

Rosen, Jay. "Community Connectedness: Passwords for Public Journalism," *Poynter Papers* 3. St. Petersburg, Fla.: The Poynter Institute for Media Studies, 1993.

Rosen, Jay, and David Merrit Jr. *Public Journalism: Theory and Practice.* Dayton, Ohio: Kettering Foundation, 1994.

Rothman, David J. *Politics and Power: The United States Senate, 1869–1901.* Cambridge, Mass.: Harvard University Press, 1966.

Russell, Charles Edward. "At the Throat of the Republic," *Cosmopolitan* (December 1907, January, February, April 1908).

———. "The Cry of the Slums," *Everybody's* (December 1907).

———. "Trinity: Church of Mystery," *The New Broadway Magazine* (April 1908).

———. "Trinity Corporation: A Riddle of Riches," *The Broadway Magazine* (May 1908).

———. "Tenements of Trinity Church," *Everybody's* (July 1908).

———. "The Break Up of the Parties," *Success* (January 1909).

———. "The Slum As A National Asset," *Everybody's Magazine* (February 1909).

———. "Trinity's Tenements—The Public's Business," *Everybody's* (February 1909).

———. "What Are You Going To Do About It?" *Cosmopolitan* (July–October and December, 1910).

———. *Why I Am A Socialist.* New York: George H. Doran, 1910.

———. *Business: The Heart of the Nation.* New York: John Lane Co., 1911.

———. *These Shifting Scenes.* New York: George Doran Co., 1914.

———. *Bare Hands and Stone Walls.* New York: Scribner's Sons, 1933.

———. *A Pioneer Editor in Early Iowa: A Sketch of the Life of Edward Russell.* Washington, D.C.: Ransdell Inc., 1941.

Schlesinger, Arthur M. *The American as Reformer.* Cambridge, Mass.: Harvard University Press, 1968.

Schudson, Michael. *Discovering the News.* New York: Basic Books, 1978.

———. *The Good Citizen.* New York: The Free Press, 1998.

Schultz, Stanley. "The Morality of Politics: The Muckraker's Vision of Democracy," *Journal of American History* (December 1965).

Semonche, John. "Teddy Roosevelt's Muck-rake Speech: A Reassessment," *Mid-America* (April 1964).

———. *Ray Stannard Baker: A Quest for Democracy in Modern America, 1870–1918.* Chapel Hill: University of North Carolina Press, 1969.

Sinclair, Upton. *The Jungle.* 1906; reprint, New York: Bantam Books, 1976.

———. *Cup of Fury.* Great Neck, N.Y.: Channel Press, 1956.

———. *My Lifetime in Letters.* Columbia: University of Missouri Press, 1960.

———. *The Autobiography of Upton Sinclair.* London: W. H. Allen, 1963.

Sloan, William David. "American Muckrakers, 1901–1917: Conservative Defenders or Liberal Reformers?" Paper given at the Association for Education in Journalism and Mass Communication Southeastern Regional Colloquium. March 29–30, 1985.

Stead, William T. *If Christ Came to Chicago*. Chicago: Laird and Lee, 1894.

———. *The Americanization of the World*. New York: H. Markley, 1901.

Steffens, Lincoln. "Enemies of the Republic," *McClure's* (August 1904).

———. "Rhode Island: A State for Sale," *McClure's* (February 1905).

———. *The Shame of the Cities*. New York: McClure, Phillips & Co., 1904: reprint, New York: Hill and Wang, 1957.

———. *The Autobiography of Lincoln Steffens*. New York: Harcourt, Brace and Co., 1931.

———. *Lincoln Steffens Speaking*. New York: Harcourt, Brace & Co., 1936.

Steel, Ronald. *Walter Lippmann and the American Century*. New York: Little, Brown, 1981.

Stein, Harry H. "American Muckrakers and Muckraking: The 50-Year Scholarship," *Journalism Quarterly* 56 (spring 1979).

Stidger, William L. *Edwin Markham*. New York: The Abingdon Press, 1933.

Swanberg, W. A. *Pulitzer*. New York: Charles Scribner's Sons, 1967.

Tarbell, Ida. *History of Standard Oil*. New York: McClure, Phillips & Co., 1904.

———. *All in a Day's Work*. New York: Macmillan, 1939.

Thelen, David P. *The New Citizenship: Origins of Progressivism in Wisconsin, 1885–1900*. Columbia: University of Missouri Press, 1972.

———. *Robert M. La Follette and the Insurgent Spirit*. Madison: University of Wisconsin Press, 1976.

Tomkins, Mary E. *Ida M. Tarbell*. New York: Twayne, 1974.

Tucher, Andie. *Froth and Scum: Truth, Beauty, Goodness and the Ax Murder in America's First Mass Medium*. Chapel Hill: University of North Carolina Press, 1994.

Unger, Irwin, and Debi Unger. *The Vulnerable Years: The United States, 1896–1917*. New York: New York University Press, 1977.

White, William Allen. *A Theory of Spiritual Progress*. Emporia, Kans.: The Gazette Press, 1910.

———. *The Old Order Changeth*. New York: Macmillan, 1910.

———. *Some Cycles of Cathay*. Chapel Hill: University of North Carolina Press, 1925.

———. *The Autobiography of William Allen White*. New York: Macmillan, 1946.

Whitlock, Brand. *The Thirteenth District, The Story of A Candidate*. Indianapolis: Bowen-Merrill, 1902.

———. "The City and Civilization," *Scribner's Magazine* (November 1912).

———. *Forty Years of It*. Westport, Conn.: Greenwood Press, 1968.

Wiebe, Robert H. *Businessmen and Reform: A Study of the Progressive Movement*. Cambridge, Mass.: Harvard University Press, 1962.

———. *The Search for Order, 1877–1920*. New York: Hill and Wang, 1967.

Wiesenthal, Simon. *The Sunflower*. New York: Schocken Books, 1976.

Wilson, Harold. *McClure's Magazine and the Muckrakers*. Princeton, N.J.: Princeton University Press, 1970.

Winter, Ella, and Granville Hicks, eds. *The Letters of Lincoln Steffens.* 2 vols. 1938; reprint, Westport, Conn.: Greenwood Press, 1974.

Wolfinger, Raymond E., and Stephen J. Rosenstone. *Who Votes?* New Haven, Conn.: Yale University Press, 1980.

Wright, Esmond. *The American Dream—From Reconstruction to Reagan.* Cambridge, Mass.: Blackwell Publishers, 1996.

Index

About the Editor and Contributors

MICHAEL DILLON is an Assistant Professor of Communication at Duquesne University. He is an award-winning newspaper reporter and was a columnist in Pennsylvania. His journalism has appeared in *New York Newsday*, the *Philadelphia Inquirer*, the *Pittsburgh Post-Gazette*, and the *Dallas Morning News*.

BRUCE J. EVENSEN is Professor in the Communication Department at DePaul University. He was a journalist and bureau chief on both sides of the Atlantic. He is the author of three books, including *When Dempsey Fought Tunney: Heroes, Hokum, and Storytelling in the Jazz Age* (1996) and editor of *The Responsible Reporter* (1997).

HOWARD GOOD is Professor of Journalism at the State University of New York at New Paltz. He has written six books about journalism, media, and popular culture. His most recent book is *The Drunken Journalist* (2000). He was an editor for newspapers in Michigan and North Carolina.

AGNES HOOPER GOTTLIEB is an Associate Professor of Journalism at Seton Hall University in South Orange, N.J. She has written numerous articles and presented a variety of scholarly papers on the role of women in journalism history.

JAMES KATES is a longtime journalist who has worked for the *Philadelphia Inquirer* and is currently an editor at the *Milwaukee Journal Sentinel*. His book, *Planning a Wilderness: Regenerating the Great Lakes Cutover Region,* will be published in 2001.

THOMAS LEONARD is Professor and Associate Dean of the Graduate School of Journalism at the University of California, Berkeley and author of *Power of the Press: The Birth of American Political Reporting* (1986) and *News for All: Coming of Age with the Press* (1995).

ROBERT MIRALDI is Professor of Journalism at the State University of New York at New Paltz. He is the author of *Muckraking and Objectivity: Journalism's Colliding Traditions* (Greenwood Press, 1991) and is also an award-winning newspaper columnist. He was a Fulbright scholar in the Netherlands in 1992 and a reporter in New York City for ten years.

STEPHEN WHITFIELD is the Max Richter Professor of American Civilization at Brandeis University, where he has taught since 1972. He was a Fulbright professor at the Hebrew University of Jerusalem and the Catholic University of Louvain, Belgium. He is the author of eight books, including *In Search of American Jewish Culture* (1999).

AEA-0993

WITHDRAWN